THE
SUNSET
MURDERS

LOUISE FARR

POCKET BOOKS

New York   London   Toronto   Sydney   Tokyo   Singapore

POCKET BOOKS, a division of Simon & Schuster Inc.
1230 Avenue of the Americas, New York, NY 10020

Farr, Louise.
    The Sunset Murders / by Louise Farr.
        p.   cm.
    ISBN 0-671-70088-X : $21.00
    1. Murder--California—History.   2. Sex crimes—California—
History. I. Title.
HV6533.C2F37   1992
364.1′523′0979493—dc20   91-43558
                                                                            CIP

First Pocket Books hardcover printing April 1992

10 9 8 7 6 5 4 3 2

POCKET and colophon are registered trademarks of
Simon & Schuster Inc.

Printed in the U.S.A.

Author's Note

This book is based on trial transcripts, Los Angeles Police Department files and logs, appellate court briefs, and tape recordings and transcripts of those recordings, as well as interviews with over eighty people. As always in a story as complicated and emotionally tangled as this, there were discrepancies. I have pointed them out when they were material. Otherwise I have told the story as it corresponded to the evidence.

Nothing has been made up. Dialogue is taken from transcripts or interviews and wherever possible has been double-checked. Ellipses indicate where I have cut dialogue. No thoughts or observations have been put into people's heads that they did not actually think, or say that they thought. The murder scenes have been re-created as told to Carol Bundy and recounted by her in police statements and trial testimony. Many details are backed up by the physical evidence. Douglas Clark's and Carol Bundy's letters include their misspellings and grammatical errors.

During 1980 and 1981, I interviewed Douglas Clark when he was in Los Angeles County Jail awaiting trial. In late 1990 and in 1991, I also spoke to him by phone when he called from San Quentin. Immediately after her arrest, Carol Bundy refused to be interviewed, but between 1989 and 1991, with the cooperation of the California Institution for Women at Frontera, she spent days discussing her case with me.

During that same period, Detective Leroy Orozco was available for hours of discussion and insight and was always good-tempered about digging into his files and rehashing minute details of the case. His only interest was accuracy, which included pointing out that in a case like the Sunset Murders, the detective work is done by a group and never by one man.

Of course, I'm grateful to Roger Pida as well as those Sunset Murders Task Force members who added their memories to those of Leroy Orozco, particularly Helen Kidder, Mike Stallcup, and Frank Garcia. I'm also grateful to Carol Bundy's psychiatrists for their insights. Dr. Dorothy Lewis, a consultant for Douglas Clark's appeal, wanted it made clear that she refused to be interviewed for this book. Other members of Douglas Clark's defense team were, of course, bound by the attorney-client privilege. Judge Ronald Coen merits a special note of thanks, as does Joseph Walsh.

Jeannette Murray, Robby Robertson, Vicky Peters, Art Pollinger, LeAnn Lane, Janet Marano, and Richard Geis were unstinting with their help.

Obviously untold numbers of people help with a project like this, even though they don't show up in the story. I'm speaking of my late mother, Georgina Kemp, who had the idea for the book, Stephen Adams, Colston Young, Ashley Bowler, Richard Hunter, Tennyson Schad, Estelle Nicol, Lillian Cole, Ruth Gregory, Frank Haflich, Pierre-Gilles Vidoli, Jessie French, Robin French, Katherine Pearce, Harlan Ellison, Connie Bruck, Timothy Carlson, Andy Klein, and Doctors James Way, Helen Grusd and William Weinstein.

The Novato *Advance* and Orange County *Register* were helpful with news clips. Ivy Kessel, formerly of the California State Attorney-General's office, was generous with transcripts and files. Mike Carroll, Craig and Joseph Jorgensen, and Geoffrey Cowley were equally generous with background material on the late Robert Jorgensen.

Maureen and Eric Lasher have always been more than agents. They were there from the beginning, and without Maureen's insight and sensitivity and Eric's weekly doses of common sense this would have been a much more difficult project—if it had been a project at all.

My editor, Claire Zion, made wonderful suggestions.

I especially want to thank the Sunset Murders children, now grown, who so clearly saw the shortcomings of the adults in their

AUTHOR'S NOTE

lives and needed to have their pain acknowledged. They are Christopher Bundy, who insisted that his real name be used, and Spike Bundy, Judith Marano, and Theresa, whose first names have been changed.

Eleven years after the murders, a number of people were still afraid. To protect their privacy, some names have been changed.

Preface

It was almost one o'clock in the afternoon on Wednesday, June 12, 1980, and the weather in Burbank, California, was humid and sunny. Highway worker Francisco Vasquez was cleaning papers and beer cans from a steep slope by the side of the Ventura Freeway when he discovered the bodies of fifteen- and sixteen-year-old stepsisters from Huntington Beach. They had been shot in the head and, perhaps as a malevolent joke, dumped beneath shrubs and bushes near the Forest Lawn Cemetery on ramp to the freeway.

Within the next few weeks, three more bodies were found, all of them young blond women who had been shot with the same gun. Because they had spent time on Hollywood's Sunset Strip, their killer became known as the Sunset Strip Slayer.

There were few clues at the discovery scenes. The investigation into the murders dragged on into the heat of July while the team of detectives in charge of the case pursued the killer and waited for him to strike again.

PART
ONE

1

DETECTIVE LEROY OROZCO DIDN'T KNOW HOW HE CAME TO BE called Leroy, which he never thought of as a Mexican name. People asked about it, and Orozco told them that his father's ship had been torpedoed in World War II. After the cook, Leroy Washington, rescued his dad from the icy waters, Orozco's story went, he wrote to his wife at home in the Mexican barrio of Los Angeles and told her to name the new baby after the hero.

People always said, "Huh. Is that right?" And Leroy Orozco would nod solemnly.

The fact was, Orozco was making a joke out of what had been a sad beginning. It was true that his dad was in the navy when he was born. But when he was only a couple of months old, and while her husband was still at sea, Leroy's mother had run off. Leroy never knew why, and he didn't see her again until he was seventeen years old.

His paternal grandmother, who was barely five feet tall, had rescued him and his older brother when their mother abandoned them. After that he lived with her and his step-grandfather, two aunts, and an uncle in a three-room house near Los Angeles County Hospital. Leroy slept on a shelf in the closet and bathed in a standing tub. The curtains dividing the rooms were made of string and bottle caps, and his first memory was of waking at four or five in the morning to a slapping sound as his grandmother made tortillas, which she dipped in hot sauce and handed to him as a pacifier.

His real grandfather, who was his grandmother's first husband, had been a general in Pancho Villa's army. When for some reason Villa ordered him out of the country, his granddad made the right Orozco move. He crossed the border at El Paso riding a horse with his wife walking alongside him. On his mother's side, Leroy's grandparents were from Arizona. Somewhere along the line, he was convinced, he had picked up Apache blood from Geronimo.

When his dad got out of the navy, he and his boys stayed on with the family in the small bungalow surrounded by the music and teeming streets of the Mexican ghetto.

Of course, Leroy Orozco didn't know he was living in a ghetto. He didn't even know what a ghetto was. The house was in an alley near the railroad tracks. A man came to deliver ice, and for fun everyone sat around watching the radio. Leroy and his older brother played kick the can and hide-and-seek, and Leroy was especially fond of catching tarantulas by pouring water into their holes.

One day, when Leroy was nine, a man who lived next to the elementary school invited him and his brother into his house. The boys watched TV and drank hot chocolate and found another world. There were curtains at the windows and pictures on the walls, a fireplace and a separate room for everyone. Leroy wanted a different life, he decided. The life he saw here.

At that time, the hope of the Orozco family was Leroy's uncle, a heavyweight boxer who worked at Alcoa Aluminum with Leroy's dad and every other male Orozco. When his uncle was electrocuted at the foundry, the grieving family's hopes fell upon Leroy. He was to become the first in the family to graduate from high school— unlike his brother, who had already dropped out to get married. Leroy, with crisp, dark curly hair, pale olive skin, and chiseled Indian features, fulfilled his family's dreams, he thought later, by living up to a bunch of negatives: he didn't drop out of school, didn't get anybody pregnant, and didn't become a punk.

There were gangs when Leroy Orozco was a boy. In those days, though, they weren't baby sociopaths. They were kids with attitudes, knives, and a code of silence. At Garfield High in East Los Angeles, Leroy was the first to get an Ivy League haircut and wear khakis and button-down shirts. But even though he didn't have a duck's-ass hairdo like they did, he was popular with the cholos.

THE SUNSET MURDERS

In twelfth grade, where he did just enough work to get by, Leroy decided to run for student-body president; his competition was a brilliant geek. Before the election, Leroy's mini-gangster friends walked around the school sticking their faces in people's business. "Who are *you* voting for?" they said. When the vote was tallied, it was Leroy Orozco 1,470, with thirty for the geek.

That was the year Leroy decided he was going to find his mother and show her what he was like. He had been thinking about her all his life and he was convinced that she would be proud of him. When he tracked her down, she was working as a cook and dietitian at a school in East Los Angeles. But when he and his brother went to meet her, they discovered his brother looked like her, and Leroy looked like his dad. Leroy's mother hugged his brother, then she shook Leroy's hand. She didn't seem that proud. And that was the extent of his relationship with his mother.

By that time, Leroy had decided to be a professional baseball player, even though the odds were against his dream. He was broad-shouldered, but he was too short—only just over five feet nine. Plus he was Mexican, which in the 1950s would have made it too damn difficult. But Garfield High was city champion while he was on the team, and he was able to win a baseball scholarship to Humboldt State University in the northernmost reaches of California.

The Orozco family upgraded its dream. Now Leroy was going to become the first college graduate in his family.

Humboldt County was a shock. It wasn't that Leroy Orozco didn't like redwoods. They were pretty, and so was the Victorian house that he lived in with Humboldt's handful of black and Mexican students. But the quiet on the streets of the coastal village of Arcata made him uneasy. The big hit song the year he went up there was "Purple People-Eater." And that's what Leroy felt like in the quaintness and the fog and the barking seals: he might as well have been a purple people-eater from another planet. All the locals were looking at him, he felt, saying, "Sure looks strange to me."

After two years at Humboldt, Leroy still wasn't used to the silence and boredom of small-town life. His grades weren't too good either. He dropped out of college and went back to Los Angeles, where, at a buddy's wedding, he met a girl he'd known in high school. Her name was Patsy and they'd been partners once in a three-legged sack race. They'd won the race, but they'd never dated.

5

Now he and Patsy fell in love and got married, and Leroy tested for the phone company and the gas company. The phone company told him he had a bad back, which was news to him, and the gas company told him he didn't pass the test. The idea that they might not want him because he was Mexian crossed Leroy Orozco's mind, but he didn't dwell on it. Instead, he applied to the police academy. There he was accepted, and when he discovered he was one of five Mexicans and five blacks in his class, tokenism crossed Leroy Orozco's mind. He didn't dwell on that either. Instead he decided to get through the academy without drawing attention to himself.

"You'll never make it; you're nothing but a piece of shit," Leroy's counselor yelled at him one day, in standard 1960s' academy style.

Some kind of counseling, Leroy thought, expecting all the time to be booted out.

Out of more than a hundred guys, about two-thirds finished the year. Some walked away terrorized. Others were ousted from class through the huge rattling doors, never to be seen again.

A couple of days before graduation, a geek who was number one in the class heard his name called. A buzz filled the room. If the geek went, no one was safe. The geek picked up his stuff and left, tears streaming down his face. It was a joke. They brought him back to graduate amid much manly laughter. He must have joined the FBI, Leroy thought, where all good police-academy geeks go.

Leroy graduated too. He became a cop on February 5, 1962, beginning with two years on foot patrol in Watts followed by two years in Vice. He now knew what a ghetto was. And he had acquired a nickname. He had been standing with his foot up on a fire hydrant on his first stakeout when a mean-looking dog trotted along and peed on his ankle. His lieutenant named him "the Plug," and the name stuck. He even had it on his business cards, which were misprinted "LeRoy 'the Plug' Orozco."

A cop was supposed to have ten years in uniform before he could apply for detective, but Rampart Division needed someone who spoke Spanish. Leroy got the job. In 1968, he was transferred to the elite downtown Los Angeles Robbery-Homicide Division at the Parker Center skyscraper. His first assignment was the Robert Kennedy assassination: there were Mexicans working in the kitchen at the Ambassador Hotel, where Kennedy was shot.

Twelve years after Kennedy's death, by the time of the Sunset Strip killings, Leroy Orozco had worked at least three hundred murders and thought that nothing could shock him. He was a hardened member of Homicide who still thought a cop was someone who hit the streets and didn't stop until the bad guys got caught.

In the early days, he'd had nightmares of blood and bodies, of fear and danger, but they'd stopped. A man couldn't go home and not sleep. A man couldn't go home and dump it on his wife and his kids. Patsy Orozco and their teenage son and daughter knew no details of his work beyond what they saw on the occasional television news clip. Now Orozco said that homicide work was just a job to him. A strange job, but just a job nevertheless. He no longer had nightmares. The only thing that awakened him at two in the morning was his ulcer, burning his belly like the Mexican food he loved and no longer was allowed to eat. When he got to work, the pain always went away.

After he heard about the young stepsisters, identified as Cindy Chandler and Gina Marano, discovered dead on the Ventura Freeway in mid-June of 1980, Orozco took his vacation. The murders belonged to Northeast Division, not his. As usual, to his wife's disappointment, they hadn't made any plans to go away. Leroy puttered around the house and tended his garden—just in case something should come up.

On June 23, his partner, John Helvin, called him at home to tell him about twenty-year-old Exxie Wilson, a prostitute found dead next to a Dumpster in the parking lot of the Studio City Sizzler restaurant. She had been decapitated and her head was missing. He and Helvin discussed what to do. It was a single homicide. There was no need to upset his wife and go back downtown for that.

But on the twenty-seventh Helvin phoned again. At about two-thirty that morning he had examined a wooden box found by a Studio City motorist. Inside the box had been the missing head of Exxie Wilson, wrapped in a pair of jeans from which the crotch had been cut and a pink T-shirt imprinted on the front with "Daddy's Girl." At the left rear of Exxie Wilson's skull, Helvin had noticed a gunshot wound with no apparent exit. By the time the coroner had arrived at about three-thirty, the outside temperature was sixty-eight degrees Fahrenheit, but sixty inside the box. The coroner inserted a thermometer into Exxie Wilson's neck. The temperature was only thirty-five degrees. It seemed that her head had been frozen.

"Jesus," Leroy said.

At the coroner's office at eight o'clock on the morning of June

27, Dr. Joseph Choi had begun his examination of Exxie Wilson's skull. In the center he discovered a .25-caliber copper-jacketed slug. By eleven-fifteen, the Firearms Unit had called Helvin at Parker Center with the news that the bullet had six lands and grooves with a left twist, markings created by the gun barrel when the bullet was fired. Between twelve and twenty-five makes of .25-caliber automatics fit that description. But this gun was probably a Raven. Definitely, Firearms said, it was the same gun that had killed the stepsisters.

In the early hours of the same morning as the grisly discovery of the decapitated Exxie Wilson, the body of Wilson's friend, twenty-four-year-old Karen Jones, had been found lying in the street near the Burbank Studios. Police did not, at first, think she was a prostitute. She was too well-groomed and dressed. It turned out that Jones, too, had been shot in the head with the gun that had killed the other women.

There was a dilemma. Wilson's body had been assigned to Downtown while her head belonged to North Hollywood. The stepsisters' case was still in Northeast Division and Karen Jones belonged to Burbank. All the murders had to be consolidated into one case and moved to Downtown, where Robbery-Homicide was already stretched to its limits.

The Los Angeles murder rate was reaching a record high, which would peak at about 1,040 dead by year's end. Too, the largest number of accused multiple murderers to be caught in the city at one time were awaiting what would be high-profile trials.

There was Hillside Strangler Kenneth Bianchi and his cousin, Angelo Buono; Lawrence Bittaker and his accomplice, Roy Norris, the torture killers of young women; and Freeway Killer Randy Woods, who had strangled a series of young men. With the Alphabet Bomber and the Skid Row murderer, Los Angeles had begun to seem like the serial killing capital of the world.

Robbery-Homicide's dapper Lieutenant Ron Lewis, nicknamed Little Ronnie Homicide, would coordinate the Sunset Strip investigation. He had assigned two other sets of Downtown partners to the case besides Orozco and Helvin. A pair of women detectives from Northeast would join the task force to continue their work on the teenage stepsisters' case.

No one—whatever their heritage, gender, or perceived sexual persuasion—was exempt from Orozco's barbs. Often his insults were a sign of his affection. In truth, Orozco did not believe that he had anything against women. Still, he didn't like the idea of the female detectives as part of the task force. He'd seen men eaten alive by the work. They retired and shot themselves in the head or drank themselves to death. In his opinion, homicide wasn't women's work. Nothing to be done about it, though. The women had all the clues on the teenage stepsisters.

Because Helvin had been the first from Downtown on the Exxie Wilson murder scene, the Wilson-Jones killings were given to him and Orozco. As Patsy Orozco hovered in the background, recognizing the signs leading up to another ruined vacation, Leroy made plans to leave with Helvin on Monday for Little Rock, Arkansas. There, the hometown of Exxie Wilson and Karen Jones, the detectives would gather background information.

These crimes were weird and interesting and Orozco was glad he was going to be in on them. He had no way of knowing that eight months before trial, the Sunset Strip murder book of clues and evidence would land on his desk and he would be put in charge of preparing the case for court.

The weekend of Helvin's call, Orozco caught up on work around the house and, in a feeble attempt to make up for the lost vacation, took his wife and children out for hamburgers.

On Sunday he packed for Little Rock. In one corner of his bag he put a fresh bottle of Mylanta for the ulcer. In another, he tucked his favorite cassette tape: a compilation of Ravel's "Bolero," which he had seen his idol, George Raft, dance to in the movie, and Glenn Miller hits that reminded him of his days in the barrio when his dad would put on a zoot suit to go out jitterbugging. If he and Helvin had to drive down dusty Arkansas roads to find Exxie Wilson's family, Orozco didn't want to have to sing along to country and western hits. The part of him from his mother's side that was descended from Geronimo hated cowboys and their music almost as much as he hated killers.

On Monday, while he and Helvin were getting directions to the trailer home near Little Rock where Exxie Wilson's mother lived, a hunter looking for snakes in a north San Fernando Valley ravine spotted some blond hair sticking out from beneath an old mattress. Using his snake stick to push away debris, he discovered the mummified body of a young woman. It seemed that the fifth Sunset murder victim to be found had been the first to die.

2

THE MASQUERS CLUB WAS IN AN OLD SYCAMORE AVENUE HOME around the corner from Grauman's Chinese Theatre in Hollywood. In the golden days of the movie industry, in the 1930s and 1940s, John Barrymore and Errol Flynn went to the Masquers to get whacked. By the 1970s, the club reeked still of what passed for tradition in southern California. Frank Sinatra was a member; so was Rudy Vallee. And less illustrious Masquers—out-of-work comedians, say, or singers or magicians—could knock back a beer in the Olde English bar on a hot afternoon and still feel part of the most inconstant business on the face of the earth.

One early summer day in 1973, John Robert Murray, more commonly known as Jack, wandered into the Masquers. He spotted a sign on the bulletin board asking for volunteers to perform at a telethon in nearby Huntington Beach.

Jack, who had been born in Glasgow and taken to Sydney by his parents when he was three months old, had been known in Australia as "Scotland's Man of Song." Now he was thirty-eight, and he had arrived in Los Angeles determined to become a star. With him he had the requisite eight-by-ten glossies and newspaper clips to prove that he, a swinging pop vocalist, had appeared across Australia, even by popular demand, with the Fabulous Jeff Doyle Trio; with Mr. Entertainment himself, Norm Cole; with none other than

10

Ron McCulloch's Bluebirds; and with the Incomparable, Top of the Pops, Little Pattie.

Jack also proudly displayed a blind item from an Australian newspaper whose headline blared TRUTH TO TELL. "Who was the the well-known Brisbane entertainer who did an impromptu strip-tease act the other day in front of the landlady?" the clip read. "He stepped out of the bath into full view of her after he had forgotten to close the front door." Those who would read this clip later in Los Angeles could be forgiven for guessing that if the well-known entertainer was Jack, Scotland's Man of Song probably left the front door open by design to titillate the landlady in question.

But that day at the Masquers Club, Jack Murray's past was not on his mind as much as his future. Coincidentally, the producer of the Huntington Beach telethon sat at the bar, a bear of a man named Robby Robertson, prematurely gray and good-natured. Jack introduced himself. He'd been the Tom Jones of Australia, he explained.

Soon he stood next to the piano. Accompanied by a Masquer, he sang a song called "I'd Rather Die Young," a country and western dirge in which a lover chooses early death over loss of his woman.

As he sang, Jack Murray's slight body and almost delicate features took on an aura of strength. Robby Robertson was listening to the sweetest, purest voice he had heard in years. You charismatic son of a bitch, he thought, deciding that he'd rather listen to Jack than Tom Jones any day.

He'd written the song when he was a professor of music in Melbourne, Jack volunteered.

Robby went home and told his wife, Diane, that he had just auditioned a great new singer. A handsome SOB and a sharp dresser.

At the telethon, Murray was magic. He was also hard up for money. Robby, head of the guest-relations department at Hollywood's KTTV Channel 11 television station, liked the guy and believed in his talent. He and Diane were Canadians and they knew it could be difficult getting started in a new country. He let Jack hang around the studio and help handle game-show audiences.

"I'm Robby's partner," Robertson heard him say. He ignored it. He had become instantly fond of Jack. If the man's ego needed the boost of using him and the studio, Robby wasn't going to make a deal of it.

It wasn't long, though, before Robby wondered why he put up

with Jack. The man lived in fantasyland and spun out stories of past accomplishments that Robby soon began to realize were nothing but hot air. Anything anyone mentioned, Jack could do better.

The first time Robby heard his war stories, Jack had fought in Vietnam in the Australian army. The second time around, he had been in the Special Forces. The third time Vietnam came up, Jack said he had been involved in undercover operations for the CIA. Assassinations, that kind of thing. Robby bit his tongue.

When Jack took credit for writing "Waltzing Matilda," the time had come to challenge him.

"Come on, Jack," he said. "That was written before you were born."

"Well, originally, yes," Jack said. "But we revised it and put it in its final form." He didn't say who he meant by "we."

Robertson shrugged. Nothing fazed the guy. When Robby had wondered why, when Jack had written a song as compelling as "I'd Rather Die Young," he had since written nothing, Jack spun an elaborate story about his music portfolio being stolen. Battered and bloody, he had fought the robbers and lost. It would be years before Robby heard George Jones sing "I'd Rather Die Young." Jack, he then realized, had nothing to do with its creation.

At forty-three, Robby was only five years older than Jack, but sometimes he felt old enough to be his father. As easily as he acquired bits and pieces of other people's lives, Jack, charming and amoral, acquired the women he called "birds." It seemed he could talk any of them into bed at the motel room he kept at the ready a few blocks from KTTV. Astounded, Robby watched as Jack cased each new show audience.

"Look at the bazooms. Look at the buns," he said, a wolf eyeing the flock for the most succulent sheep.

Robby didn't tell his wife about Jack's conquests. If she had known he was sexually insatiable, she would not approve. Jack was a satyr; but he was also, after only a few months, Robby's best friend, and Robby didn't want to stop seeing him.

The man could be a star if he didn't alienate everyone by behaving like an asshole, Robby thought. Jack cadged drinks and bad-mouthed people as soon as they left the room. He liked to flash a wad of bills, a hundred on top, singles underneath. When he'd lost at poker, paper replaced the singles. He turned up at the Masquers with women who, to Robby's eyes, were bimbos. And he bragged to anyone who would listen that he was the best singer in the goddamn world. Johnny Cash, Frank Sinatra, or whoever was the topic of discussion, was a "bloody wimp" as far as Jack Murray was concerned.

Red Hippler, a sheriff and Masquer, lectured Robby about his new friend. "He's nothing but a con man and a leech," he said.

"I know," Robby sighed. "But he's a nice guy."

Over Labor Day weekend, the year Robby Robertson met Jack, he let him help with the Hollywood segment of the Jerry Lewis telethon, which aired from Las Vegas over KTTV. Robby was an audience warm-up man. Jack was to circulate with other volunteers, carrying a plastic box for donations. The show had been going on for a few hours when Jack, as usual ogling women, spotted a Pacific Telephone volunteer.

"Look at the legs!" he said to Robby, asking him to introduce them. The woman's name was Jeannette Houtz.

Jeannette followed the guest-relations man down some stairs, then along a tangle of dark corridors as the echoes of band music, applause, and raised voices followed them and receded. She was flattered to be invited backstage and did not know that a man named Jack Murray had been watching her.

In the greenroom the distant sounds from the show gave an intimacy and gaiety to the party of people gathered there. They'd been working hard, a small battalion of volunteers, in an almost combatlike atmosphere that lent a giddiness to this moment of relaxation. It was the first break they'd taken in hours. Everyone was punchy.

The group looked up expectantly when Jeannette came in. As Robby introduced her, she noticed that one of the men had an unusual accent. He was no Paul Newman, but he was no dog, either. He had charisma. Whenever she took a sip of wine or crossed her legs, Jeannette felt his eyes boring into her back. He didn't say anything. He just listened intently as she regaled the group with tales about her days as a marine. This always got a reaction. A woman of twenty-five with a Modigliani neck and wide eyes did not fit anyone's preconception of the military.

After a drink or two, Jeannette was still enjoying herself, but she had to get back to the phones. She turned to the man with the accent. He was the only person in the room not engaged in conversation and she was afraid of getting lost on the way back to the soundstage.

"Could you show me how to get back upstairs, please?" she asked. Her voice was demure.

Jack Murray agreed. In the early morning, as the phones quieted down, he told Jeannette that he had been a star in Australia but had had terrible luck in America. After a singing engagement at a local Hilton Hotel, he explained, his manager had absconded with the profits, forcing him into a behind-the-scenes career in television.

Jeannette thought that was a shame, but still she was impressed with Jack. Just three months before, her widowed mother had died of cancer. Jeannette, who had nursed her through her illness, had felt empty afterward. "Where's my someone?" she had actually heard herself say out loud one day. Now she was beginning to think that that someone might be Jack Murray. The thought frightened her, and she made a point of telling him that she did not plan ever to marry.

"Neither do I," said Jack, who claimed to have been married once in Australia but refused to talk about it. "The past is past," he said then and would always say later. "This is here and now."

When the telethon ended, Jack and Jeannette left together, telling each other they were going out to breakfast. On the way they stopped at Jeannette's apartment so that she could change. Instead, Jack followed her into the bedroom, where they made love.

The Wednesday evening after the telethon, Jeannette sat in the audience at a Hollywood comedy club watching Jack sing "I'd Rather Die Young." As he glided into "I Can't Help Falling in Love with You," a spotlight shone on her.

"Will you marry me?" Jack cried from the stage, while Jeannette blushed and the audience erupted in cheers.

"When?" Jeannette shouted, not believing that Jack was serious.

Anyway, how could she have said no? Jack was a dreamboat, she thought. And with his accent and indefatigable sexual appetite, he seemed completely different from her cold, naval officer father.

There had been three girls and two boys in the Houtz family, and Jeannette's dad used to hold bedroom inspections. He had worn his uniform and white gloves to run his fingers along the shelves and tables. If there was a speck of dust, a child was grounded. If Dad, who drank, couldn't bounce a quarter on the small beds, he tore the beds apart. If the children didn't eat their peas at the dinner table, he whacked them. If they did eat their peas but reached for more without asking, he smacked their hands with a knife.

To keep the peace, Jeannette had been obedient and neat, but still she got a dislocated shoulder once from being banged against the wall. When she dropped a plate one day as she and her sister set the table, they got their heads knocked together and Jeannette got a concussion. Their father told the children he was raising them to be marines. Which Jeannette had become.

Some family members thought that her dad had killed himself at the age of forty-two because he couldn't recover from the trauma of fighting in the Second World War. He had been on a submarine in the Pacific three days out of Pearl Harbor on his way to join the USS *Arizona* when it was bombed. He had lost friends and never got over the guilt of being a survivor.

Jeannette was twelve when he died. But it had not been until her mother's death that she was able to put the pieces of her life's puzzle together. Her father had seen his children as his possessions, she realized. She had been an abused child, and she decided that she would never let anyone raise a finger to any children she might have.

Later on during the week that Jack proposed, Jeannette invited him to go with her to Las Vegas. She had won a free trip for two through her telephone-company bowling league.

Jack accepted. "We'll get married there," he said.

Yeah, right, Jeannette thought.

Ten days after they met, Jack and Jeannette were married in a tiny, glittering wedding chapel. Diane Robertson told Robby that she thought Jeannette was marrying because she wanted children. Robby knew that Jack had fallen for Jeannette, but he suspected he was marrying to get a green card. At that moment Robby felt particularly sour about Jack. During the telethon, he had walked into a back room, where he discovered Jack with four other men splitting a pile of cash they had collected from the studio audience.

Robby had stared. "Shove the goddamn money back in the boxes," he said.

"We're just taking a few bucks. No one'll miss it," Jack said. He was holding several hundred dollars himself and he held out a fistful of bills to Robby.

Robby's stomach turned. Of course he didn't take the money, and he made Jack put it back. But because Jack was his friend, he didn't report him.

3

In 1911, SHORTLY BEFORE THE SHEEP FARMS AND WHEAT FIELDS OF the San Fernando Valley began to give way to orange and walnut groves and midwestern settlers, and two years before Owens Valley water began its more than two-hundred-mile journey south to irrigate the dust, someone dreamed of building in the newly created town of Van Nuys a boulevard named Sherman Way. It cost half a million dollars and was meant to resemble Mexico City's Paseo de La Reforma. Miles of grand palm trees were imported to line sidewalks dotted with tiny, tile-roofed stucco bungalows and shops, which by the 1970s, with the exception of an occasional stubborn holdout, had given way to pseudo–Cape Cod, Moroccan, and Bauhaus-styled apartment buildings and condominiums.

If in its early days Van Nuys was known as "the Town that Started Right," nearly seventy years later it could be described as little more than a disappointment. Something had gone wrong— although on paper everything looked fine. More than half of the houses in the by now twenty-square-mile suburb were worth over $100,000. But in summer, the Santa Monica Mountains to the south and the rocky Santa Susana range to the north were likely to be obscured by a pale shroud of smog that drained the community of what little color it had to start with. In winter, the winds kicked up enough to uncover the sometimes snow-tipped northern hills.

16

But they were prone to carry with them south to Sherman Way the unmistakable whiff of paint from the General Motors plant just north of the railroad tracks.

After marrying, Jeannette and Jack Murray had lived in the sleepy little town of Azusa, east of Pasadena. In June of 1974, when a job opened in Las Vegas for the Channel 11 game show "Dealer's Choice," Robby Robertson offered Jack the job. Jack accepted. Now he was Jack "Aussie" Murray, audience coordinator, alternating two-week shifts between Los Angeles and Nevada, where he was supposed to work the casino lines offering game-show tickets.

But soon after their first anniversary, with Jeannette pregnant and about to go on maternity leave, Jack lost the job. A so-called friend of his had offered to do it for less, he told Jeannette. Robby Robertson never had the heart to tell her that Jack had been such an overbearing pain in the ass, and had done so little work, that he was fired.

Briefly, Jack became a parts manager for the Schaefer ambulance service. Then, tipped off by a friend, he applied for the manager's job at the Valerio Gardens apartment house in Van Nuys. The pay was only $750 a month. But it included utilities and free rent for a large two-bedroom apartment opening onto a swimming pool. He could expect frequent raises, and he could make his own hours to take off for singing auditions. Jack accepted the position, and he and Jeannette moved in to the complex just north of Sherman Way two weeks after their daughter, Jessica, was born in January of 1975.

Baby Jessica won the Supreme Countess prize in the Burbank Beautiful Baby contest and the Murrays kept a picture of her in their Valerio Gardens living room, a large crown wobbling on her tiny head. Two years later, when Bryan Murray was born, Jack gave up his dream of singing professionally. Nights on the road and in cheap hotels had lost their allure.

The country was at the beginning of an immigration boom, and Valerio Gardens seemed to be at the forefront of it. In all but the worst weather, groups of young men with bandannas and cynically drooping eyelids sat on the fence in front of the apartments. Behind them sprawled five buff-colored, graffiti-spattered buildings. Hundreds of Vietnamese, Latino, Cambodian, and Anglo children ran screaming up and down the driveway, dodging cars and waiting for the sound of the ice-cream truck that played a quavering version of "Yankee Doodle."

Jack's first task had been planting flowers in the flower beds.

When children lopped their heads off, he planted more. He also helped new residents find furniture and appliances and held the building's owners at bay when they demanded large security deposits. With his toolbox and his gun—registered to Jeannette, because he had his green card but not his citizenship—he prowled Valerio Gardens like a colonial administrator overseeing his territory. To Jack it was "my building," and its residents, mostly refugees and illegal aliens, were "my people." In return, the Vietnamese pleased him by calling him "Mr. Jack." And by 1979, as long as Jack Murray's striped Chevy van with the kangaroo decal was in its parking space, the subjects in his small protectorate knocked on the door to ask for financial or domestic advice.

Robby and Diane Robertson, who visited Valerio Gardens, were appalled. The man had squandered his talent for the pleasure of being in control of the pettiest of empires. Jack had also found another arena in which to be a star: the Little Nashville Club on Sherman Way.

Anyone driving east on the boulevard would notice that the giant palm trees grew sparser and disappeared altogether to be replaced by telephone poles at Woodman Avenue. Past the old folks' home on the right, Sherman Way formed a bridge over a tributary of the Los Angeles River, which in the early part of the century had cascaded, teeming with steelhead trout, over boulders toward downtown Los Angeles, fourteen miles southeast. Now, a scattering of pigeons, joined by sea gulls that had strayed twenty miles inland, pecked nervously at the wash bed's trickle of brown water. U-Rent Furniture was on the left not far from U-Save Auto Parts. Further east a dusty man squatted by the curb each day until dusk selling plastic bags of oranges.

Little Nashville sat back in a miniature shopping center on the south side of the street. Machine-shop foremen and their workers came at lunchtime for the tender $4 steak sandwiches, cold Coors, and Conway Twitty and Merle Haggard on the jukebox. At night, the regulars, mostly single, arrived in cowboy hats and boots to trundle each other around the dance floor while Little Nashville's owner, Johnnie White, played steel guitar and sang in front of a Confederate flag about being an Okie from Muskogee.

When they heard Jack Murray sing, people stopped dancing. His latest nickname was "the Australian Cowboy," and his voice was so pure and strong that every woman in the club felt as if Jack were singing just to her.

Now four and two, Jessica and Bryan were golden-haired, blue-eyed, and unusually beautiful. But Jack was beginning to seem more and more like Jeannette's father. Rather than a family, the Murrays resembled some obscure vaudeville act: The One and Only Jack Murray and His Three Possessions.

At the Little Nashville Club's Sunday baseball games, everybody's kids played in the dirt while Jack nagged Jessica and Bryan to stay neat. Jack smacked two-year-old Bryan on the stomach to make him stand up straight, saying he wanted him to be like a little soldier. When the family went to restaurants, the children were not allowed to spill anything or raise their voices. Jeannette sat trying to keep them clean and quiet while Jack got on with his meal.

It fed Jack's ego to leave the house with Jeannette on his arm, dressed in a short skirt with her full violet eye makeup on. But Jack didn't worry about Jeannette's ego. He liked leggy blondes and didn't hesitate to say so. Jeannette, enviably leggy, had brown hair, which Jack continually urged her to bleach. At last, exasperated, Jeannette settled on having her hair streaked.

"The blond part is for you," she said, "and the brown is for me."

Early in their marriage, Jeannette had realized that he had chosen a partner with even more nervous energy than she had.

"My God. Can't we stay home?" she had begged Jack. But if Jack did stay home, he couldn't stay still. If he wasn't stripping wallpaper he was putting new washers in all the faucets. He changed his clothes several times a day, freshening himself in between with a splash of Pierre Cardin cologne and a clean pair of socks under his cowboy boots.

At first Jeannette had bragged to her friends that Jack could keep going all night in bed, insisting that she be satisfied. Eventually she would yell, "I'm satisfied. I'm satisfied. Now can we get some sleep?"

Gratifying as it was that Jack seemed to want her so often and for so long, by the time Jessica and Bryan had arrived and Jeannette was rising at five-thirty to get herself to Pacific Telephone—and the children to their expensive little preschool so that they could rise above Valerio Gardens—Jeannette would have welcomed a little dampening of his ardor. The trouble was, she could rarely say no to Jack with any conviction.

Eventually an exhausted Jeannette made a pact with her husband. On weeknights Jack could go out to the Masquers or the

Playboy Club on the Sunset Strip and to Little Nashville. She would stay home and join him on weekends at Nashville to dance and socialize.

Soon after marrying, Jeannette had wondered if Jack was unfaithful. She hadn't seriously begun to worry until she was pregnant with Bryan. The pregnancy was difficult and one night she'd had to be rushed to the hospital to save the baby. Later she found out that Jack had had another woman at the apartment while she was gone.

Jeannette blamed his attitude on his Australian values. Jack just had a roving eye, that was all.

Discussing it among themselves, some of the Little Nashville regulars were more blunt. Jack's eyes had nothing to do with it. The man had a permanently stiff dick.

One of the club bartenders came right out with it one night. She told Jeannette that Jack had adopted redneck American values.

"They think what the wife doesn't know won't hurt her," the bartender said.

Because of his temper and the rumors of other women, Jeannette took the children and left Jack. Once she stayed with Robby and Diane, and once, after Jack broke her elbow, she checked into a motel. Both times Jack found her. At the motel, while the children watched, he sang "I Can't Help Falling in Love with You." Jeannette's resolve crumbled, as it always did. It was just like at Christmastime when Jack sang "My Way," then segued into "Silent Night." Tears sprang into Jeannette's eyes and she couldn't see straight, even after six Christmases.

After Jeannette's broken elbow, Jack's Masquers Club friend, Red Hippler, spoke to him. If he ever hurt his wife again, Red warned, he and a couple of the Nashville bartenders would go after him. Jack still became angry when he got drunk. But after Red's talk he hit the wall instead of Jeannette.

Leaving Jack seemed impossible to Jeannette. She would need more than a thousand dollars for rent and security deposits on a new place and she never seemed to be able to save enough. Jack had expensive taste in disco shirts and pants, not to mention his continuing propensity for losing at late-night poker games.

If she left him, he threatened, he would steal the children from school and take them to Australia.

"You'll be at work, you'll come home, and we'll be gone," he said.

Jeannette was trapped and she knew it. But at least there was still Jack's prowess in bed. He came at her when she was furious with him and still he managed to get her aroused, even if he had to sing to her to do it.

When it rained in Van Nuys, the intersections along Valerio Street flooded within minutes. In January 1979, the rain fell from a pale, dirty sky, and plumes of water made a wake behind a taxi that turned into the driveway of the Valerio Gardens complex. Carol Bundy, on her way to drop off some cartons at her new apartment, couldn't see the rain through the taxi windows. Sometimes she could see shapes. Sometimes she could see dark and light. But mostly what she could count on seeing was a gray haze. She had been told by an opthalmologist that she was going blind.

Carol had been to Valerio Gardens before, sent by the nuns at a shelter for battered women. They had said the manager, Jack Murray, was known to be kind, and he had shown her an upstairs apartment that Carol had liked. She had sensed cheap carpeting underfoot, but with what little vision she had left, she had been able to tell that the place was bright—she needed the light—with good-sized bedrooms for her and her two little boys and a long balcony off the living room. Preparing her sensitive nine-year-old, Chris, and five-year-old, David, nicknamed Spike, for the fact that they would be doing now without a back garden as well as without their father, Carol had made plans to move in and already had left some boxes of toys and clothes.

She was a plump, motherly looking woman of thirty-six with heavy glasses and cropped brown hair. Now she paid the taxi driver and thanked him in her high, girlish voice, which sounded as if it had been stopped somewhere in adolescence. She knocked on the manager's door to let him know she was there with more belongings. The door opened, and the man who before had seemed so courteous told her, sounding officious, that without her permission he'd moved her to a different apartment downstairs.

It was less than two weeks since she had left her husband. Though Carol liked being dominated by men, she wanted that to be her choice. She was not ready to let another man push her around quite this soon. Because of her eyesight, she'd had to give up her job as a licensed vocational nurse at the Motion Picture and Television Fund Hospital, which catered to film personnel and actors. Her husband, Grant, also a nurse, had panicked and told her he wasn't going to support her if she was sitting around the house all day. When he came at her with his fists, an effeminate man but still threatening through the haze of blindness, Carol had grabbed the boys and escaped from her pretty little bungalow on Enadia Way, a west Van Nuys street lined with spruce and palm trees.

The other apartment was next door to the manager's and felt dark and oppressive to Carol. As she left, she stepped in a puddle in front of the doorstep, making her even more bad-tempered. Well, that's just great, she thought. I'm going to be living next to the manager and his family and he's going to know every move I make.

"Please put me back in the other apartment," she said.

Jack Murray moved her back upstairs. Still, he seemed arrogant, aggressive, and unpleasant to Carol. But her feelings would change.

A couple of weeks after she moved in, the sliding closet doors in the boys' room kept leaping off their track. Carol called Jack Murray to come and fix them. He arrived with his tools, sat down and lit a cigarette, then asked for a beer. She didn't have any beer. Would wine do? Wine indeed was fine.

Carol sipped hers carefully. To add to her problems, she was a diabetic and wasn't supposed to drink alcohol.

The wine loosened Jack's tongue. He had found what he always sought—a new audience for his old stories. Before setting to work fixing the closets, he spun Carol a few romantic tales of his days in the Australian army and his tour in Vietnam. Today Jack had also been a mercenary. Carol, intrigued, pressed for more biographical details, which Jack was more than happy to provide. He had been a famous singer and songwriter in Australia, he said, warbling a few notes to demonstrate.

Carol could see little more of Jack Murray than a blurry outline, but she began to revise her previous negative opinion of him. He was talented, and she liked to think of herself as artistic. Perhaps Jack only wanted to kill time, but Carol, blind, newly poor, and at the lowest point in a decidedly difficult life, was flattered that he seemed to want to kill it with her. The attention perked her up and she looked forward to seeing him again. When she did see him, in the Valerio Gardens office, she told him she was sorry he was married.

"That's okay," said Jack. "I fool around."

A few days later, Jack was back. Carol confided in him about Grant Bundy hitting her and belittling her. She tried to make light of her depression over her blindness but couldn't pull it off, and

Jack Murray seemed sympathetic. Already he had helped her find furniture and appliances the way he always did for new tenants. Now he wondered if she might be eligible for disability payments. Could he make an appointment for her with Social Security? He'd be happy to drive her there. And why didn't she get a second opinion about her sight? Maybe it was not as bad as she had been led to believe.

Something akin to lust began to stir in Carol Mary Bundy's lower belly. By Jack Murray's third visit, she thoughtfully provided beer. But by then, they were not about to waste time with preliminaries. They fell into bed and Carol Bundy fell into what at the time she decided was love.

Carol was careful to keep her affair from the children. She didn't think she was the world's best mother, but she wasn't the worst either. Sentimentally, she thought that she had loved every stage with her kids, from the moment they discovered their toes until the time they began discovering the world. Chris and Spike, she had rationalized, made anxious by their father's occasional violent outbursts, had wanted her to leave him. But now that she had, they were complaining and defiant.

Feeling as out of control of her life as she had at any time in the past, Carol found herself shrieking at the boys. She didn't like herself for it. No wonder they were unhappy: the Valerio Gardens children fought with each other and stole toys. To get to their new school safely in the mornings, Chris and Spike gathered in a pack with twenty of the gentler children. Together they sneaked along a ditch to protect themselves from older kids who might attack them on the main route along Sherman Way.

The boys felt the loss of their safe little neighborhood with its summertime corn stand and nearby park. But Grant had worked such long hours at his nursing job that he had not had much time for his children. Although he was often affectionate, at times he had been cruel to them. Once he gave Chris a black eye, and Carol, who believed in what she thought of as "normal spankings," had spent the afternoon in bed crying. Another time, he raised welts on Chris's back when he hit him with the track from his Hot Wheels set.

Still, the boys missed their father. They missed dinner at McDonald's on demand. They also missed riding in Carol's brown Honda, which they had nicknamed Charlie Brown and which she had to sell now because of her poor vision.

Carol's world was closing in on her as well. No one had brought the former Carol Mary Peters up to expect any particular rewards. But no one had brought her up to expect blindness, either.

Later, when Carol reminisced about her childhood, she always at first focused on the good. Like her brother Gene, seven years older, and her sister, Vicky, three years younger, she would have trouble facing the reality of her past.

Her father, Charles, had been an alcoholic who moved his family from state to state for his work as a movie-theater troubleshooter. Gladys, her mother, was a stand-in for tap-dancing star Ruby Keeler, and later became a hairdresser.

When Carol was a preschooler, the family lived briefly in Los Angeles. Her brother Gene was in fourteen movies, and in *Miracle on 34th Street* Carol sat on Santa Claus's lap. She had to be dragged screaming from the studio lot where, she thought, she happily would have stayed for the rest of her life.

Money was short. Always at Christmas, though, the children found notes on the tree that led them on treasure hunts. One year Vicky found a bicycle in the garage and Carol found her own Muntz television. When she lost her front teeth, her father dipped a doll's feet in mud and left fairy footprints in a trail from the window to the side of her bed.

Years afterward, Carol would talk about watching the deep red glow of her mother's cigarettes sketch patterns in the dark as Gladys Peters spun bedtime fairy stories. Carol could sense her mother's magic as much as she could sense her own lack of it. Gladys, she thought, was beautiful, and Vicky took after Gladys. Even Vicky realized that Carol, a gorgeous baby but a bulky and awkward child, fell short of Gladys's ideal of a daughter.

When Carol was eight, Gladys cut her off, for some reason that Carol was never able to fathom or remember. The family was living in Louisiana. On a swelteringly hot day, Gladys was inside the house. For what seemed like hours, Carol ran around banging on the doors and windows trying to get in.

"Go away, little girl. You don't live here. You aren't my little girl," Gladys called from inside.

Carol had cried until she hiccuped. She would admit crying over the incident into her twenties. At last she ran two miles to her father's work. Charles Peters brought her home and fought into the night with Gladys. After that, Carol thought, she did not exist for her mother.

But she was the stars in her father's eyes, Carol always insisted: Charles Peters's favorite. And if her sister, Vicky, didn't agree, the truth of the matter would have been hard to define. As a grown woman, Carol would admit that nothing touched her. Where other people saw ugliness, she was able to blot out what she did not wish to see and instead see only beauty.

Affectionately, Gladys and Charles had called Carol "Petunia" while she was in the womb. But from the beginning, Gene thought she was a demon baby. When the family brought her home from the hospital, the car door slammed on his hand and he decided it was Carol's fault. When she and Vicky were little, he buried all their dolls in the sand. Their heads came off and Carol was grief-stricken. Gene never stopped seeing his sister from the vantage point of a jealous seven-year-old. He would detest her into adulthood.

All the Peters children were intelligent, and their parents planned family vacations to coincide with what they were studying in school. When Carol took American history, the family visited the Smithsonian in Washington and drove through the quaint towns of New England. That was why it was difficult for Carol to think of herself as abused.

She would remember that Gladys was not allowed to administer any beatings. If once allowed to take belt in hand, her mother would go berserk and have to be pulled off the children. But Vicky would think that Carol had detached herself from that, too. As a child, Vicky had watched Carol sit in a wing chair, calmly reading a comic book as Gladys beat her fiercely about the face and body with a belt. When it was over, Carol got up and grinned and went to her room.

Charles Peters demanded complete control over his family, and Gladys kept a watchful eye on Charles. But because he had a lighter hand than his wife, in Carol's mind there was a clear distinction between whippings and beatings: whippings were with a hand or a paddle, left nothing more than welts, and were necessary discipline. Beatings were administered with a belt. They drew blood or caused bruises and constituted abuse. Her father had made fairy footprints on the wall and had not beaten her but only whipped her, never using more force than the offense required; therefore most of the time Carol did not consider herself an abused child, but a loved one.

As an astigmatic and walleyed nine-year-old, Carol was fitted for her first pair of glasses. Now she felt like the dog in the family even more than she had before. Her hair was lank and brown. Her body was like a dumpling. At school, the children called her Miss

Encyclopedia and Four Eyes. She slunk around, her nose buried in a dictionary, which she read every day for pleasure. Through her thick, round glasses, Carol also read science fiction, which transported her to worlds on the surface more alien, but decidedly less threatening, than her own.

At Valerio Gardens, Carol had found yet another alien environment to conquer and she had made an instinctive choice. She had attached herself to Jack Murray, who, in those limited surroundings, gave off an aura of power.

At first Jeannette Murray had felt pleased that her husband was running Carol to her doctor's appointments and the Social Security office. Poor blind thing, alone in the world with two little boys, thought Jeannette, who in spite of her sympathy wasn't altogether sure that Carol needed that white cane. Chris and Spike seemed like nice, polite kids and Carol appeared to be a good, concerned mother, if somewhat overindulgent, Jeannette and Linda, the assistant manager's wife, agreed. She was intelligent, with a raunchy sense of humor, but aside from that appeared to be simply the stereotypical Valley housewife down on her luck.

When Jack told Jeannette that Carol claimed to have been a prostitute up in Oregon, Jeannette scoffed.

"God. She'd have to pay the guys," she said.

After a couple of months, Jeannette Murray began to get irritated. Carol hung around Jack all the time. If he was working on an apartment, there Carol would be, standing silently. When he was in the office on rent day, so was Carol. Perhaps it should have seemed ominous to Jeannette, but she was no more than annoyed.

"What's she doing there?" she asked Jack about Carol. "What does she want?"

"I don't know. She just sits there," Jack said.

In the driveway, talking to Linda, Jeannette sometimes watched Carol tap with her cane down the steps that Jack had painted red to help her see them. She walked to his empty parking space and, discovering the van wasn't there, tapped her way upstairs again, where she sat on a chair on her balcony, waiting and listening for the sound of his van. Once Jack returned, the phone calls began. The dishwasher wasn't working. Could Jack come up and fix it? There was something wrong with the light switch. Would he mind? One of the boys had dropped a GI Joe down the toilet. Did he have a plunger?

If Jeannette hadn't known that Jack liked blondes with legs, she might have thought some funny business was going on. Luckily, though, Jack had never hankered after overweight brunettes with limp hair, hoot-owl glasses, and stretch pants. Carol Bundy had a crush on Jack that bordered on an obsession. But she was not the first woman to be interested in him, and at least she was short, fat, and harmless. When Carol showed up one day with her mousy hair streaked blond just like Jeannette's, Jeannette stifled her irritation.

At Little Nashville, the regulars' nicknames ranged from Bozo and Dirty Eddie to Jennie the Jew Broad. There was even Token Nigger (a real nice guy, everyone took care to point out). They called Carol Bundy "the Blind Bat." She showed up so often and made so little attempt to cover up her infatuation with Jack Murray that whenever he sang one of his favorite songs, "Release Me, and Let Me Love Again," people nudged each other. When Jeannette was there, they gave her covert glances.

Everyone at Little Nashville knew about Jack, his sweet talk and his one-night stands in the Chevy van. It seemed almost a compulsion with him to leave the club with a woman on his arm. But for the most part, the regulars had always tried to protect Jeannette as much as Jeannette tried to protect herself.

"Jack's an asshole, Jeannette," Patti, one of the bartenders, unbent enough to say one day, standing in front of the tiny American flag and the plaster bust of Elvis and the club's baseball trophies. "But he's a likable asshole. And he isn't any more of an asshole than the other assholes who come in here."

Ron, another bartender, had a different point of view. He didn't find Jack that likable. Underneath the macho pose, Jack Murray was a coward, Ron thought. If there was a fight, the Australian Cowboy ran the other way. But the Blind Bat seemed oblivious to his faults. She loved the man. She followed him like a whipped dog, and Jack Murray treated her like shit.

That summer and fall during the year of Carol Bundy, Jeannette was not sure about Jack's affair but she *was* sure that as much as she had loved Jack, she was now beginning to hate him. As long as she hated him, she reasoned, their marriage wasn't over, because she still had feelings. Where there were feelings, good or bad, they could work things out.

Carol took ten steps down, glimpsing dim slashes of shadowy red on the apartment stairs. At the bottom she turned right, then took a few more steps to Jack's parking space. The van wasn't there. But she knew that when Jack returned he would come to see her.

Sometimes he called from an empty apartment that he was preparing for new tenants. Sometimes he sent one of the Valerio Gardens children to collect her. As casually as she could, Carol would walk over, and within minutes they would be in bed. After Jack drove her to her doctor's visits, they made love in the red interior of the Chevy van. "Made love" was perhaps not quite the way to describe it: Carol found Jack sexually unimaginative and interested more than anything in his own pleasure, which meant being on the receiving end of a great deal of oral attention. Luckily, this was Carol's specialty.

Of course, Carol had needs of her own: specifically, half an hour to an hour of oral or manual stimulation if she were to have one of her own infrequent orgasms. If she expressed her needs, Jack lectured her on Australian culture. There men were men and women were put in their place. Jack's hand was always ready to push her head down toward what he seemed to think Carol's place was: with her mouth hovering in the vicinity of his penis.

One of the Little Nashville regulars criticized her one day to Jack, saying how unattractive she was.

"Yes," said Jack. "But she gives great head."

Jack was so kind to her, Carol thought. One day she apologized to him for her breasts, which she considered too large to be appealing. He thought for a moment before he said, "Yes, but you have pretty nipples." It was one of the nicest things a man had ever said to her.

When Carol considered herself, at least, she was under few illusions. Generally she felt average to dumpy-looking, blossoming when the temperature or circumstances were right. In the early months of her relationship with Jack Murray, unable to see herself clearly in a mirror, she began to feel beautiful. Knowing that it was a cliché, she told herself that she glowed. In wild moments, with time hanging heavily and with no focus to her life, she longed to have Jack's baby. But she was fantasizing, as she often did. After Spike, she had been surgically sterilized.

Lying there spent, following one of their assignations, Jack managed to muster the energy to tell Carol that he would like to borrow some money. He wanted to get his singing career going again, and he hoped Carol might be able to help. Carol loved his voice. His range was extraordinary, dipping from a sweet tenor to a deep bass. If it hadn't been for Jack, she told herself, she would not

have discovered that she was entitled to retroactive disability benefits and a housekeeper funded by the state.

Her image of herself was of a guileless, warm, and giving person.
"Stupid me. Good-hearted me," was often the way Carol described
herself. As a warm and giving person, she would happily lend Jack
small amounts of money. There was, too, behind these loans, an
unspoken desire to be in control.

But soon Carol began to feel insecure. She was the other woman,
and because Jeannette Murray lived across the driveway, Carol
couldn't pretend that her rival didn't exist. Indirectly, she instigated
a discussion with Jack about marriage.

"Do you think we'll ever be together?" she asked, unable actually
to bring herself to say the word "marriage."

Marriage, she heard Jack say, would be a couple of years down
the line after their respective divorces were final. Separations were
expensive and he and Jeannette had no money to spare.

Carol, who generally misread people's intentions and was given
to great leaps of imagination that fed her fantasies, believed him.
After all, he had demonstrated his love. If he hadn't insisted, she
would not have obtained a second opinion about her eyesight. At
the Foundation for the Junior Blind she discovered that the condition an ophthalmologist had told her was untreatable retinopathy
was simple cataracts. Her sight could be surgically restored.

In June of 1979, when Jack drove her to Valley Presbyterian Hospital for her first operation, Carol felt as if she were being given
back her life. Then, when her ex-husband, Grant, began making
noises about selling the house and it looked as if Carol was about
to get a royal screwing over, Jack introduced her to a real-estate
agent named Gloria. The woman thought there was something odd
about Carol and was convinced that she overheard her say something about killing. Nevertheless, Gloria did not drop her as a client
and told Carol she could expect to receive about $25,000 as her
share of the profits once her house was sold.

Jack was taking care of her, and Carol enjoyed the secret pleasure
of thinking that she was closer to him than his own wife was. At
first Carol had liked Jeannette, then jealously she decided she was
too skinny and a bit snaky.

Carol thought she was handling the affair well. Jack had asked
her to be discreet, so she had learned not to go looking for him or
to hang around the office too much. Once in a while, when he
worked on his van, he allowed her to come out and socialize and
bring him a cold Budweiser. Sometimes he phoned her and she

would walk the long block to Sherman Way and Van Nuys Boulevard, where Jack would pick her up in the van for a coffee date followed by sex.

One of their most treasured evenings was in August. Carol still wasn't driving, so she took the bus all the way into Hollywood and back to buy tickets for *Apocalypse Now*. It was a forty-five minute journey one-way, but Jack, haunted by his memories of Vietnam, wanted to see the movie. The same evening they returned in the van to the Cinerama Dome theater. After the show they made love in the parking lot, thrilled by the possibility of discovery as the lights from other cars flickered through the gaps in the Chevy's shades.

Because of her diabetes, Carol's moods had always fluctuated wildly. When she was depressed, which was often, because Jack didn't seem any closer to leaving Jeannette, she slopped around in old pants and tops and didn't bother much with herself. To push Jack into action, she increased the number of presents she gave him.

In October, Carol had her second eye operation, for which Jack drove her to the hospital and picked her up. Now that she could see again she realized that she was not quite so glowing and beautiful as her affair with Jack had made her feel. She had no waistline, but her hands and ankles were slim and pretty. Her neck was short, her mouth was small and narrow, and her nose spread a little too broadly across her round face. But Jack, she found out, was possessed of as much charisma as she had sensed before. He may not have been classically handsome, but he had a rugged appeal.

Carol's vision would always be distorted, but she was on the way to an independent life again. Her retroactive disability payments had amounted to about $2,500, and when escrow closed on the Enadia Way house she and Grant had owned, her share of the profits came to the $25,000 her real-estate agent had anticipated. With the monthly checks that had been arriving from disability and welfare because of her vision—improving but still hazy—Carol felt rich. Now the woman who always thought she belonged in the front of the cavalry yelling "Charge!" with Teddy Roosevelt was able to go on the biggest cash spending spree of her life.

During her marriage, Carol's credit-card extravagance had caused problems. One Christmas a few years before, she had bought $700 worth of toys and clothes for the boys. The sum was around a month's take-home pay from her LVN salary. As she watched Chris catch his first glimpse of a black Huffy bike and Spike pounce on a Tyco train set, Carol felt it was worth it. But there were so many gifts, the boys grew restless and bored. By nightfall, gaily wrapped presents still lay under the tree, and her husband was annoyed.

Carol had been in the kitchen. From his chair in front of the television, Grant called out that he wanted to see her credit cards. Carol fished them from her purse and handed them to him. He cut them in little pieces, first Penney's, then Ward's, then MasterCharge. Carol wept. Christmas day had fallen far short of her plan to evoke the magical holidays of her childhood.

Some children might have thought that the magic ended on the day they were locked out of the house by their mother.

Even later, though, Gladys humiliated Carol, Vicky thought. When Carol got her period, her mother stood on the front porch as Carol left for school. In a voice loud enough for the world to hear, Gladys yelled, "Today you are a woman!"

But the turning point for Carol had come on a hot July afternoon when she was fourteen. Her mother was polishing the floor at home in Garden Grove when she stopped and took to her bed, saying she felt ill.

"Phone your father at work," she called to Carol. "Tell him to come home." Her voice sounded weak.

Soon Carol's father arrived and took Gladys to the doctor.

After a couple of hours he returned alone.

"Your mother's dead," he said. Gladys had suffered a heart attack.

The first episode of sexual abuse happened that very night. In an extraordinary stroke of verisimilitude, the movie *Sentimental Journey* played on television. It was about a dying woman who adopts a daughter as companion to her husband.

Vicky and Carol, who knew nothing of sex until that night, would tell different stories. Both heard Charles saying that he did not wish to sleep alone. Instinctively, neither girl wanted to go to her father's bed. They played a game of "Skunk," with the loser to make the sacrifice. Vicky lost, and was initiated into oral sex. Her father, Vicky thought, died on the same day as her mother, and a monster came home in his place. Vicky's abuse would continue for several months.

Carol would remember her father calling her as she followed his voice into the bedroom.

"You have to take over for your mother now," he said.

31

Then Charles took her nightgown off and accomplished his goal of seducing his older daughter.

Carol, who thought Vicky was molested only once, the following night, had not understood that what Charles was doing was called oral sex. Why would he want to put his mouth there? She had cried, terrified and revolted, but he didn't stop. That night, grief over the mother she had first lost so many years before when Gladys shut her out of the house was replaced by fear and confusion.

As far as Carol would remember, for the next year her father didn't touch her, although he did expose himself to her once. Then he took her to his bed again for what she believed was the second and last time. Within eight months of Gladys's death, her father would remarry and begin humiliating Carol as well as beating her. Charles called her fat and he called her stupid, and Carol felt both those things and ashamed besides.

Gene, who had long since left home, explained later that their father drank and that Gladys had been able to hide it by telling the children that he was resting or not feeling well. Her father was a good man, Carol insisted to herself, but he did not know how to grieve or take care of his grieving children.

On the day that he sent Carol to the store to buy bread, Charles's new marriage was only a few months old. When Carol returned, the house was empty, the cat was dead behind the curtain, and her father's shotgun case lay empty in the bloodstained living room. Carol, terrified, waited until Charles appeared. He had planned to kill the whole family, he told her, starting with his wife. But she had tried to wrest the gun from him and he had caught his thumb in the gunsight, accounting for the blood in the house.

Charles was arrested, but when his wife, who soon divorced him, refused to press charges, he pleaded guilty to disturbing the peace. Carol and Vicky were sent to foster homes, then to Carol's "angry old harridan" of a grandmother in Michigan. Within a year, Charles reclaimed them from an uncle in Indiana. He drove the girls back toward California, weaving erratically on the highway as if trying to scare them.

When she was fifteen, at one of the three high schools she attended, Carol wrote an article for the school newspaper. It was titled "Being an American Citizen," and it was about wanting to be the first woman president. But in high school, she also discovered the power of flesh and her own large breasts. She buried herself in promiscuity. For the moments she spent having sex, at least she felt a glimmer of something. But high school boys—and the occasional bus driver—hurt her feelings and did not bring her sexual satisfaction.

By the time Carol dropped out of ninth grade in the wake of a false rumor that she was pregnant, she added everything up. She had been to twenty-three different schools in ten years, and always had felt the outsider.

In front of relatives one day, Vicky confronted Charles about the molestation. Carol denied that it had happened. She was dependent on her father and had to protect herself, Carol told Vicky later.

To get away from Charles, at seventeen Carol married and then left a 56-year-old man named Leonard. Leonard, Carol said, had been a drunkard and wanted her to prostitute herself. Although, if she were being honest, she would admit that she had taken small sums of money from men before she even met him.

Carol was still seventeen and the writer Richard Geis was thirty-two when they bumped into each other in the hallway of the Venice, California, apartment house where Geis lived. Geis found her a convenient companion, pathetically eager to please, but bubbling, he thought, with intelligence and wit. He also had no complaints about her large breasts. If her father hadn't made her enroll in beauty college, which she had not finished, she could have been anything she wanted to be, Geis decided.

The year Carol met Dick Geis, her father had given her a typewriter. She had decided to write a book. She got as far as page twelve. But with Geis, who wrote pornography and published the science-fiction fanzine *Psychotic*, she wrote a short story. Dick revised it for her and helped her publish in the mainstream magazine *Adam*. Carol's heroine was a policewoman who rode to work on the bus. The hero of her story was named Jack. While she lived with Geis, Carol also put out one issue of her own science-fiction fan magazine. Then she tried to become a cartoonist. She had talent but gave up.

In 1962 Charles Peters hanged himself, and Dick Geis thought Carol blamed herself for her father's suicide, as if it were her fault that he had sexually abused her. Not long after Charles's death, Carol took a creative writing course in which she developed a character named Strawberry, a fruit picker with a daughter named Virginia. Strawberry's hands bore the permanent red stains of juice from the fruit that he picked.

Carol would remember waiting until her father died to try sex with women. When she discovered that they could hurt her feelings as badly as men, she returned to her on-and-off relationship with Dick Geis, and after that was serially bisexual. If a man hurt her feelings, she ran to a woman. When the woman hurt her, she returned to men. Her problem, she knew, was that with men or women she never was one to speak up for herself. As she had been with her father, she was servile and obedient. She kept quiet, took whatever abuse was offered, and said nothing until it was too late.

Dick Geis and Carol Bundy moved to Oregon. They were living together again when he discovered that sometimes she slept with other men and took money from them. One was in his seventies and paid Carol twenty dollars plus all the books she could haul away from his bookstore to spend Thursday nights with him.

Because of her hideous childhood, Geis accused, Carol had to dirty herself. But although he was older than she was, Dick Geis would later think that he had been trapped in youth's self-centeredness. When all the terrible violence happened, he would blame himself for not urging Carol to get help for her emotional problems.

They moved back to Santa Monica. One day, as they lay on the beach, Carol asked Dick to put her through nursing school. He agreed, on the condition that she maintain good grades. At Santa Monica College, after passing her GED, Carol was class valedictorian. She took her state boards in 1968. Although Dick Geis wondered if she would ever recover from the trauma of her childhood, what worried him the most was the possibility that Carol might emulate her father and commit suicide. As an adolescent, she had tried to ingest iodine, and in her thirties, married to Grant, she indeed would make two more unsuccessful attempts on her own life.

In 1962 Carol had forever lost the chance to speak her mind to her father. But by the time she was at Valerio Gardens, recovering from her second cataract operation and coming into the money that would boost her self-esteem, the strains of the song "Sentimental Journey" still came unbidden to her mind. In that way she had of transforming fear into pleasure and ugliness into beauty, Carol had made the song one of her favorites. She found herself humming it, even though it would instantly carry her back to that night in July 1957 when she had walked unsuspectingly into her father's bedroom.

The fall of her affair with Jack, Carol spent $4,000 on Early American living-room furniture, bunk beds for the boys, and a dishwasher and side-by-side refrigerator. She bought new clothes and she visited the vast Moroccan-style beauty salon at an upscale Bullock's department store deep in the Valley, where one day she left a $100 tip for the startled electrologist. Between shampoos, because her fine hair went limp, she treated herself to comb-outs at local beauty shops. She also bought Jack a VCR and a new desk for his office.

Still believing that she and Jack would be married, on the first of November Carol opened a joint safety deposit box with him and deposited $13,000 of her remaining cash. If anything ever happened to her, Jack said, he would use the money to take care of the boys. Then he told Carol the terribly sad news. Jeannette had cancer. He would not be able to leave her until he had paid the doctor bills.

"Let me help," Carol said.

She lent Jack $10,000. And to make him jealous, she had a fling with Jeannette's twenty-three-year-old brother, Warren, to whom she confessed her love for Jack. Delighting Warren, who was always being told everything he did wrong, Carol passed on through the Valerio Gardens grapevine that Jeannette's brother was more accomplished in bed than her husband was.

"Gee, Warren," Jeannette said, an edge to her voice. "If you're better than Jack, you must be some kind of superstud."

Warren brushed her comment off. He couldn't really tell if Jeannette believed that Jack and Carol were having an affair or if she were testing him. He did know that he did not want to be the one to enlighten his sister, or mention that Carol had told him she planned to do everything possible to split Jack and Jeannette up.

One night Warren and Jack went to the Masquers for a drink. At the bar, Jack flirted with a woman, and as he and Warren left through the front door, Jack spoke.

"I may play around, but I love my wife and kids," he said.

Not long after that, Jack took Warren aside and warned him to stay away from Carol.

"She's no good for you," he said.

But Warren, pleased if he got lucky every four years, had no intention of staying away from Carol.

4

Robby and Diane Robertson were disgusted. They'd been invited to Valerio Gardens to a party at the Murrays' and it turned out to be the usual thing. Jeannette scurried around pouring drinks and keeping food on the table while Jack, gun tucked into a cowboy boot, sat playing gracious host and spinning yarns for a group of unsavory-looking men who didn't know him well enough not to believe him. The Robertsons sensed menace in the air. Jack, who had worn out his welcome on the other side of the hill in Hollywood, was hanging around with small-time Valley hoods. He was even, Robby knew, carrying around a policeman's badge to give himself the illusion of authority. It was pathetic in a man of such talent.

Earlier Jack had pulled Robby aside and told him that he had a broad on the hook who was giving him money.

"What about Jeannette?" Robby asked.

"What about her?" Jack said.

As he watched his friend that night, Robby thought that his life was going down the toilet. If Jack wasn't careful he was going to get himself killed.

The Robertsons left the party as early as they could without being rude. Later Robby phoned Jack from his house in Burbank.

"Come here any time," he said. "You're welcome. But I'm not coming there again."

After he hung up the phone, Robby wondered about the woman who was giving money to Jack. She'd have to be awfully naive to trust him.

Not long before Christmas, Carol planned a Las Vegas trip. It would be another reward for Jack to repay him for all his help—and a chance for her to spend some romantic time alone with him. She arranged for Grant to take care of the boys, and Jack told Jeannette that he had business to take care of in Santa Barbara for the owners of Valerio Gardens.

Carol did not want to be seen getting into Jack's car. She left her small blue suitcase outside her apartment and paid one of the Valerio Gardens children to intercept it and drop it off to her a couple of blocks away, where Jack picked her up.

All went smoothly. They left from Burbank airport and checked into the Continental Tower Hotel. That night they watched some seminude dancers flash their feathers and sequins. But then Jack's mood turned sour—over what, Carol was never sure. He stomped off by himself to gamble. That was the last she saw of him until it was time to catch the plane back.

It was an unusually quiet journey for Carol, generally a nonstop talker. Jack dropped her off at the corner of Sherman Way and Van Nuys Boulevard and she began to trudge home. She had been back for a few minutes when she thought about unpacking her suitcase. Oh, my Lord. She had left it in Jack's car. There was a timely pounding on the door. Who else could it be but Jeannette?

"Do you have a little blue suitcase?" She was steaming.

As long as Jeanette was suspicious, maybe being somewhat open with her would hurry things along, Carol thought. She decided to tell Jeannette that she knew about her cancer.

"I had a little cyst removed, that's all," Jeannette said.

Carol said, "What about the lump on your back?"

"I don't have a lump on my back."

Later a stunned Carol confronted Jack. It was true, he admitted. There had been no medical bills. He had used Carol's $10,000 to pay off his beloved Chevy van.

Carol, usually slow to catch up to her own anger, this time was furious. And when she complained bitterly to Jack, he told her to "get laid."

Perhaps realizing his vulnerability to Carol—he had, in effect, stolen $10,000 from her—Jack changed his approach and urged her to be patient. Just because he had lied about Jeannette's cancer, he said, that didn't mean he wasn't going to leave her. He was. They just couldn't afford it right now.

Carol, pacified, chose to believe him.

For her part, Jeannette was no longer able to deny that Jack and Carol were having an affair. She began paying a little boy a quarter a day to sift through the Dumpster behind Valerio Gardens looking for Carol's letters to Jack. In case she decided to file for divorce, Jeannette wanted evidence.

Carol wrote:

Can't you be just a little possessive? I need to know that you care enough to be "boss." Be firm with me. If you allow me a free head, I'll just manage to get into trouble again.

I don't know why, but I need to be dominated. The best sex I've ever had? Well, I suppose there are men with greater technical skills than you, but you've got a natural instinct about how to handle my body. I literally glow when you touch me.

I don't ever want to risk that for any lover, real or imaginary.

Don't EVER tell me to 'get layed.' I know your intentions were kind, but I resented it so bad that I wanted to hurt you. It's now a week later and I'm still angry. Can't we manage with a little old-fashioned faithfulness for awhile? Let me enjoy giving it. I screwed it up once with Warren. I don't want to be pushed into an affair because you think it's for my own good. When things really go sour between us . . . then I will probably fool around. But for God's sake let it be MY idea!

I want to belong to somebody (you). Not everybody.

I'm perfectly capable of screwing the entire west coast, so I don't need a push.

Yes, he's slept with Bundy, Jack finally admitted to his wife. But only because they were thrown together and because he had thought that if he made love to her, it would shut Carol up. Instead she had wanted more and more of him. But it was over now.

As the holidays approached, Carol continued to hope.

At Christmas time, she bought Jack a Seiko watch and a gold chain with his Taurus birth sign on it. She chose a doll for Jessica and a toy garage for Andrew and left them discreetly in the office, telling Jack to let the children think they were from him. With a bottle of Chanel for Men, she enclosed a card signed from the boys to Jack.

Jack promised to come over on Christmas Day. Carol waited, trying to make the best of the holiday with Chris and Spike. But knowing all the while that Jack was across the driveway with Jeannette made it too difficult. She was getting tired of waiting. How long was a woman supposed to wait?

Late in the day, she heard the sound of Jack's cough in the driveway, but he was not on the way to see her. The Chevy rumbled as it left Valerio Gardens.

Carol walked downstairs and across the courtyard, past the flowers Jack had planted. As Jeannette let her into the apartment, she thought that Carol was slightly unsteady on her feet, as if she'd had a drink.

Under the Christmas tree, Bryan slept peacefully on a white flokati rug. Jessica was in bed, her doll and Jack's cologne discarded among the litter of gifts and wrappings. There was an Australian flag on the wall. A rack near the door held Jack's collection of cowboy hats. On the coffee table, in a gilded frame, sat a new family portrait of the Murrays wearing Christmas colors.

As she settled into a love seat, Carol wobbled slightly. Jack had told Jeannette about the gifts, and, polite but cold, she thanked Carol and offered her a cup of coffee. As Carol sipped it, she told Jeannette what she wanted. She wanted Jack. She was in love with him, and she was willing to give Jeannette $1,500 if she'd let him go.

Jeannette snapped at her. "Just because you get rid of me doesn't mean you'll get Jack."

"I'll step right into your shoes," Carol said. She sounded as if she meant it.

"It's Jack's choice," Jeannette said. "He's the man. If he wants you, fine. Let me have my kids and I'll go."

That Christmas night, as Jeannette waited for Jack, she picked up the wrapping paper and gifts and put Bryan to bed. When Jack came back, Jeannette did not waste time.

"Bundy wants to pay me fifteen hundred dollars to leave you. Should I take it?" Jeannette said.

For a moment Jack just looked at her. He smelled of the Chanel for Men he had splashed on after he opened Carol's gift.

"What?" he said.

Jeannette repeated herself. "She says she's in love with you and you guys had an affair. She's sure she can step into my shoes."

Jack turned and slammed out of the house. Carol was hovering anxiously in the driveway.

"Stay out of my life," Jack yelled at her. "No woman is going to come between me and my family."

39

5

Carol pushed her way through the crowd at Little Nashville. Everyone else seemed to be part of a two-stepping couple in blue jeans and plaid shirt, and she was conspicuously dressed up and slightly out of place in her navy velveteen pants and lace-trimmed blouse.

After her scene with Jeannette three days before, she had felt depressed but had rallied for the birthday cake, ice cream, and neighbor kids at Spike's sixth-birthday party the day before. Today she'd plummeted again, which was why she had dressed extra carefully before she headed to the club to look for Jack. She hoped he would tell her that he had been putting on an act for Jeannette when he told her to stay out of his life. She also hoped that Jeannette had been lying when she said that he didn't plan to leave her to marry Carol.

Carol peered around through her big glasses. There was a festive air to the club. She squeezed a place for herself at the tinsel-trimmed bar and ordered her usual tall vodka and 7UP, short on the vodka. Suddenly, on the other side of the bar she spotted Jack dancing with Jeannette. It was easy for Carol to romanticize the Murrays' relationship as she watched Jack smile and whirl his wife around. Carol sipped carefully at her drink. She'd had more booze in the year that she'd known Jack than she'd ever had in her life.

A little buzz of warmth spread through her body from the liquor forbidden because of her diabetes. It was enough to make her feel even more sorry for herself.

As she watched her fantasy of marriage to Jack disappear into the blur of kicked-up sawdust and cigarette smoke, Carol got the uneasy feeling that someone was watching her. She glanced up at a tall blond man who wore an expensive-looking dark blue suit and tie. They were the only two in the place dressed up. It made it seem as if they were meant for each other. The man came toward her smiling. His left front tooth was chipped, giving an informal edge to the formality of the suit.

"Would you like to dance?" he asked. His voice was cultured and Carol liked the way he looked.

She said, "Yes."

He held her, and there was something soothing about it. At the same time, she knew Jack could see her and she was intensely aware of every move Jack made. See, she thought, I can get someone else.

She had never before met anyone quite as charming, Carol decided. Douglas Clark held her close but not too close. As he spoke, telling her that he was thirty-one and an engineer, he pulled back to look at her with an unusually intense gaze from pale blue eyes whose pupils were deep and dark and oddly flat. He seemed smitten. But he made no attempt at sexual advances. He didn't need to. The hypnotic tone of his voice alone was enough to make Carol's plump knees buckle.

After he bought her a drink, Douglas Clark whisked her next door to the Playtime Club for more dancing. Generally, Carol felt compelled to try and seduce every man she met. Tonight there was no opportunity. Soon Douglas Clark had to leave, apologizing because he had promised to be at a holiday party.

"I'd like to see you again," he said.

Carol read sincerity in his eyes and gave him her phone number. Later, she tried to remember what they had talked about. She remembered that there had not been one boring minute.

A few days later she was scurrying around the kitchen at Valerio Gardens when the phone rang. It was Douglas Clark, wondering if he could come over.

Her children were there, Carol told him. She was cooking their dinner. That was all right, Douglas Clark said. He would join them. They had a companionable meal after which Doug played Battleship with Chris and Spike in the living room. Later, the boys,

41

suffering from a lack of fathering, climbed on his lap to be cuddled. Then at bedtime Douglas Clark tucked them in and, at their bedroom door, put his arm around Carol's waist.

"By the way," he said, "I'm spending the night with your mother."

Twice in the past Carol had been careless and her sons had caught her engaged in sex, once in an episode of domination. She had, though, succeeded in shielding them from her affair with Jack Murray.

As Chris giggled and put his head under the sheets, Carol deferred to Douglas Clark's openness and took him into her bedroom. That first night he touched and stroked and murmured, his voice again as much an aphrodisiac to Carol Bundy as the glittering of his eyes. Making love with him, she would decide later, was the most superb sexual experience she had ever had.

There was, though, one awkward moment when Douglas Clark apologized for the size of his penis. It was unusually small for a six-foot-tall man.

"When you're not as well endowed, you compensate," he said defensively.

Much to Carol Bundy's further delight, he did. They made love most of the night, with him whispering to her how beautiful and intelligent she was. Jack's repertoire with her had been limited and self-centered, and it was, of course, a comment on Carol's masochism that she had chosen to view him as the love of her life. But most men, she had discovered, tried to please her in bed, if not out of it. Somehow she felt they were making a colossal effort for which they needed to be heaped with praise. This male need for approval was a tedious distraction from the business at hand.

Douglas Clark didn't appear to be trying, with knitted brow and gritted teeth, to please. He seemed genuinely to enjoy pleasing her. Or so Carol thought. Other men could lunge away for hours at a time, but very few were willing to engage in sexual activity that didn't directly stimulate their penises. It was not so much, though, what Douglas Clark did to her body for so many hours with his lips and tongue. It was the effect he had on her mind. It was the continued soft purring of his voice, his total consideration for her feelings, his ability to build little fantasies.

When she awoke, Douglas was looking down at her. He seemed worried. A lost little boy. It turned out that his landlady was giving him trouble. Could he move a few things in with Carol? Carol said she thought that would be just fine.

42

She made coffee and tried to get Douglas out of the apartment before the boys got up. At the front door he turned to her. There was just one thing. Could he have a pair of her underpants?

Carol was hardly naive, but this was one quirk she wasn't used to. It must have shown on her face. Quickly Douglas explained that he wore his lovers' underwear to remind him of them. Somehow he made it sound rather sweet and romantic. Carol went to rummage in her bureau.

How embarrassing. Along with her 40DD canvas bras was a selection of basic iron bloomers, size eight. This was not how she wanted to be remembered. On the other hand, did she want to appear prudish? Certainly not. And with her history, she could hardly afford to. Brazening it out, she marched from the bedroom carrying a pair of dowdy white cotton pants.

Douglas Clark looked at them and held them up.

"I think they'd be too big," he said. He handed them back to her and left.

Carol felt humiliated yet strangely positive. She knew he'd be back, and she wondered how she could have found someone that nice. She was not about to call it love. But she would certainly call what happened with Douglas Clark technically superb sex. She could hardly wait to see him again.

Later she would say that they spoke of guns almost from the moment they met.

For now, though, Carol still considered herself to be in love with Jack Murray. Instead of staying out of his life, as he had asked, she had secretly tape-recorded a phone conversation between herself and Jeannette in which Jeannette again matter-of-factly stated that if Jack wanted to leave her and the children, he could leave and she would not stop him.

When Jack heard the tape he was furious. But Carol's plan backfired. Instead of leaving Jeannette, Jack told Carol to leave Valerio Gardens.

"I did not do it to make trouble," Carol wrote to him in an unconvincing letter about the tape. On the surface temporarily abandoning her plans to marry Jack, she tried in a rather manipulative and grandiose manner to show herself as the catalyst necessary to nurture the Murrays' true love.

After knowing you and getting to know Jeannette, I came to realize that you two are still very much in love. Your marriage is a little frayed around the edges, but it has a good foundation in

43

that love. [. . .] You need help now. If it doesn't work out, well, we'll see. You don't know it yet, but I'm about the best friend that you've ever had. I can let go when it's in the best interest of all concerned.

You listened to her side. You listened to me, but what you wanted to hear was her side. Don't take the negative and let the positive get lost. Now it's your turn. You MUST be willing to let her hear you. Not just the petty gripes that build up, but the deep, hidden side that is so vulnerable. Talk to me. Or make a tape with me. I will not EVER make one on you for any reason without your permission. I helped her reach you. Now let's reach out for her! You want that family.

If you want, I will stick around long enough to see if you still want a relationship with me.

I'll give you the space you need right now. But I'm going to want some answers soon. Not about us now, but about us in the past. I've been good to you, I think that I've earned that much respect.

> With concern and affection,
> Carol

In January of 1980, she found a two-bedroom apartment on Lemona Avenue, less than three miles southwest of the Murrays. It was a step away from Jack but a step up. The buildings were smaller and cleaner than Valerio Gardens, and the circular driveway was landscaped with trimmed spruce trees and tropical plants.

When she moved the first of her things in, chatting to one of her new neighbors, Carol cracked a dirty joke and from behind her heard the clear, high laugh of a child. She turned in time to hear a plump little blond girl crack a dirty joke of her own.

"I *like* you," Carol said. She laughed back, and the little girl looked pleased. Her name was Theresa and she was eleven.

A few days later, Jack and his assistant manager, Tony, helped Carol load a rented trailer with her belongings. As they drove toward her new life, Carol glanced in the rearview mirror. A few car lengths behind, Jeannette followed in her Granada.

Carol was livid. How could Jeannette be so rude? It seemed like such an invasion of her privacy. When they arrived at the new apartment, Jeannette parked a couple of buildings away and sat in her car watching. Carol was ready for another confrontation with her rival.

Jack held her back. "I'll take care of it," he said.

Tony and Jack unloaded the trailer and moved Carol's furniture in, then Jack kissed Carol good-bye, promising to call later. He did not.

After the move, Carol wrote to Jack, her tone that of a doormat in love.

January 26

My darling:

Can tender thoughts be conveyed on typewriter paper and written with a Smith-Corona? Well, I'm going to try.

I don't really have anything to say. No tears to cry, pains to bare, hurts to protect.

Just a simple statement. I love you. I've said it before. Usually when I'm demanding attention or crying over real or imagined hurts.

Now a question. What can I do to please you? What can I do to make you happy? At this moment I feel very warm and giving. I want to share with you some of the glow I feel when I'm either with you or thinking of you.

I'm feeling very good about things these days. I only regret that I had to leave Valerio. Yet it was necessary. Someday will you let me come back?

When I look back at everything, it seems that even if you aren't really aware of it, that you do love me in many ways. You've given back to me as much as I've tried to give to you. You don't express tenderness, but it's there.

Jack, around the holidays you told me to put my emotions on hold. Can I take them off now and relax?

Of course, I now realize why I don't like this apartment. It is across town from you.

I wonder why my life is so filled with thoughts of you and why I take so much pleasure from knowing you?

I won't turn this letter into an erotic statement, but I hope you do understand that I treasure those special moments that we've had.

I know who my "master" is, and I'll follow your lead. Why I want you to control me, I don't know. But it feels good when you take command, and you've never abused your authority with me. I don't know if its just a game, but it is a good feeling. I trust your judgement and you seem to respect mine.

I wish there were more ways to show you how much I care. Will you give me a pet name?

> Affectionately,
> Carol

If Carol felt good about things, it was, as usual, because of misplaced optimism brought on by her ability to see good instead of bad: Jack was not aware of it, but he loved her. He did not express tenderness, but Carol knew that it was there.

Her pet name was not forthcoming, and Jack, Carol would later insist, was not interested in her invitations to indulge in sadomasochistic sex. He did not want to be her "master" or her "boss." After the move to Lemona they no longer went together to Little Nashville or out in the van for coffee dates, although he did visit her at the new apartment for sex, sometimes as often as three times a week.

They had been seeing each other for a year. But with the distance of a few miles, Carol began to notice that there was a price tag attached to their meetings. Before or after making love, Jack mentioned something he wanted. Invariably, Carol bought it for him. She was also not above an occasional small overt bribe to get his attention:

"When will Amalgamated come up with my security refund" she wrote. "We could use it to go out with if you were willing."

She wondered if he had ever been to a girls' gay bar and thought he might find it an interesting change. If all overtures failed, Carol could grovel.

"Would you come and stay the night with me? You don't need to do anything to me, but I would enjoy your company."

Jack did not stay the night. He did, however, ask her for $150 so that he could join the Masons. When her bank statement arrived, Carol's check had been endorsed by Little Nashville. He had used her money to pay off his bar tab.

As she usually did, Carol made excuses for him. Perhaps she had misunderstood and he had really told her that the money was for someone named Mason who was a Little Nashville bartender. Carol was convinced that she still loved Jack Murray, but she was finding it more and more difficult to rationalize his behavior.

"All I expect is honesty," she told Jack after the Nashville bar tab incident. "Don't tell me you're going to buy a gold-plated feather duster, then show up with a leather Hula-Hoop."

The community was littered with gold-plated feather dusters and leather Hula-Hoops that she had been foolish enough to buy, Carol thought.

But if she was beginning to realize that her relationship with Jack Murray was falling apart, the relationship with Douglas Clark was growing. She had been right. He had come back. Periodically, and with little consistency, he and his belongings, including his teddy bear, Mozart, moved in and out of her apartment. When he was there, he was out at night barhopping. Sometimes they went together to Little Nashville, where he and Jack took a violent dislike to each other, gratifying Carol, who was flattered to think that she was the cause of such jealousy.

When she confided in Doug about her gifts to Jack, he became angry, particularly about the Chevy payoff.

"No more freebies from Mama," he advised in his smooth, cultivated voice. "Look, you're buying ass. It's okay to pay a guy to fuck you, but not ten thousand dollars a throw."

Carol still had thousands of dollars from the house sale in her joint safe-deposit box with Jack.

"Get that money in a savings account or a checking account where he can't get his hands on it," Doug said.

Carol didn't get around to doing it.

The fact that Douglas seemed to want to protect her rather than use her for her money pleased and surprised Carol. Of course, he indulged in some petty scamming: He would grandly present her with a check for his share of rent, telephone, and food. Then he would borrow the check back before she had time to deposit it. But this was minor compared to Jack. And it wasn't as if Carol wasn't self-sufficient. Her eyesight had gradually improved, and in January she had returned to work as a vocational nurse. She was employed in the laser-care unit at Valley Medical Center near Valerio Gardens, tending mostly geriatric patients with bedsores and ulcers. The patients had to be photographed for insurance purposes, and it seemed to Linda at Valerio Gardens, who still babysat the boys, and to Jeannette's brother, Warren, that Carol enjoyed showing the unpleasant pictures to people.

If the theme of Carol's relationship with Jack Murray was pleasing Jack, the theme of her relationship with Douglas Clark was turning out, not surprisingly, to be pleasing Douglas Clark. At the time, she viewed it as a mutual eroticism.

Doug talked nonstop, barely allowing her to get a word in. He shared his philosophy of life, the details of his days, and snippets

of his background: his father, Franklyn, was a former navy lieutenant commander and executive with Kaiser Steel who had lived all
over the world with Doug's mother, Blanch.

Carol was impressed by his sophistication and intellect: his conversation was sprinkled with French phrases. Of course, it was not
surprising in one who had gone to school at the Ecole Internation-
ale de Genève, a Swiss boading and day school founded in 1924
by a group connected with the League of Nations. Doug (he preferred that to Douglas; his father had called him Douglas and he
found it patronizing) hadn't graduated from the school but had
gone from there to the strict and expensive Culver Military Academy in Indiana. After that, adding to his mystique, he had been a
cryptographer during a two-year stint with the air force. He'd been
married to a woman with whom he was still friends. And the
"landlady" who was giving him trouble when he first met Carol
turned out to be a girlfriend with whom he had lived for several
years and had squabbled.

Carol didn't think to wonder why, with his background, he was
working as a steam engineer tending a boiler at the Jergens soap
and lotion factory in nearby Burbank. She considered herself to be
an underachiever and she understood that in someone else.

Doug did not seem interested, though, in hearing about, let alone
understanding, Carol. Even though he took to calling her "Motor
Mouth," most of the time she felt as if she couldn't get a word
into their conversations. In an effort to reveal to him her artistic
side, she tried to show him a story she had written. Instantly, he
produced one of his own, a two-inch-thick stack of purple prose
about dungeons and torture.

One night Doug lay next to Carol in her queen-size bed. The
boys slept deeply in their room. Although he wasn't interested in
Carol's real-life background, after reading a magazine article about
true love having to do with fulfilling your lover's fantasies, he had
been encouraging her to open up, and he had been opening up
himself.

It was dark in the bedroom. Doug's voice purred in Carol's ear
as he told her he'd like to subdue and capture a young girl, then
take her to a country house with a torture chamber where the girl
would become his sex slave.

Carol thought this was a neat fantasy. But she had always, herself, rather wanted to be the captured slave. For years she had
dabbled in light bondage and domination, and she had persuaded

Doug to help her further explore the pleasure of being restrained during sex.

Douglas appeared to enjoy seeing how far he could take her, she thought, and how far she would let herself go. It was as if he wanted to determine her sexual limits—if indeed there were any.

Carol would always swear that Doug was the first to fantasize about murder. After they made love one night, he pointed out that throughout history, people had shown no reverence for human life and had slaughtered each other wantonly, which Carol had to agree was true. It was fun to kill, he told her, and he thought that any woman who loved him should be willing to kill for him.

Their fantasies deepened.

One evening a short time later, Carol would claim, she sat at the Lemona Avenue dining-room table reading the newspaper. Douglas stood casually by the kitchen bar. He had become inexplicably annoyed with the uncle of a former girlfriend.

"I want you to fly to Denver," Doug said.

That was where the uncle worked, across the street from a department store. If Carol, posing as a shopper, went to the store, she'd find a high-powered rifle in a drawer in one of the women's departments. She was to take it, go to a display window, and shoot the uncle while he sat at his desk across the street.

"What time should I get off the plane?" Carol asked. She peered up at Douglas through her Coke-bottle glasses. "What should I wear?"

Doug thought for a minute. "A black pillbox hat," he said. Carol nodded. He never again brought up the plan and did not tell her why he was upset with the uncle.

But he did bring up killing. They were lying in bed talking as usual, before they went to sleep, when Doug explained that he was a low-level hit man for the Mafia. Minor stuff. Three hundred dollars for a kill. Secretaries who wanted to do away with the boss's wife. That kind of thing.

He lay propped on an elbow. In the dark she sensed him trying to judge her reaction. She was unfazed. She had known other men who had bragged about being hit men. Now, as then, Carol could have run. Now, as then, she stayed.

Weeks later, Doug told her about an episode with a former lover who had asked him to climb inside a freezer to chill his body. Afterward, he had powdered himself until he was white and let the woman make love to him while pretending he was dead.

49

The story strained credibility, Carol thought. She giggled. Sometimes with Douglas it was difficult to sort out fantasy from reality.

Soon after the move to Lemona, young Chris Bundy sat on the floor in front of the television. Washington State serial killer Ted Bundy was on the news.

"Mom," Chris said, looking up. "Mom, are we anything to that man?"

Carol told Chris that they weren't related. "We don't associate with that kind of person," she said, Miss Priss when she wanted to be.

But soon she and Doug were discussing the serial killers who seemed to dominate Los Angeles crime news in 1980. Angelo Buono, accused accomplice and cousin of Hillside Strangler Kenneth Bianchi, used to have an upholstery shop, and Doug told Carol that when he was married and had his own upholstery business he had gone to Buono's shop to buy fabric. They had never, Doug assured her, discussed anything but work, although he claimed to have dated the roommate of one of the strangler's victims.

When news aired on television about Lawrence Bittaker, who with his partner, Roy Norris, captured young girls and then tortured them and tape-recorded their cries, Doug appeared outraged.

"Bittaker's just a vicious, cruel bastard," he said. He also thought Bittaker was stupid to have left so much evidence.

In the spring after she moved from Valerio, Carol applied for a driver's license for the first time since her last eye operation. Wearing contact lenses and glasses, she failed the exam with one eye but passed with the other, which was all that was required.

Now that she had her license, she decided to buy a car. Douglas phoned her to tell her he'd found a station wagon, perfect for hauling the boys and groceries around. Carol went down to look at it.

It was a tank of a 1973 Buick, light blue and bigger than anything she'd ever driven even when she had some peripheral vision, which now she did not have. Simply looking at the Buick made her feel insecure. Carol bought it anyway, claiming later that she had no idea what Doug planned to do in it.

6

HE WAS CALLED DANNY, AFTER HIS MIDDLE NAME, DANIEL. THEN, in Berkeley, California, when he was in the third grade, he walked into class, sat down, and wrote his name out: D-U-G. And he announced to his teacher, not amused by the little towhead who could not spell, that from then on that was what he wanted to be called.

Douglas had been born in 1948 in Pennsylvania where his father, Franklyn, was stationed in the navy. He was the third son of five children: Frank, Jr., Carol Ann, Walter, Doug, then Jon Ronlyn. When Carol Ann, seven years older, thought back as an adult, the only thing that she could remember about Doug that was different, aside from his delightful ability to tell tall tales, was his long fingernails. He'd grab hold of you and dig in, like a girl. Not that there was anything effeminate about him.

One of Doug's psychiatrists would credit Walter Clark, less than two years older than Doug, with saying later that the brothers had competed furiously, even for their parents' attention. Everything Doug did was all right with Blanch and Franklyn, it had seemed to Walter, who described his brother as a pathological liar.

Even Doug would admit that when he was nine, his mother had caught him dressed in her own and his sister Carol Ann's underwear. But Blanch Clark would swear that Doug gave her no trouble, exhibited no behavior problems, and was the most considerate of all her children when she was suffering one of her migraine headaches.

With a father in the navy, it became routine for the Clark children to give away their toys and books and stuffed animals, to travel abroad and try to make new friends. There were benefits. If they found themselves in difficult situations with playmates or at school, there was no need for them to take action. Wherever they were, they knew that soon they'd be moving on and whatever problem they had would disappear.

In 1959, after time in Pennsylvania, Seattle, Berkeley, and Japan, the Clark family moved to Kwajalein, an atoll in the Marshall Islands, which are sprinkled over half a million square miles of Pacific Ocean. Missionaries landed there in 1803, bringing Christianity and clothes. Then in 1944, the United States marines arrived and seized the islands from Japan. Later they became the testing ground for U.S. atom and hydrogen bombs.

By the time the Clarks arrived, the atomic tests had ended and Kwajalein was an interceptor pad for test missiles being shot from Vandenberg Air Force Base in California. Set improbably on this half-mile-wide atoll was an idealized American suburb with broad, paved streets, bungalows, baseball diamonds, and a school for the children. There was grass and there were coconut palms, but the trees were contaminated with cesium 137 and the Marshallese were afflicted with increased cancer rates and spineless fetuses they called "jelly babies," a result of the atomic fallout.

Franklyn Clark had been in the Pacific before, during World War II, when he'd served as a supply corps officer. He'd retired in 1958 as a lieutenant commander. In Kwajalein, as a civilian, he ran the supply department for Transport Company of Texas, and Blanch worked as a radio controller.

For two years the family stayed in the Pacific, living a life of colonial privilege. They bicycled along the safe roads and snorkeled and swam in clear, blue-green water off white sand beaches. Then life in this tropical paradise came to an end, and the family returned to their house in Berkeley. There, Doug would boast, he had played with the grandchildren of Admiral Chester Nimitz.

The family moved on to India, where Franklyn worked with the Engineers International division of Kaiser Steel. In Renukoot, in the jungle halfway between Calcutta and Delhi, a steamy locale as exotic in its own way as Kwajalein, Kaiser was erecting aluminum plants. The family lived in a compound of cement-block houses with a swimming pool. They shopped in Delhi and went to cultural events at the American embassy in Calcutta where, in the mornings, the bodies of the poor who had died of exposure were shoveled off the streets.

The American children learned through Calvert's correspondence courses and were taught by Indian teachers. They were the elite. At home, where there could be seven or eight servants, a child could snap his fingers and in would run a bearer to fetch him a drink.

No matter where the Clarks were in the world, there was always church on Sunday. On a grassy Indian hillock in the middle of nowhere, a missionary couple sang hymns, the woman pumping away enthusiastically at the organ (which was also a talent of Franklyn's) as the Clark family joined in "The Old Rugged Cross."

There was an incident—made hazy by the years and the miles and the need to preserve family secrets. Young Douglas admitted to buying liquor for the servants and getting them drunk in their quarters, annoying his father.

One American couple who lived in the same compound would remember the Clark family as pleasant, but not mixers. Another couple, who would remember Franklyn and Blanch as wonderful people who kept to themselves, also remembered young Doug Clark doing nothing worse than flipping his towel at their son and refusing to stop until he was decked. The son thought Douglas Clark, bigger than his older brother Walt, was a bully, always trying to start some kind of ruckus. Franklyn Clark stood up for Doug so aggressively that the other boy's parents thought it odd and decided that the Clarks were overprotective.

As a simple practical matter—and for the boys' languages, the Clarks would later claim—Walter and Douglas, beneficiaries of Franklyn's new position in life and Kaiser's largesse, were packed off to the International School in Geneva, Switzerland.

The Ecolat, as it was known, still had its share of children of U.N. diplomats along with the offspring of international celebrities and European and Middle Eastern royalty. Yul Brynner's son, Rocky, attended at the same time as Douglas. So did Burt Lancaster's son, Jimmy, who would not remember Doug but unwittingly offered him a chance to name-drop.

On weekends some students flew to Riyadh or Paris, intimidating those not used to international-jet-set life. But most of the American students were simply from comfortably off—but hardly rich—corporate executive families stationed in Europe.

Doug seemed disappointed and somewhat resentful that he had not landed at one of those notorious Swiss slack-off schools for rich kids, one of his classmates thought. He was sullen. His attitude was arrogant. He also seemed to like getting into fights that Walt, popular and outgoing, thought he could have avoided.

"We're quite rich, you know," Doug boasted one day to a group of classmates not interested by the news.

Another day he was spotted complaining loudly as he paced the hallway outside the cafeteria.

"My dad's a millionaire," he said. "I shouldn't have to eat this crappy food."

Doug's class, 3CB1 (the equivalent of ninth grade in America) produced several National Merit Scholarship winners and a Rhodes scholar. It was not unusual for students to score 800 on their SATs. But Bob Shade, 3CB1's English and homeroom teacher, a Scotsman of military bearing, thought that Douglas Clark was the sort of lad who didn't seem to want to try. He wasn't a discipline problem— no one was a discipline problem for Shade, a tall man with a loud voice and the point of view that authority was authority and not to be questioned. It was just that Doug Clark seemed as if he would rather be anywhere else than at school. He didn't work. He was perpetually late. He never handed an assignment in on time. In Shade's opinion, he was an unpleasant character with a malicious streak who damaged other people's property for fun. Nothing major. Just schoolbooks. But then he wouldn't own up like a man. He lied and blamed other people.

In Geneva, there was no such thing as street crime. The old section of town had winding cobblestone streets and basement discotheques. Ecolat kids roamed there at will as long as they had their parents' permission to be off campus. Belying Geneva's reputation for stuffiness, all that any sybarite (let alone a fifteen-year-old boy) could want was there for the taking. It was 1963. The year John F. Kennedy died. The beginning of the Beatles and the mod and pop sensibilities. Dope and free love came later to the world, yet this was where Doug Clark would always claim he discovered kinkiness. Thereafter, he said, he was unable to look at sex straight on.

Although he was not part of the Ecole in-group, Doug did not think of himself as lonely, because there was so much to make up for it. He listened to other guys say, "I got my hand up her skirt," and he thought, How lame.

Doug had found what he thought of as older women. On campus

54

girls didn't glance his way. But on ski trips to Davos and Klosters, where the powdery snow was as high as his kneecaps, he had fun with the daughter of a Hollywood producer and her best friend, or so he bragged. They latched on to him, he thought, because he was this young kid, big for his age, with a vast collection of American rock and a taste for good whiskey.

There were also the town girls. When he talked about Switzerland later, Doug told stories that might have been teenage fantasies. Still, they demonstrated his distaste for women even at that early age. He told of waking up on an apartment floor one morning after a party. Two town girls were there, one of them on the couch wearing a T-shirt and panties. She sat on his chest. He'd never been that close to a female before and he realized that the rumor about French and Swiss girls not bathing as much as Americans was true. Still, Doug Clark boasted, that was the day that he first experienced oral sex.

There was another incident in which Doug claimed he stole Walt's girlfriend. Doug was in the infirmary and she went to visit him, a homely-looking broad, he thought. A mutt that the other kids called "Funny Face." But after the visit she didn't go with Walt anymore because, Doug guessed, she wasn't getting any sex with him.

All Doug had to do, Walt told Carol Ann, was talk to his girlfriends, and they were gone.

Doug was suspected of drunkenness. A bicycle was stolen and the spokes destroyed, but Doug claimed someone else did it. He wrote a letter full of deep, dark, unpleasant thoughts to a female math teacher. Blanch Clark traveled to Switzerland to discuss her son's problems. The problems continued, and Douglas Clark was expelled.

CULVER CODE OF CONDUCT FROM THE 1930s

That I may be an honor to my country, to Culver and to my comrades, I voluntarily adopt as my rule of conduct this Culver code:

In all matters concerning self to speak truthfully and deal openly; to seek no advantage by favor or deceit; to face duty without grumbling and to bear discipline without complaint; to respect authority; to hold manhood above victory and self-respect above failure and in every circumstance to play the man.

In all matters concerning others to be fair, considerate and kind; to be silent rather than belittle or betray; to keep myself, in mind and body and habits, fit company for the youngest boy who looks at me as an example and to carry on with courage and devotion the best traditions of Culver and of American manhood.

Not greatest he, by merit quickest found
The cunning cheat is often falsely crowned,
But greatest he, who scorning sham or lie
Or the cheap practice which all tricksters try
Stands shoulders square, face front and head erect
Lets triumph go, but keeps self-respect!
Yet greatest, who faithful to his post
Seeks not the prize itself, but to deserve it most.

Edgar A. Guest

Doug's parents were half a world away, first in Venezuela, then in Perth, Australia; Frank, Jr., and Carol Ann were grown and on their own; Walt was at boarding school in Arizona, where he was joined by Jon Ronlyn; and Douglas Daniel, Danny, Duggie, Doug, was in Indiana at military school, partly because, Franklyn Clark would say later, he talked too much.

Franklyn, who grew up in Indiana, had named Doug after a friend who died fighting in World War II. He had always wanted to go to the Culver Academy himself, and when he and his wife at last had the means, that was where he wanted to see Doug.

Culver was a military academy, but it turned out more than colonels. Past alumni included novelist Ernest Gann, actor Hal Holbrook, Broadway director and playwright Josh Logan, and movie critic Gene Siskel. George Steinbrenner, owner of the New York Yankees, was a Culver graduate and so was Ohio congressman J. William Stanton. The list of illustrious Culverites filled pages.

The campus itself sprawled on fifteen hundred acres of midwestern beauty at the edge of Indiana's Lake Maxinkuckee. In springtime white blossoms covered the trees, the grass turned a brilliant green, and the sun bounced off the lake to warm the curlicued spire of the Victorian chapel and the old brick school buildings, some of which dated back to Culver's founding in 1894.

Working somewhat against the heartbreaking beauty of sunrise on the lake was the sight of almost one thousand boys in blue cadet uniforms marching everywhere, beset by rules and regulations and tormented by a governing network of bells. Reveille was at six-thirty. Staying in bed until the three-minute-warning bell rang or until someone of authority marched sharply through the barracks had become over the years a hallowed Culver custom.

Every evening, the boys studied in the library or at their desks in their rooms. Lights out was at ten, and beware anyone who had not made his bed properly. Punishment for various infractions meant marching in circles with an M-1 rifle on your shoulder in the company of the other naughty kids. During his years at Culver, Doug Clark would do a great deal of marching.

But just as marching boys and the insistent sound of bells created an uneasy alliance with the campus's physical beauty, so did the cultural side of life at Culver contrast with its rampant militarism. There was nothing quite like an inspirational lecture about Shakespeare to point up the inherent absurdity in having to disassemble an M-79 grenade launcher blindfolded in three minutes or less.

At sixteen, Douglas Clark, fresh from Switzerland, was older than his fellow tenth-graders. They noted that he was bigger and had to shave more than they did. Doug did not study any harder at Culver than he had at the International School. He was intelligent, though, and was able to get by without working, spewing out in half an hour last-minute two-thousand-word snow-job essays.

He took wrestling, football, crew, and rifle. He played saxophone in the dance band and he belonged to the firearms club. The usual prep-school hazing system prevailed. Seniors beat the juniors, who in turn would beat the younger students. Terror bonded the boys and helped form lifelong friendships. But not for Doug Clark, who didn't have a best friend. Rather, he hung around with a group of kids who passed for friends and tolerated him.

It was odd. People tended to leave the room when he approached, except for a handful of students known as the Bad Attitudes. Doug, like most BAs, was someone with potential who didn't like authority and didn't give a damn. The others admired his energy and found his lies entertaining.

"You want to get a laugh?" A BA would say. "Let's see what Clark's got to talk about today."

What Clark had to talk about was his parents' wealth and his sex life, until eventually even the BAs became sick of his bragging. If Doug left school for a weekend, everyone knew his stories of his sexual exploits would carry him for a month. Prevarication was Doug's second nature, one of his schoolmates would reflect years

57

later, going on to decide that when a kid lied so consistently, might it not have been more helpful to insist that he see a psychiatrist instead of marching him in circles with a rifle on his shoulder?

In fact, Doug did see the school therapist, who felt he had trouble with his schoolwork because of problems with his peers. His counselor, Colonel Gleason, wrote more bad-conduct letters than usual to Doug's family. The family didn't seem bothered, Gleason thought. In the three years that Doug was at Culver, Blanch visited once and Franklyn once during vacation, when Doug wasn't there.

In the middle of the 1960s, even in a military academy the Vietnam War seemed like a television show. By 1966, "Star Trek" on Thursday nights was more entertaining. Television watching was not encouraged, though. Instead, top-notch opera and theater groups visited to perform Cole Porter or Greek classics. Culture may have been a priority for some students. For others, outwitting authority took precedence.

It was a little too early for Superintendent Delmar T. Spivey, Major General, U.S. Air Force [ret.], to have to worry about drugs. Drinking, though, meant immediate expulsion. Flirting with danger, one boy set up a minifactory that spewed out fake IDs. Another reckless cadet had a still in his room, where he produced foul-tasting but effective whiskey.

As the outside world began to change with the beginning of the peace and student-protest movements and the hippies with their beads and free love and marijuana, a cadet began smuggling dope into Culver to supply his friends.

But Doug Clark was not interested in drugs. His interest still was women. Townies from the country village of Culver found academy boys too uppity rich, and the Culver boys in turn felt contempt for the townies. Except for Douglas Clark, around whom some of the other boys began to feel envy, awe, and discomfort. Everyone tried to sneak girls into the dorms after dances. Doug went farther than that. Somehow he got them into his room on Saturday nights and had sex with them. When most boys of his age would have been grateful for that, Doug needed more. He wanted to use them and control them, then expose them to the world for the gratification of his ego.

He set up a large, old-fashioned reel-to-reel tape recorder under the bed or in the room next door. He taped the cries and moans of the girl and then played the tape for the other students. His attitude was that of the sophisticated ladies' man, and some other boys saw it as nothing more than that: Doug was doing what they all fantasized about. Yet it was almost as if he were a director, thought one of his roommates, both fascinated and repelled. It was as if Doug had scripted in advance the raunchy things he wanted the girl to say. People muttered about how he got the girls to go along with it.

There was an older girl Doug wanted to date. He wrote her rambling and incomprehensible letters on legal paper, which he folded carefully into thick, tiny packages, as small as he could get them.

There was always a kid like that at school, thought the girl. Someone ahead of the others with sex. She wasn't interested. Doug had zits. Once when she was in the bathroom at someone's house, he came at her, his mouth wide open as he lunged, a typically inept adolescent. She pulled away, disgusted. There was something sinister about him, she thought, wondering if she felt that way only because she had heard stories of his exploits. Twenty-five years later, though, she would still remember his eyes. They had looked right through her, she thought.

To one adult who watched Doug with a mixture of anger and sadness, it seemed that the more girls he could conquer, the happier Doug Clark was. His girlfriends were acquisitions, the woman thought. Although Doug visited his family at Christmas, first in Venezuela, then Australia, the boy was lonely and putting on a macho front. And no wonder he seemed so lost, when his family had virtually abandoned him. Deep down, the woman suspected, he was angry. She had heard rumors about what went on with Doug Clark and girls in the dorm. But she did not report it, because she felt sorry for him.

Later Doug told about meeting the love of his life at a Culver dance when he was seventeen. Her name was Bobbi and she was with another boy who was treating her like a dog. Doug, bold, had walked up and interrupted.

"Come on, honey, we've got to go," he said. She had looked at him as if he were her savior.

They went back to the dorm, Doug not realizing that she was a virgin. In bed, when she shook so that he couldn't get her underpants off, he stopped.

But later he took photos of himself having sex with Bobbi. His roommate could not tell whether all the photos were of the fourteen-year-old or of more than one girl because in the pictures, Doug took care to cut the girl's head off. As he passed the photos around the school, he seemed to enjoy the notoriety.

Students left Culver feeling as if they'd had the equivalent of a college education. Douglas Clark was nineteen when he graduated, and the only class he'd enjoyed was Military Science and Tactics. For the final, he had brandished a machine gun that shot blanks as he led his platoon through a forest and across a stream to take a hill and capture the enemy.

There was supposed to be an outside graduation ceremony with a big parade and military band music. Traditionally, Culver graduates walked through Culver's iron gates, which symbolized walking out into the world. But in 1967, for the first time in years, it rained, and the ceremony had to be held indoors.

After Culver, Doug took time off to hang out with his parents, who by then had retired to their country home near Yosemite. The Vietnam War was raging. When he was drafted, even though he was a conservative Richard Nixon fan, he didn't want to end up in the army front lines. He enlisted in the air force. His best bet, he thought, was radio intelligence, because they protected their people.

He looked forward to seeing the world again, Ankara, Turkey, perhaps, or back to Japan. But he ended up in Texas and then Anchorage, Alaska, where they gave him a top secret clearance and put him to work decoding Russian messages. His title was Intercept Analyst Specialist.

Being in the service in Anchorage was like being back at Culver, and the guy running the barracks and giving him crap about not having his shoes shined reminded Doug of Colonel Gleason. But the city had its benefits. There were hookers there, and a proliferation of dancer bars. It boosted his ego to walk out of a bar with a woman on his arm who minutes before had been naked and an object of desire for all the other men in the place. He liked a woman who had the courage to say, "You can look, but don't touch."

His air-force rank was E-3 when something happened. Doug Clark left the air force before his term was up but with an honorable discharge, a National Defense Service Medal, and his benefits intact. The details of what led to his early departure would remain murky, as Doug told different stories at different times and the air force wasn't letting on.

One of Doug's versions had him threatened with Leavenworth because of trumped-up charges: a superior officer hated Doug's guts for naming him a security risk. In a second version, white officers plotting to kill a black enlisted man tried to cover it up;

when Doug found out and threatened to expose them, they got him into trouble.

Luckily, though—and this part at least must have been true—with a father in the service, Doug had grown up with the Uniform Code of Military Justice as his bible.

"You fuck with me, you're fuckin' with God," Doug claimed to have told the air force.

The rest of the story, whether true or not, was at the very least provocative.

While Doug waited to be court-martialed, so his tale went, the air force placed him on snow-shoveling detail seven days a week. But since he was not stupid, Doug paid another enlistee twenty bucks to do his job while he went into town to "take care of business." By the time Doug met Carol Bundy, this would mean going out to look for a woman to kill. In 1970, it may have meant nothing more than going out to look for a woman.

Whatever his plan, Doug later claimed to have found a taxi driver willing to take the night off and let Doug drive his cab. He was tooling around Anchorage when he heard shots, Doug's story went. A white man had murdered a black man in a green Corvette. With no desire to be a material witness to a homicide, Doug killed the lights on the taxi, then sped off. Which was what he would do in Hollywood in 1980 after a prostitute named Charlene escaped from a station wagon he was driving.

That night in Anchorage, someone wrote the cab number down. The cops found the owner, who confessed that he wasn't driving on the night of the murder and told the cops who was. When Doug found the note on the barracks door telling him to report to Anchorage Homicide, he decided to get out of state by noon the next day.

With nine hundred dollars travel pay and savings of $4,500, he got in his car and he drove. He had always wanted to be able to tell his grandkids that he'd driven from Alaska to the Mexican border. In California, though, he moved in with his sister, now Carol Ann Mackenzie, in Van Nuys.

He couldn't seem to find anything to latch on to. Carol Ann, sympathetic, thought that it was difficult for young people to make transitions. But Carol Ann had her own problems. Her husband abused her.

The man reminded him of himself, Doug said one day. He felt sorry for him.

In a North Hollywood rock-and-roll bar Doug noticed Beverly, blond, heavy, and four years older than he was. He followed her around, talking in her ear, moving after her from bar to bar until she stopped and listened to him go on and on about his big dreams in that melodic voice of his.

That's what I want, Beverly thought. A man with ambition. She felt fat and ugly and belittled herself. But Doug always tried to build her up.

Doug was almost twenty-four and Beverly twenty-seven when they married at a Valley chapel. It was a small wedding with a homemade wedding dress, because Beverly had been married before and her mother wouldn't spring for a second one.

She worked as a bookkeeper, but they bought a car-upholstery business, Doug consulting with his father before they laid out any money. On weekends Beverly did the books for him, and after work she rode the bus from her job to meet Doug so that they could drive home together. But it seemed that every time they got ahead he'd reinvest the money in the shop or squander it. There was no way of telling him anything, because he always made it clear that he knew he was the intelligent one.

The marriage was not ideal—everyone in the family admitted that Doug was strong-headed and self-centered. Beverly, as loyal as Doug's other women, would remain close to Doug's parents after the split and would be reluctant to say what brought the marriage to an end beyond little things, like his laziness about the house. They made a deal once that she would paint their living-room walls in North Hollywood and he would paint the ceiling. She did her share, and the ladder and paint can stayed in the middle of the room for one week, then two weeks, and the ceiling never did get painted.

But to begin with they were a nice little married couple. They worked together on their budget and one day wore each other's underwear to work and thought of each other all day. It was true that Doug wanted to try wife-swapping and three-way sex. But, thought Beverly, what man hasn't had those fantasies at one time or another? And the women's underwear: well, he said it was more comfortable. In the 1980s, when manufacturers began making fancy underwear for men, Beverly would think that Doug had just been ahead of his time.

During the marriage, Beverly gained more weight and got even more down on herself than she had been before meeting Doug. Doug didn't seem able to spend time alone, and she wondered if maybe that was why he went to bars all the time, so that he'd have someone on whom to unleash his endless flow of words.

Of course, he did like to drink, as well. He became overanxious and angry after a few beers, Carol Ann thought. And although Beverly would say only that he became lovey-dovey when he drank, she persuaded him to join Alcoholics Anonymous as a condition to save the marriage. He stayed sober for more than two years.

Doug had told Beverly about his love for prostitutes, saying after the wedding that he was finished with that behavior. Anyway, it was more a thing of helping them out when they were in trouble, she decided, as did Carol Ann. Later, Doug claimed that he had been running hookers through Beauty Upholstery, his employees the happiest work force in town.

During the 1970s oil embargo, they had trouble ordering materials. The business went sour, and Doug would also later blame his drinking. He didn't want to let the business go. He and Beverly considered bankruptcy, but as both of them were morally opposed to it, they ended up selling out for a couple of thousand dollars. Doug worked in a gas station and as a security guard to pay off debts. Then he bought merchandise at auctions and sold it at swap meets. Beverly's job, because she was no salesperson and he was, was to load their Ford camper-shell truck with car parts or unassembled rattan rocking chairs or Hollywood bedcovers or whatever Doug was selling that week.

Still Doug had dreams of being the big businessman, or even a lawyer. Still he wanted it all *now*. Working toward it through business school or law school was out of the question. Tentatively, Beverly suggested that he apply to the city. He did and passed exams to train as an animal-control officer, storekeeper or steamplant trainee. He chose steam, which was a job his father had once held in the navy.

"Look forward to career in expanding field of neuc.-steam generation particularly," he wrote on his application to the Department of Water and Power, mentioning that he had taken "fresh. adjenda" through University of Nebraska correspondence courses. (Doug's expensive education had not improved his spelling.)

In 1976, after four years, his marriage came to an end. Again, he would blame this failure on his drinking. But Beverly stayed friends with Doug, who occasionally used the Ford pickup truck.

When the allegations of violence began, Beverly would have trouble believing that they were true. Doug had loved her cat as if it were a baby. And when they'd gone fishing with her father, Doug had recoiled at the thought of chopping off a trout's head. The police would make much of the door handles being off the inside of the truck, as if they thought, when Doug borrowed it, long after the divorce, he had taken them off to stop someone escaping. Those damn door handles had been falling off the pickup since the day they bought it, Beverly would protest. Still, she would sell the truck.

At Jergens, the Burbank factory where Doug now tended a three-story-high boiler, he sat in a twenty-by-sixty-foot room while the boiler churned and bubbled and the sweet smells of soaps and lotions wafted from nearby. At his desk fitted with dials and instruments, Doug could control the heat, which reached as high as two thousand degrees.

There was power in the boiler. But the job of stationary engineer, for which he had trained through the Los Angeles Department of Water and Power, was blue collar and did not fit his early education or his family's aspirations.

Actually, he was lucky to be at Jergens. In 1975, a manager who thought he was a disrupting influence had wanted to fire him from his steam-plant-assistant job at the DWP Valley Generating Station in the northeast San Fernando Valley. Although most of his fellow workers found him a tolerable blowhard who didn't mind making other people look bad in order to boost his own image, at least four employees said he had verbally abused them or threatened them with assault.

No one got around to firing him. So in 1977 he was still on the job, exhibiting what appeared to be far more ingenuity with his excuses for being absent—he was gone 15 percent of the time—than with the job itself. First he blamed an inoperable car. Reasonable enough. Then having to drive an injured friend to work and his wife to the hospital. On another occasion suspected hepatitis or mononucleosis kept him home. And one two-week period spent "recovering from knife wounds," which apparently was true, he followed by time off to go to the LAPD "to look at mug shots."

In 1978, an absence for a simple "bad headache" in February gave way to more "unreliable rented transportation," which led to a "sprained ankle," which led to "must transfer funds from Credit Union to bank." Which led eventually to Clark's resigning after making a series of complaints about job safety. The next day he tried to get his job back, but he had gone too far. The DWP fired him for insubordination, the plant superintendent noting in a memo that because of the possible risk involved, his discharge papers would be sent by registered mail instead of delivered in person: on the day Clark was notified that he was to be terminated, Valley Steam security was told by the LAPD that Douglas Clark, in possession of a shotgun, was possibly heading their way. No one knew how the police received the information, and luckily Doug and the shotgun didn't turn up.

In September of 1979, when Douglas Clark applied for the Jergens stationary engineer job, he claimed to be earning $1,750 a month in his job at Pacific Coast Packaging. His reason for leaving DWP earlier, he told Jergens, had been "$ plus lack of advancement possibilities."

At about two-thirty in the morning on February 27, 1980, outside the Jergens factory while Doug worked the graveyard shift, his Pacer automobile erupted into flames. The driver's side window was broken inward, and a can of lighter fluid sat on the front seat. Doug grabbed two Jergens fire extinguishers and rushed to put out the fire, but the car was totaled. Although he said the car had been locked, the driver's door was unlocked. But Doug collected on his insurance and wrote an apologetic letter to Jergens offering to reimburse them for the price of the extinguishers.

The car was no good, so he had set fire to it himself, he told Carol Bundy at the time, although later he would tell her a different story: that he had burned it to cover up evidence.

By that time, of course, Doug's sexual speciality had become insinuating himself into the lives of fat, lonely women. It had worked well for him, he admitted. At different times in his life, he had charmed his way in with one woman after another, not paying his share of the rent, then moving on if the woman dared complain or speak of love.

His stray-puppy routine had worked once again with Carol Bundy. He had asked her to dance, laid his line on her, and now had what he described as his own Stepin Fetchit: a hot and cold running maid, a virtual slave. Carol cooked for him, cleaned the house, did his laundry and the dishes, and even kept trying to buy him new jeans, which, to his annoyance, never fit. She was hung up on him, there was no doubt about it. Every time he turned around she was like a dog with her mouth open and her tongue hanging out, willing to do anything to get him in the sack. With Doug, sex was always a whole big rigamarole, even if it was only a one-time thing. But with Carol he was looking at the sex as a cash deal, coming out ahead a couple of hundred dollars a month on rent or food.

In retrospect, in many of his relationships the women had been pigs, Doug thought. He'd had his share of tight-ass society bitches from embassy row when he was in the air force. Women who wore too much makeup or fussed with their hair made him sick. Now he was drawn to the earthiness, the almost naked need of homely women, who seemed grateful for his small attentions.

Of course, he reflected, in one of his rare moments of modesty, any man would become a love object for women of the caliber he chose.

"The door to your room is locked, mine is open," he would offer at first. "I can give and not receive."

That way, he remained the one in control. And if nothing else, as roommates, the women provided security.

"I have this sort of involvement," he could say to a woman at whatever bar he happened to be working from that week. And the new woman would know that she couldn't stay overnight and couldn't dream about getting too close.

When Doug first saw eleven-year-old Theresa, early in 1980, she was roller-skating in front of the Lemona Avenue apartment house, her long blond hair flying. He watched her stop in a skid on her tipping skates as she put up her hands to break her fall against his chest. She smiled, apologetic.

The little girl lived across the hall from Carol with her mother, who worked long hours in a hospital. Theresa visited Carol and played with the boys: unruly little kids, in Doug's opinion. When Carol went out and left him with them, he was taking them in hand. He had Chris and Spike running around waiting on him too.

Sometimes Carol baby-sat Theresa and sometimes the little girl stayed over. Her parents should be shot for letting a kid with a rear end like that go around in a pair of shorts meant for a nine-year-old, Doug thought.

Jack Murray and Carol were sitting on the maple-and-plaid Early American sofa in the Lemona Avenue living room. He nuzzled her ear. It was the beginning of April 1980. He would be forty-five in May.

"There's a camera lens I want," he said.

"No," Carol said. For the first time she meant it. Afterward she would guess that that was when he went to the safety-deposit box to make a withdrawal of her cash.

Doug was trying to wean her from Jack and seemed threatened by the degree of control he still had over her. In turn, Jack seemed threatened by Douglas. Carol, pleased, thought it was because they were both in love with her. Doug had brought a red Kawasaki motorcycle and told Carol about his fantasy of drilling a little hole in Jack's gas tank. He would follow the Chevy on his bike, drop a match on the trail of gasoline, and watch it explode as it reached the van. For his part, Jack made it clear that he didn't want Doug near the Little Nashville Club, which he considered Murray territory.

Carol carried pictures of both men in her wallet and displayed them proudly. At the Bullock's beauty salon, employees wondered at the ability of this homely woman to attract two such photogenic men. Thumper, a Little Nashville waitress whose dad was a psychiatrist, took a look at Doug Clark in person. He was good-looking, she decided, and he obviously came from a good family, but something about him was weird.

Doug continued to move in and out of Carol's life and apartment. He enjoyed keeping her on edge, she thought. First he seemed to want to draw her close, then he encouraged her to sleep with other people and tell him about it. If she began to get close to anyone else, he would reappear and warn her to watch out for strangers who might hurt her.

During one of Doug's absences, Carol had answered a *Singles Register* ad placed by a stereo-company executive named Art Pollinger who was looking for a decent and marriageable woman. Art weighed four hundred pounds and knew all the restaurants in town that gave second helpings. He was so fat that recently a commuter airline had made him fly in the baggage compartment, strapped in by a net.

The boys liked him. Art bought them toys and played with them and took them to museums. Chris, especially, felt as if he had a dad again when Art cautioned him about being too rough. The boys loved their own father, Grant, who loved them. But he was a nurse at a convalescent hospital and worked night and day. As always, he did not have much time for his children.

Art tried to let Carol know that she was a worthy person. He saw her as intelligent and an immaculate housekeeper, with clean, beautifully dressed children. It became Art's goal to wean Carol from the devious and unsavory people she still mixed with on the three days a week that he was out of town. He wanted to create a righteous life for her. They spoke of marriage, and Carol opened up to Art, telling him that when she was blind and dependent upon him, Jack Murray had sexually abused her, sodomizing her even though she did not enjoy it. Carol was passive, thought Art, who was not interested in unwholesome sex. She allowed men to do whatever they wanted simply because she needed to please.

One April evening Art and Carol were driving to dinner without the boys when Carol announced that the previous year she had opened a joint safety-deposit box with Jack Murray.

"Carol," Art said. "That's the oldest game in the book. You've probably already been ripped off."

Jack would not do that, Carol protested. But the next day Art met her on her lunch hour and drove down Sherman Way to the bank to inspect the box, which should have contained at least $12,000. According to the signature cards, Jack had been there twice. There was $6,300 left.

Carol tried to rationalize the loss and said that Jack had taken care of her when she was blind. But Art thought she was covering up the devastation he had seen on her face when she opened the box and saw that her money was gone, taken by someone she had trusted. She closed the safety-deposit box and put what was left of the cash in a checking account. Jack, she later told Art, had admitted paying off gambling debts and angrily accused her new boyfriend of wanting her money for himself. But Art made over $100,000 a year. What he was interested in was making a decent family woman out of Carol.

Soon Carol and Art stopped seeing each other. Her roommate, Doug, seemed to have a hold over her, Art thought. In his opinion, with Doug and Jack she had two perverted men controlling her life. Art had tried to straighten her out. It had been a contest between good and evil, Art felt, and evil had won.

Art, Carol decided later, saw only the good side of her, which was the side she chose to show him. But she would look back wistfully and think how different life would have been if she had chosen Art instead of Doug.

Also through an ad, Carol had met another man, nicknamed Phil the Mafioso. He visited Valerio Gardens to bang on Jack Murray's door, frightening Jack enough that he hopped a plane to Australia. He thought he could sell family land to pay Carol back, but he could not find his family and returned empty-handed.

It was still April as Carol maneuvered the Buick through the Valley on her way to work, doing her best to avoid bushes and parked cars. To her surprise, a buck knife fell from the sun visor and into her lap. She pulled the car over and found a jagged hole in the vinyl where the knife had been hidden. Later she asked Doug about it, and he said he kept the knife as protection from strangers. As a matter of fact, he suggested, as she lived in a sleazy neighborhood, she should buy a gun for her own protection.

Carol agreed.

On April 24, Doug went to the Diamond pawnshop on Van Nuys Boulevard to select Carol's weapon. As long as she was getting one, he suggested, why didn't she buy two? They could have one each. Doug, who wanted the guns registered to Carol in order to distance himself from what was to follow, told her that he couldn't buy his own. He had done time for robbery in Indiana, he lied, and was a convicted felon.

Carol believed him. The idea that he was a felon added to Doug's mystique. The next day she went down to apply for the pair of guns he had chosen. She would pick them up in three weeks.

7

I‍T WAS A SUNDAY EVENING LATE IN APRIL WHEN THE MAN PULLED his station wagon into the supermarket parking lot on Sunset Boulevard near La Brea Avenue. Charlene Andermann, twenty-two, was waiting for a trick, but when she strolled over she noticed that the man was playing with himself.

"You don't want nothing," she said to him, and she turned to walk away.

But he called after her and she listened to him, finally agreeing to give him some head for forty bucks. She got in the blue car, and they rode south to De Longpre Avenue, where he parked.

He said his name was Don. Or maybe Ron. She wasn't sure. He had blue eyes and blondish hair and a mustache and he wanted to get in the back of the car, but she wouldn't.

His hand was on the steering wheel and she leaned over. There was long, smooth hair on his hands. His penis was little. Real little, and it didn't get hard, thought Charlene Andermann, laughing to herself and maybe out loud as she looked.

She had barely started, with him still not hard, when she realized he was holding her down and had a knife at the back of her neck. She grabbed at the passenger door to unlock it, but he caught her and kept stabbing. He cut and cut. Then she managed to get hold of the knife blade herself, and for three or four long minutes they

70

lay there, the man on top of her and Charlene Andermann trapped underneath.

"What's your name?" he said.

"My name's Charlene."

He wondered if she had a family and if they cared about her.

She guessed they did, she said.

"You're all wet. What's the matter? Did you wet your pants? You scared?"

"No, mister. That's blood. You're hurtin' me."

He laughed and said, "I know."

Then he said, "Neither one of us are going to let go of this knife, are we?"

"I can't, mister."

That was when he put his fingers on her windpipe and, pressing her throat, made her see stars.

He spoke, saying, "This is your last round, baby." Which was when Charlene Andermann pushed as hard as she could with her feet and propelled herself out of the car. As she lay on the sidewalk bleeding, yelling "Help," the man tossed her jacket and shoes after her and sped off down the street with his headlights off.

One afternoon Chris screamed at his mother, "Get Doug out of here."

Carol slapped his face.

His mother had changed. She was not a perfect mother. Chris knew that. But she had always been on his side. Jack Murray had got mad at him once for messing around with Jessica. He had waved his gun and told Carol to whip Chris, but she had taken him in the bedroom and told him to yell while she hit the bed with her belt. He had cried "Ow, ow" loudly as his friends gathered outside. When he told them that she'd hit the bed and not him, his Vietnamese friend said, "You have a really nice mom."

Chris still loved her. He always would, because she was his mom. But he didn't think she was that nice anymore. Before, Carol had been physically modest around her children, but since Doug had moved in, she walked around the apartment naked. Chris didn't mind Doug nagging him and Spike about doing their chores, because that was how a father would act. And he felt proud after Doug taught him to play backgammon and told him he was so good he was going to take him to Las Vegas for luck. What he didn't like was Doug controlling his mother. Worst of all, Chris could tell that his mother enjoyed being totally dominated.

One night, at bedtime, Chris had watched from the end of his bed, staring through the open door as Doug staggered into the apartment covered with blood. He had blood on his blue denim jacket, blood in his teeth, blood all over his hands. Quickly Carol pushed him into the bathroom and told Chris to go to bed. He scrambled under the sheets, his heart skittering. Spike, pretending to be asleep, had seen it too.

It was a motorcycle accident, his mother told them later. But Chris had seen his mother clean Doug's bloody knife.

Doug came home with blood all over him another night. The second time, Carol told Chris that Doug was a hero. A man had been trying to steal the car and Doug had been hurt fighting him off. Afterward, privately, Doug told Chris he'd killed a guy in a bar and slit his belly up to his breastbone. Then Chris heard him tell Carol that he was going to kill Chris. Doug didn't know Chris had heard, and sent him off to find his knife.

Chris wandered through the apartment. He pretended to look for the knife, then he came back to the living room and said he couldn't find it.

Doug was sitting on the sofa. He picked up a comb and held it to the left side of Chris's spine.

"If I put the knife in here," he said to Carol, "it would go right through to his heart and kill him."

Carol said, "Yes, it would," her voice quiet and matter-of-fact.

She should have bellowed, Chris thought. She should have bellowed, "Leave him alone. Don't touch my kid."

Chris escaped from this new and terrifying world by visiting Theresa, who one day told him that Doug let her see him naked and let her touch his penis. After that, when he went to play, Chris took Spike's little bad-guy action doll with him and his own Pulsar good guy, who had a button on his back that Chris could push to make fake blood come out. The bad-guy doll would kidnap Theresa's Barbie while Theresa screamed, "Oh, Pulsar, save me! Save me!" in a little high pretend Barbie voice. Chris always saved her.

After the knife incident with Doug, Chris withdrew emotionally, crying easily and complaining of headaches. Doug hated him so much, Chris figured, because he knew that he was the only man who could come between Doug and his mom.

Like Art Pollinger, Chris saw things in terms of good and evil.

He thought that he and Doug were in a battle for his mother's soul. A battle that Chris knew he was losing.

Carol realized that things had taken a serious turn in late April when Doug had staggered, bloody, into the apartment. She had tried to cover it up for the children. Doug's explanation, which she had almost believed, was that he had met a girl at a bar and was having oral sex with her in the Buick. Her boyfriend, a rival of Doug's, was a hit man named Nick who appeared, attacked Doug, and engaged him in a fight. Doug wasn't injured, and Nick's girlfriend got away. The next time Carol was in the Buick, she noticed blood spots. Then a week or so later, the incident replayed as Doug again staggered into the apartment, this time telling her that he had killed Nick.

On May 16, Carol returned to the Van Nuys Boulevard pawnshop to buy the guns. They were .25-caliber Raven automatics, small guns solid in the palm of the hand, yet like toys. That's what Doug and Carol called them: "the toys."

Carol bought three boxes of ammunition from sporting-goods stores, then they drove to Balboa Park in nearby Encino. Doug sat in the wagon and Carol stood twenty-five feet away while he test fired the toys into a telephone book. The sound they made was no louder than the pop of a child's balloon.

Later, as Carol watched Doug stick a gun in the back of his jeans and walk away from her toward the front door, she felt washed with a wave of pride. He looked like a hero in a movie.

By this time, Carol was thoroughly immersed in the idea of being Doug's slave. When she did ordinary things—work, shopping, taking the boys to McDonald's—she felt free of his influence. When she was around him, she told herself, she was his. She had never before met anybody whose mind so completely mirrored hers.

Oddly, though, she no longer felt at all good about herself. When she asked Doug why he was still interested in other women, he accused her of being "underwhelmingly attractive." He didn't want to have sex with her anymore and it hurt Carol's feelings.

One day she drove with him to Hollywood. They picked up a young prostitute and took her to a parking lot. Carol paid thirty dollars and then watched from the back seat while the young woman tried to get Doug aroused. When she was unable to, they gave up and went home.

Using the names Betsy and Don, Doug and Carol answered an ad placed by a couple who wanted to swap partners. Again, Doug was unable to become aroused, although he worked hard and enthusiastically to satisfy the other man.

Another night, at a party house in Hollywood, Carol sat in a darkened room and watched blue movies while she waited for Doug. Once someone asked her to dance, but no one wanted to sleep with a matronly looking woman with heavy glasses.

8

DOUG WOULD LATER JUSTIFY HIS MOVES IN AND OUT OF CAROL'S apartment by saying that she was a mood destroyer, a lousy drinking lady, and far too possessive. He had wanted to be away from her clinginess, her emotional swings, and her controlling attempts to buy his clothes. As different women reported their alliances with Doug, the dates would overlap and the exact chronology would remain unclear. At one stage, he moved in with a woman named Linda. But after a few days, even though he'd taken some furniture over, Linda turned him out. Well, she was an "all-down slut," anyway, Doug rationalized, and the situation had deteriorated rapidly from what should have been a hundred-dollar room rental to the usual sex deal of which he claimed later, haughtily and unconvincingly, he wanted no part.

Luckily, though, Linda had told him about a large-busted friend of hers named Daphne. Intrigued, Doug agreed to meet her with a view to three-way sex. Daphne was as pretty and dimpled as she was overweight. Instead of the threesome, Doug dumped Linda and took up with her friend.

At first Daphne wouldn't let him stay over, and Doug complimented her.

"I'm glad you're not a loose woman," he said.

Daphne wasn't a loose woman, and she wasn't sure why she was going out with Doug Clark.

75

But then again, there was no reason not to. He was a perfect gentleman. After a couple of dinner dates, for which Doug picked Daphne up in a blue station wagon, and an orgy at a house in Hollywood where she sat at the bar as Carol Bundy had done before her, Daphne allowed Doug to stay.

But at the sight of a two-hundred-pound man wearing green silk bikini panties, she howled with laughter, and Doug couldn't become aroused. He stayed over anyway and in the morning, perhaps as some kind of symbolic compensation, he left a small gun on top of the television.

Daphne saw him again—she had to return the gun—and one night volunteered that she was afraid of her ex-boyfriend. She was startled when Doug offered to kill him for her.

"We'd have to go in on it together," he said. They were out to dinner and he had ordered steak. Doug, most likely fed up with Carol Bundy and trying to draw a new woman into his fantasies of murder, still had a hearty appetite.

Daphne did not take Doug up on his suggestion, or his offer to move into her apartment. But one night later they went to visit Carol Bundy and sat on the living-room sofa talking. From across the room, Carol watched silently, riveted by Doug's every word. She seemed possessed by him, Daphne thought, as if he had put her under some kind of spell.

After an hour Doug told Carol to go in the bedroom. Silently she rose and went in and shut the door. By then, Daphne had decided that even if Doug Clark was a perfect gentleman, he was weird. She dropped him.

At the Viking Bar in North Hollywood, Doug's eye fastened on a bouffant-haired blonde named Lydia Crouch who was there with a friend. Later he told his story of that evening, the date of which was at odds with Lydia's version:

Lydia weighed nearly three hundred pounds. Idly, Doug had gone into his usual routine of intense eye contact combined with the vulnerable air of one of Peter Pan's Lost Boys, all the while wondering what it would be like to have sex with a woman of that size and shape.

He asked Lydia to dance and held her close but not too close, all the while murmuring in her ear. He bought her a drink. They danced two more dances. Then they made their way to Lydia's small but neat apartment, where she went to slip into something more comfortable.

In the front room, Doug sat and wondered what something more comfortable could possibly be for a woman of Lydia's dimensions. To his amusement, out came Lydia in skimpy underpants and a bra.

The evening progressed until it became Doug's customary first-night gala performance. First he suggested that Lydia might like to relax in a tub of warm water. He offered to run it for her, then to wash her back. His main intent was not to have an amorous fling in the bathtub, but to make sure that Lydia was clean. Lydia tried but was unable to squeeze her large body into the tub.

She was temporary-roommate material, he had already determined. He had also determined that Lydia hadn't had many strokes in life. She fell in love with him, or at the very least fell in lust, he thought, when he offered to brush her hair. Later he would write her a check, and according to Lydia, he would move in with her, eleven-year-old Kevin, and four-year-old Amanda on the third of June.

But for Memorial Day, which fell on the twenty-sixth of May, he took off up north on his Kawasaki with Carol's chrome gun and his former teenage girlfriend, Bobbi, now married, who had flown out from Indiana. They were going to visit his parents near Yosemite. Over the weekend, a depressed Carol had dinner with Warren, Jeannette Murray's baby brother. If she hadn't been fat, she grumbled, Doug would have taken her to meet his family. She told Warren she hoped the motorcycle would crash. She also said she was thinking of sending the boys away.

The Lemona apartment-house garage was always packed with cars, and sometimes when Carol came home tired from work she couldn't find a parking space. One day, deciding to take the risk of sneaking into the lot next door, she miscalculated and scraped the entire right side of the Buick along a brick wall.

"You're incompetent. You have no business driving," Doug told her.

She couldn't understand why he was so upset.

"I can't control it. I can't handle the car," Carol said. She assured Doug that she would get the Buick painted.

But the wagon simply was not working out. Because she had such trouble handling it, Doug seemed to drive it more than Carol did.

On the thirty-first of May, sick of struggling with the Buick, she bought a blue 1976 Datsun 710, keeping the station wagon for Doug.

That night, Doug took the new car, saying that he wanted to test-drive it. When he returned it the next morning, the gearshift was fractured and there was an indentation on the passenger-side door panel. He'd been cleaning his gun, he explained to Carol, and it had discharged, ricocheting off the shift and the door. Carol did not believe him.

The same night that Doug borrowed the Datsun, Marnett Comer, a blond, seventeen-year-old Sacramento runaway and prostitute, disappeared from the Sunset Strip.

PART
TWO

9

On Saturdays, Janet Chandler used to line them up in their high chairs in the family room of her house in Anaheim. While Michele, Cindy, and Jenny watched Road Runner cartoons, Janet washed and curled their hair, then gave them baby manicures and pedicures, clipping and smoothing the thirty pink little fingers and thirty toes as if she were a worker on a live assembly line. Her girls were a year apart. All their birthdays fell in March and April, and Janet was only twenty-one by the time they were born. Later, she had a son, Benjy, but the girls were her little blond dolls.

Janet was a beautiful woman, proud of her trim figure and cascading chestnut hair. She would have liked to have been the perfect Christian wife and mother. She cooked and baked and prayed and gave her girls big birthday parties. One year she made a giant sheet cake covered with ballerinas. Another year, she and her girlfriend spent weeks making Barbie doll clothes, filling four large boxes with teeny little leather purses, fringed suede boots, miniature gowns, and long coats trimmed with fake fur.

Janet called Cindy, her middle daughter, her sunshine. The child had a Prince Valiant haircut, wide-set hazel eyes, and a generous smile. When she was ten, Cindy painstakingly wrote a special Mother's Day card in which she expressed her desire to be more thoughtful and caring. She wanted to give Janet another child; she wanted her to have all the secret wishes Cindy didn't know about fulfilled.

"If I could give my mother anything," she wrote, "I would give her green, yellow, and pink [. . .]. I'd like to take away her problems so she could always be happy. I would give her things to remember of me, like this saying I made up."

Although she was devout, Janet's prayers did not ensure the perfect life for which she had hoped, and Cindy was not able to take away her mother's problems. Janet was divorced from the children's father, but between marriages, she tried to live as she thought a normal, all-American woman should. This meant no sleep-over guests and no drinking in front of the children. Serial monogamy was more Janet's style. Her and Elizabeth Taylor, she joked.

By the time she was in her thirties, her name was Janet Marano and she lived with her new husband, Andy, his two daughters, Gina and Judith, and her four children in the Orange County lakeside community of Mission Viejo.

The Chandler children were not thrilled by their mother's marriage, and neither were the Marano girls. But on the surface, life looked good. Cindy was picked for a children's choir and the family went to watch her sing at Disneyland. Gina, a year younger and a straight-A student, won ribbons on swim team and accompanied the younger Judy to her own swimming lessons.

On weekends, Janet and Andy loaded the car with chairs and an ice chest and drove through Laguna Canyon to the beach, where they listened to the waves and watched the kids boogie-board until sunset. Sometimes on Sundays the whole family attended the Calvary Chapel in Costa Mesa, where the children belonged to the youth fellowship.

Still, for some time Janet Marano had had a feeling of impending doom, which one sunny day became so strong that she knew whatever terrible thing she sensed must be drawing closer.

"If anyone ever comes after you," she said to her children, "run. Scream."

Doug had moved in with Lydia Crouch as planned. But soon, as he later told the story, he had his usual situation on his hands: a woman who was a friend, a convenience, and in this case an excellent cook, but who began to become possessive, causing his feelings to cool considerably. A lusting, quivering three-hundred-pound Lydia banging on his door wanting to sleep with him was more than Doug could handle. It was fun encouraging her to gain an extra sixty pounds—he took photos of her in the kitchen and showed them to Carol—but making love to Lydia was like making love to a waterbed.

He was wasting money on a rental garage in Burbank near the apartment of his old girlfriend Joey, the "landlady" with whom he had been having problems when he met Carol, and he wanted to get his things into somewhere more permanent. Linda hadn't worked out. Daphne hadn't worked out. Lydia was now a problem. It looked as if he and "motor-mouth" Carol Bundy were going to be bunking together again. He told Carol to look for a place near the Jergens factory so that he could walk to work.

From the Huntington Beach pier, in 1980 nothing more than a cement strip dotted with fishermen and bait-and-tackle shops, visitors could see the squat palm trees and telephone poles that made up the town's near skyline. On weekends inland teenagers arrived from miles around to surf and roller-skate, and to head for the boardwalk to buy and sell, smoke and snort marijuana or cocaine.

As school let out for the summer, teenagers arrived and stayed. Some didn't wait for vacation. They ditched school and came to the beach where that new verb, "to party," seemed to have been born. They found beds where they could, east of the rows of pink-painted oil rigs that pumped in unison along the shoreline.

About half a mile inland, the narrow, twisting streets turned into four- and six-lane thoroughfares, their sidewalks lined with tall cement-block walls that enclosed the newer housing developments. This was where Andy and Janet Marano moved so that Andy could be closer to his office in Vernon.

Cindy and Gina were the closest of the Chandler and Marano children. Together they learned the meaning of what Calvary Chapel youth pastor Bill Dobrener liked to call "that big word, 'regeneration.' " They made a commitment to the Lord and gave their lives to Him so that they could learn to walk a beautiful Christian path.

In the summer of their fourteenth and fifteenth years, Gina and Cindy's secret from their classmates had been that they still played with their Barbie dolls. Now, nearing fifteen and sixteen, they seemed to want to be Barbie herself. Gina's baby fat had melted and she was long-limbed and brown-eyed, with the beginning of an adult, exotic beauty. Cindy, in a quest for popularity brought on by change in schools, had become the perfect little blond California beach bunny. She had also begun to stay away from home and school for days at a time to hang out by the pier with an in-group of friends. Gina, influenced by Cindy, had also started to cut class.

"Tell Mom it's nothing to do with her. Tell her I just want to have fun," Cindy said to her older sister, Michele.

But when Gina began running away too, Judy Marano, then eleven, knew it was because of the constantly changing rules at home and the whippings with the switches that Janet would have the children choose from the tree in front of the house.

Throughout the year that the family moved to Huntington Beach, the sounds of Pink Floyd's *The Wall* blared through the house. Janet became sick of hearing the defiant young voices declaring, "I don't want no education. I don't want no thought control." The sound symbolized to her the growing lack of authority she and her friends seemed to have over their children. She had always been able to take her girls anywhere, in little matching outfits with matching good manner. Now, like their friends, they just wouldn't listen. Both Cindy and Gina were failing their classes at Ocean View High School, and neither of them had been home for Christmas Day in 1979.

Sometimes Janet climbed a ladder up the back of the house. She let herself in through the bathroom window, hid in her bedroom and waited, hoping to catch the girls. One day she heard the front door open and Cindy's feet coming up the stairs. She opened the door, pounced on her, and paddled her on the bottom. Cindy always took her punishment, then ran away again.

In the spring of 1980, Janet's hopes had risen. The entire family was to be baptized in a Calvary Chapel ceremony at Corona del Mar beach. Cindy and Gina made sure that they stayed home that week and were good. With several hundred people, they waded into the ocean and rededicated their lives to the Lord. The next week they ran away again, and Janet and Andy, desperate, spoke of capturing them and tying them up to keep them at home.

After Cindy impaled her foot on a shard of glass and had to walk with crutches, her grandmother spoke to her severely. The news was full of Ted Bundy, the Hillside Strangler, and Lawrence Bittaker, whose victims were from California beach communities.

"Maybe this foot will stop you running away," Cindy's grandmother said. "There are monsters out there, Cindy. They'll get you."

Cindy looked surprised. "Grandma," she said. "Why would any-one want to hurt me?"

On Sunday, June 8, the girls met Andy in a Huntington Beach coffee shop. They were tired, they said, and wanted to come home. They did not tell Andy that Gina had been raped at a party. But by the time Janet arrived to help negotiate what would be expected of them, the girls had turned sullen and pouty, and they did not return.

On Wednesday, the eleventh of June, Janet and Andy Marano were out once more looking for their daughters. They drove north on Pacific Coast Highway, then south, then north again as the ocean turned from blue to black and the worried parents gave up for another night.

Doug was at the Lemona Avenue apartment all the time, even though he was supposed to be living with Lydia Crouch. He had always got along well with Spike, a blond, noisy, outgoing boy. But Chris was something else. He was as handsome in his own way as Spike, but dark-haired like Carol, and shy. Doug called him a little faggot, and Carol put Doug's attitude down to annoyance at Chris's disgust when Doug showed the boys his pornography collection.

At first when Doug hit him, Chris cried. After the knife incident he had withdrawn, only occasionally coming to Carol to cuddle up, and toward the end not wanting to be at home or around her.

Carol, who once broke a wooden spoon on Spike's behind, told herself that she didn't want to hit Chris and was picking up the belt only to spare the child Doug's brutality. Later Chris would not remember either Carol or Doug hitting him. He hated Doug, but he would think that aside from the blood, and the knife, and the way Doug kept Carol totally under his control, he had been a straight-up guy with him and Spike. But Spike, only six when he watched it happen, would remember seeing Doug punch his older brother in the kidneys and the stomach. He would remember Doug's biker belt, black leather with studs, which he had used to beat Chris. He would remember being frightened when Doug tried to teach the boys to knife fight. And he would remember what appeared to be knife marks on Doug's abdomen.

On the first of June, the day after Doug test-drove the Datsun and returned it with a broken gearshift, Carol had applied to have custody of Chris and Spike transferred to Grant. School let out on the thirteenth of June, but on the ninth, letting the boys think they were going for a vacation, Carol handed them over to their father, who put them on a plane to the Midwest country home of their paternal grandparents. She was afraid of Doug, Carol told one friend, and wanted to protect the boys. But to someone else she said the boys were getting in the way of her life with him. She sold the children's bunk beds and began to look for a new apartment near Doug's work. Whatever the reason, she was not ready to give up on having a life with him.

The exact sequence of events over the next two months would become confused in the telling and the retelling, lost somewhere between the high drama of the moment and the self-protective and self-serving recesses of the minds of Carol Bundy and Douglas Clark. One psychiatrist would call what happened "shared paranoia," a newer term for a psychological state once called *folie à deux:* a contagious madness that afflicts two people who are close. Other psychiatrists would disagree and say that madness had nothing to do with it. Whatever the cause, Carol said—and still says— that her involvement in the murders began this way:

On the eleventh of June, which Carol would sometimes confuse with the twelfth because of misleading newspaper reports, she came home from work and found an innocuous note on the dining-room table at the Lemona Avenue apartment. It was from Doug and it read, "Sorry to have missed you. Talk to you later."

That same night, deciding that she needed the Buick station wagon to go shopping, Carol drove to Lydia Crouch's Van Nuys apartment to exchange cars with Doug. Each of them carried keys to both vehicles.

The Buick was parked on the street, and on the back seat in the dark Carol spotted what looked like dirty laundry in a duffel bag. She opened the door and looked more closely. Her eyesight was still bad, but upon closer inspection, the bag turned out to be filled with bloodied clothes, a fuzzy blanket, and paper towels. Abandoning her shopping plans and the Buick, Carol took the bag into the Datsun. On her way home to Lemona, she noticed a laundromat. She did not yet know what had happened and she didn't want to be seen carrying bloody garments into her apartment house where, anyway, they locked the laundry room at night.

She and Doug had spoken for so long of murder. If he had finally done the deed, she would be there to help her friend, to stand by her man.

The laundromat was empty. The blanket and towels were so bloodied that Carol stuffed them into a trash container. She washed a green tube top and then a little maroon striped dress, thinking longingly that if she were thinner she could have worn it.

Claiming later that she was confused and frightened, Carol took the clean clothes home, still not sure what had happened. At 7:31 and 7:35 the next morning, she called the Jergens factory, finally reaching Doug at 7:11 at Lydia's that night. They spoke for thirty-six minutes, but she could not—or would not—remember what they discussed. Over the next few days, Carol learned some of what had happened through phone calls, the television news, and a conversation during a car ride with Doug.

He had cruised west in the Buick down Sunset Boulevard on the afternoon of Wednesday, June 11, the nickel .25-caliber Raven tucked down between the driver's seat and the station-wagon door. He hadn't even hit the Strip when he spotted them sitting on a bus bench under a tree near the red, white, and blue eagle sign of All-American Hamburger and the Screen Actors Guild: a young blond girl wearing a pink jumpsuit and an even younger dark-haired girl in cutoff jeans. He could see right up the younger girl's jeans to her underwear, but she was a homely little mutt, he thought, and because all he ever wanted was blondes, he pulled over and rolled down the window to try and talk the blond one into the car.

The girls conferred with each other. They didn't want to be separated. Eventually they climbed in, the bouncy, tanned little blonde next to him and the dark one in the back seat behind her (although Doug told Carol they both got in the front). He talked to them. He always liked to talk to them, otherwise what was it all about? And for a change, he listened as they chattered, star-struck. They'd been to singer Rod Stewart's house and met a girl they thought was his daughter and a girl named Mindy, and they'd been staying with a movie producer.

As they talked, he drove, ending up in a parking lot with nobody around. But somehow an argument started. They were little bitches who wanted his money without having to perform. It was time for him to take care of business.

He began by making the blond one go down on him.

"Look away," he said to the little mutt, pretending to be bashful. Obediently, she looked out of the window.

The blond one's head was in his lap and she wasn't any good. Angry that she didn't know what she was doing, angry that they'd argued with him, he fumbled beside the seat and got the gun.

He would have had to check in the driving mirror before he

acted. While she was still looking away, he shot the dark one behind her left ear. But hearing the shot, the blond girl raised up, so he shot her too, in the head, being careful about the angle.

Neither of the girls had time to realize what was happening. But they wriggled around and moaned, so he shot them again, the blond one in the heart this time and the dark one a second time in the head. Then they were quiet.

He slumped them over. No one had seen. No one had heard. Then he drove over the hill, taking about twenty minutes to get to his rental garage. He had a catch phrase for these situations: remember your ABC's. Always Be Cool.

By the time he reached Burbank it was about four in the afternoon. An alley led to the garage, and flanking the alley entrance, less than a hundred feet away, was the Teddy Bear Preschool and a Mobil station at the corner of a busy intersection. The garage was small and old-fashioned, about six by fifteen feet, in a row of seven others behind a stucco building. Other garages lined the alley. No one was around, but at any minute someone could come by.

Doug opened the garage door, then angled the Buick across it. With the wagon open on the passenger side and a blanket over the bodies, he dragged them out and into the garage.

They bled on the floor, and he walked right through the blood in his work boots, enjoying himself until the dark girl's arm rose up. It scared the shit out of him that she wasn't dead. He might have to shoot her again at a time when it wouldn't be cool. But she was dying, so he didn't have to.

He cut up the leg of the blond girl's pink jumpsuit. He put the girls on a bed that was stored in the corner. He mashed each one's face into the other's crotch. Then he played with them, shoving his penis into the blond one's vagina and throat and sodomizing the brown-haired one.

As Carol would always say, Doug burned out quickly on his women. At about eight o'clock he abandoned them in the garage and drove to the Lemona apartment, where he left the note for Carol. After months of fantasy, this was to be his gift to her, Carol always thought: her first direct knowledge of a hit and his way of letting her know that it was real, so that they could get involved in killing together. He must have been covered in blood, so maybe he showered at Lemona Avenue.

He had alerted Lydia Crouch that he would be late for dinner. At her house, he had a couple of drinks and hung around until ten-thirty, then he borrowed Lydia's Polaroid camera and left for the garage, where he stayed until, once more, he was finished with the girls.

He wrapped their bodies in the blanket. It was a struggle to get them back into the car. Then he drove to the Forest Lawn on ramp of the westbound Ventura Freeway near Disney Studios. There he opened the Buick doors and tumbled the bodies down an embankment where they came to rest in the dark near some high power lines.

Lydia Crouch, stirring in her sleep, heard Doug let himself into her apartment a couple of hours before dawn.

10

THE BODIES SEEMED SO OUT OF PLACE, DISCARDED IN THE GRAVEL where a state highway worker cleaning up trash had found them at 12:55 the afternoon of June 12. They had been tumbled down a steep slope at the side of the Ventura Freeway, where they'd landed facedown under some bushes near a bridle trail. Obviously they'd been killed somewhere else and dumped at the scene. Blood had run down the blond one's face and dried. No wounds showed, but there was a great deal of blood. If they'd been murdered where they lay, Detective Helen Kidder thought, the blood would have dripped forward onto the dirt.

The women—no telling how old they were—had puffed up from lying in the sun. The dark one wore nothing but a red tube top pulled down around her waist. The blond one's blood-soaked pink jumpsuit had been slit up the leg. There would be no reason for the killer to cut his victim's clothing if she had been alive and could cooperate, even under duress.

Necrophilia, thought Kidder.

But she was surrounded by crusty old homicide detectives. They weren't interested in listening to some blond broad in a Junior League dress bleating to them about sex with dead bodies.

The temperature was in the eighties, and it was a slow day for cops. Everyone had come out to take a look. What seemed like the entire detective team from Northeast Division, in whose jurisdiction the bodies had been dumped, representatives from Burbank and Hollywood, half a dozen highway patrolman, as well as the coroner's van and police photographers, were strung out along the freeway. Twenty-nine cops in all. Plus a couple of the big boys from Downtown who went back and told Detective Leroy Orozco of Robbery-Homicide about it. Sharing information between cops and jurisdictions was one of the ways cases got solved.

Kidder and her partner, Peggy York, the county's only female homicide team, would be in charge of Northeast's investigation. Now Kidder stood trying to block the view of crime-beat reporters who had sped to the scene almost as quickly as the cops. She didn't want someone's mother spotting her dead daughter on the eleven o'clock news.

One of her bosses took her arm and steered her in front of the cameras. A pair of women homicide detectives working the case of two murdered girls would be good PR, and the attention might help with leads.

While Kidder spoke to reporters, news cameramen managed to get footage of the body bags being strapped to gurneys, wheeled up the incline, and placed in the coroner's van. The news clips would play over and over that night and the following day.

By ten past four the crime scene had been cleared, and by five-fifteen the coroner's office had notified Northeast that the blond girl had a bullet in her chest, possibly from a .25-caliber automatic.

At 8:45 P.M., the department held a press conference announcing the discovery of the bodies but withholding descriptions of the clothing. Then they waited for calls to come in identifying the victims.

That morning, Janet Marano had awakened feeling an unexplainable peace. The day was clear and pretty, with an ocean breeze that kept Huntington Beach cooler than Los Angeles. Janet went to lunch, then wandered around a beauty-supply shop. When she returned home, the television news was announcing the discovery of two dead girls. She made Andy phone the morgue. He did, and spoke to a woman there.

"It's not our girls," he said. Something in him had made him block what the woman had told him: the blond girl had a birthmark on her leg like Cindy. Like Gina, the dark girl wore a green ring.

As they drove out again that night to continue their search, Janet listened in relief as a radio newscaster announced that the dead blond girl's eyes were brown. Cindy's were hazel. Then she thought: What do hazel eyes look like when they're dead?

Her knees began to jump uncontrollably and she heard her teeth chatter like a window in a storm. Still they drove, and on the coast near a Burger King spotted a tall, tanned girl who looked like Gina. They parked the car and ran to look, but it was someone else's daughter. They knocked on the doors of Cindy and Gina's friends. No one had seen the girls.

Back at home, Janet plucked a Christian book from the shelf and read where it fell open: "The Lord giveth and the Lord taketh away." She hurled the book across the room and ran upstairs to bed where, inexplicably, she fell into a peaceful and dreamless sleep. Andy had promised that in the morning before work he would drive to the morgue, just to be sure.

The next morning was Friday, June 13. A morgue employee and a policeman walked Andy Marano down a corridor where two bodies lay on gurneys. One was blond and one was brunette. A protective layer in Andy's brain still kept him from knowing. He walked past the bodies.

A voice called him back and Andy turned. The girls looked like two dolls, their faces pink where the morgue hadn't washed the blood off. He was puzzled. Why had he been called?

"No," he said. "They're not our girls."

The woman moved a sheet back from the brunette and a small hand fell out. He recognized it. It was Gina's.

The policeman tried to keep him in an office, told him he should phone Janet, but he slipped away, hopped an elevator upstairs, and drove home.

In the bedroom, Janet beat at him with her fists.

"You son of a bitch," she cried. "You lied to me. You lied to me."

At 8:45 on the morning of Friday, June 13, Detective Leroy Orozco of Downtown Robbery-Homicide made a courtesy call to Northeast to remind the division that the dead body of a woman named Laura Collins had been found in the same spot as the two current Jane Does. Yolanda Washington, a Hillside Strangler victim, had been discovered on the opposite side of the freeway. Both stranglers were in jail. But maybe a copycat killer was at work.

He also wanted Northeast to know that in April, in San Bernardino County, a thirty-seven-year-old Indian woman had been shot in the head with a .25-caliber automatic, sodomized, then left by the side of the road. There could be a link. As it was not his case, and as he still did not realize it would become his, Orozco went about his business.

By ten o'clock on Friday morning, the coroner's office had identified the two girls as stepsisters Cynthia Chandler and Gina Marano, aged sixteen and fifteen, from Huntington Beach. By 10:45, detectives Helen Kidder and Peggy York were in Huntington Beach trying to find out more about the girls. The mother, a strikingly attractive woman in her thirties, and her husband were inconsolable and wanted to be alone with their grief. Outside the family's comfortable two-story home, Cindy Chandler's friends clustered, a sea of weeping sixteen-year-olds with perfect bodies in leopard-skin bikinis. Gradually a picture began to emerge of the girls' lives.

Cindy and Gina, chronic runaways and truants and rumored drug users, had been letting themselves into their own house and the homes of friends when they knew no one was home. They showered, borrowed clothes, and left trails of cookie crumbs. Michele Chandler, the girls' older sister, had seen them a couple of days before they died when a group of girls had engaged in a physical fight over a bag of clothes they claimed Cindy and Gina had stolen. That was the last Michele had seen of them. The girls had spoken of two men they had met at the Colorado River. Kidder and York set off to track the men down, tedious work that meant knocking on doors and checking phone listings.

The autopsy was at ten-thirty on Saturday. A slug had penetrated the back of Cynthia Chandler's head and emerged just beyond her skull beneath the scalp, leaving its jacket within her brain. The bullet in her chest was a contact wound that had passed through her lung and heart. Both wounds could have been fatal. She had a bruise on her right shin that had occurred before death, but on her back and right buttock she had postmortem scratches and abrasions that indicated she had been dragged. Postmortem lividity— the settling of blood within the body—indicated that Cynthia Chandler had been dead for more than twelve hours before her body was discovered.

Two bullets had penetrated Gina Marano's head, one of them an inch and a half above her left ear canal and an inch behind. It had exited near her right eyebrow. The other bullet had entered the back of her head and emerged below the first wound. There were no obvious signs of sexual molestation, but if Kidder were right and this was the work of a necrophiliac, there would be no bruising from sex acts that occurred after death.

In the afternoon, Kidder and York headed into the field, still trying to find the girls' Colorado River friends, beer-drinking good-timers in their twenties who repaired sports cars. The men, they discovered, had still been at the river at the time Cindy and Gina were murdered.

They traced the girls as far as Monterey Park, where they had spent the night of Tuesday, June 10, with other friends. Gina had been excited as she prepared to leave on Wednesday morning, the day she had been killed. She was on her way, she told her friends, to get her hair curled for a television-commercial audition. She and Cindy had been staying with a man named Richie in Beverly Hills, and the friends thought that Richie's chauffeur, Dudley, had been coming to pick them up.

It was seven o'clock on Saturday night when Kidder and York walked back into Northeast Division's Homicide office to find two other officers on the phone, waving their free arms at them. There was a woman on the line who claimed to have information about the murders.

Officer Heinlein had taken an earlier call, which was patched in to him through the Van Nuys Police Department switchboard at about five o'clock. The woman—she said her name was Betsy—described a little striped dress and a green tube top that she thought belonged to the two murdered girls from Huntington Beach. But Betsy had hung up. She had been calling from a pay phone and became spooked when, coincidentally, a policeman walked by.

Two hours later, she had phoned again. The code name Betsy had been "a grave mistake," she said. Her boyfriend, who might be the killer, could link it to her. She would prefer to be called Claudia and would give her real name in a day or two when she felt secure with the situation.

The woman's voice was clear and girlish, her diction formal and multisyllabic, almost like a policeman testifying in court. It seemed as if she were trying to impress the officers.

"What I'm trying to do," she said, "is ascertain whether or not the individual that I know, who happens to be my lover, did in fact do this. He said he did."

Kidder picked up a phone and listened in. The Betsy/Claudia woman sounded like a nut to her. She said she had washed clothing and found a massive amount of bloody paper towels.

"Where did the bloody paper towels come from?" Heinlein asked.

"Presumably from the back of the Plymouth—" said Claudia, catching herself as if she had made a slip. "Presumably from the *car*," she corrected. She used the name "Don" when speaking of her lover, then hesitated again and substituted "he," as if she had made another slip. Later she called him John.

The officers were blasé. The woman's description of the clothing did not match what the girls had been wearing, and they told her so. But why they expected it to match, no one clarified.

"If the clothing is off, then it may not have happened in front of him at all." Claudia sounded stunned.

Her boyfriend fantasized and he "came up with a lot of bullshit," she said. But he had also come to her home before with his clothes and knife bloody and had told her that throughout his adolescence and "up into his forties," he had been killing and doing "assigned hits."

"I will tell you right now," said Claudia, "he's forty-one years old."

"Okay," Heinlein said. "Is he white, black?"

"Either one or the other," said the woman.

"Come on, which one is he?"

"He's white."

Her boyfriend, who had blond hair and blue eyes, had told her that he knew the blond girl, who had once given him a lousy blow job that wasn't worth the money. Her attitude had been so bad that he had planned to kill her.

"Okay," the woman said. "Now that's not a rational reason for wanting to take somebody's life."

Still she wouldn't identify her boyfriend.

"If he didn't do it, I've ruined a relationship that I happen to enjoy. . . ." she said. "If he did do it, I've got to be extremely cautious, because he will get me. . . . Where am I going to hide? . . . He will find me."

Betsy/Claudia seemed to have more than a passing knowledge of police procedures. Hearing her speak of booking, bail, and arraignment—and her lack of confidence in the police being able to protect her—Helen Kidder thought the woman was a flake who worked for a police department somewhere.

Officer Westbrook, also on the line questioning the caller, sounded actively hostile. "What you apparently know, a good deal of it, is what you've read in the papers. Now, I'm not saying that's right or that's wrong."

"Well, so put me down as a crackpot." Claudia sounded offended. "Whatever you do, if you want me to contact you again, don't give this to the media."

"Ma'am, there's nothing here that you've said so far that the media would even be interested in."

"That's good," the woman said. But she sounded deflated, and a couple of minutes later she tried again to arouse their interest.

"Oh, I know one thing else we did today. We washed the car. I mean *washed* the car. Inside out, scrubbed it down. He took hoses and he shooshed all that blood and all the clots and stuff out of the car. I mean really soaked the inside of that car down."

Heinlein wanted to know what happened to the bloody towels and a blanket the woman had talked about. Sounding evasive, Claudia said she had disposed of some of it but had kept the striped dress and green tube top she had mentioned.

"Do you still have it?"

"I gave it to John this afternoon."

"Jeez."

Westbrook again asked for the man's name.

"You couldn't even be sure it would be his real name. At this point there's an eighty-five percent chance that the things that I'm telling you now, because I'm scared off, are misdirection."

Claudia was still determined to get some information of her own. Had her lover been telling the truth, she asked, when he said he shot twice into one girl's head, virtually blowing the back of it away, then once into the other girl's head and once into her chest?

Westbrook sounded weary and patronizing now, a bureaucrat who would not be budged. "Well, ma'am, that's information that I'm not going to give out."

This made Claudia angry.

"Well then I can't give you any more. . . ." she snapped. "You have to understand this. Either I know the killer, in which case I may be the next one on his list . . . otherwise, if he's on a pipe dream, if he heard a newsbreak or something and he decided to roll in the glory of that, then there's no point in carrying this on anymore."

Claudia's ego seemed bruised. She seemed to be trying to convince herself that the officer took her seriously. They wouldn't have spent so much time with her if they thought she was a screwball, she told them.

Westbrook's voice dripped with sarcasm. "How do I know who's an obvious screwball?"

"The paper only said one bullet in each of those children. All right, he also stated that he used one of the girls in a sexual manner. . . . That isn't something that's going to come out until your autopsy is completed. I don't even know if he did it to the point of orgasm. Knowing him and his sexual pattern, he probably did not. He probably tried it and then just jacked himself off on her chest or something. Because a lot of his sexuality is masturbation in nature."

"Well," Westbrook said. "I don't see why you're telling us all this and will not give us his name so we can work on it."

By now, Claudia was insulted. "All right. You've had one hundred and fifty calls, okay, so check out your other one hundred and forty-nine other ones, okay?"

Suddenly Westbrook seemed to realize that his hard line might be a mistake. He said, "Well, your information is very interesting."

Heinlein butted in. "This may be the one. We don't want to overlook anything."

"All right. This may be the one or it may be a total pipe dream out of a neurotic lady. Right?" said Claudia.

"That's right," Westbrook said. "It could be. But I can't check it out if I don't have his name."

"But you're not helping me either," said Claudia. "You're not putting my mind at rest."

Abruptly, the line went dead. It seemed as if Claudia had hung up.

But Carol Bundy, calling from a pay phone within sight of the Van Nuys Police Department, had been cut off by the Van Nuys switchboard, which had routed the call to Northeast.

Later, when Detective Leroy Orozco heard the tape at Downtown Robbery-Homicide, he would curse. He would have given the woman something. Anything. He would have soothed her ego, flattered her, made her feel important and arranged to meet her. He chalked it up to inexperience on the part of Westbrook and Heinlein.

That night, just hours after Carol phoned police, Doug came home and told her to watch the news. There was a story about the murder of a man named Vic Weiss, whose body had been found stuffed in the trunk of a Rolls-Royce in the parking garage of the Sheraton Universal hotel. Carol assumed the murder had happened that day.

Doug laughed. He'd killed Weiss, he told Carol, as a voluntary initiation into a Mafia hit group. But he'd left the body lying there. He hadn't stuffed him in the trunk of any Rolls.

The next day was Sunday. Doug suggested a drive. He showed her the drop site for Cindy and Gina—he had nicknamed them "the Twins"—then doubled back east to Griffith Park, where immigrant families rode the carousel and, to escape the heat of their nearby apartments, picnicked on sun-dappled grass beneath the trees.

As always when they were together, Doug was at the wheel of the Datsun, which they were driving because of the stench of drying blood in the freshly washed Buick. One of the toys, his dull-finished nickel .25-caliber Raven, lay between them. It was cocked, with a shell in the hammer.

Near a scrubby patch of hillside, Doug gestured vaguely. That, he said, was where he had dropped Nick the second night that spring that he had arrived home soaked with blood. Immediately he changed his mind. Maybe that wasn't the spot after all. He seemed to enjoy telling Carol things that were close to but not quite the truth. That way, she interpreted, she could never turn him in. No one would believe her. The cops hadn't believed her yesterday.

As she sat next to him, Doug seemed able to read her mind. She was the only one in the world who knew about his crimes. She was aware of nothing much more than the gun that lay between them.

"You think I'm going to kill you, don't you, Carol?"

"Well," she said. "The thought has crossed my mind."

"Don't worry," he said. "I'm not going to kill you." He paused. "At least not now." He said, kindly, "Put the gun away if it'll make you feel better." Carol put the gun in the glove compartment. Again, in an expansive mood, he told her not to worry. If he had to kill her, he wouldn't dump her like the other girls. He'd make sure she got a decent burial.

They were on the freeway now, heading toward open country, the Valley spread out as far as they could see. To the north, near the foothills, he pulled the car up by a rugged ravine and pointed. This was the drop site for a hit Carol didn't know about yet. It was time to tell her.

"Down there," he said.

The night he had test-driven the Datsun, he had picked up a young blond hooker. A real little snot. He had pulled the gun on her, and when she spotted it she yelled at him in fear.

"You son of a bitch," she had said.

She kicked at him and struggled, breaking the gearshift before she died. He shot her three times (although he told Carol four, with one shot going through her elbow). Then he had driven out here, dragged her body into the ravine, and sliced open her belly with his knife to encourage what he called "the wiggly-squirmies" to accelerate the decay. No one would ever find her under the vegetation.

Because the dump site was near Foothill Boulevard, he'd nick-named the girl "Foothill," and he'd given some of her clothes to eleven-year-old Theresa, keeping the fuchsia-colored panties for himself.

As he spoke now to Carol, Doug told her that if she decided to run, there would be nowhere for her to hide. If she turned on him, the way killer Roy Norris had with his partner, Lawrence Bittaker, he would find a way to get to one of the boys and she could spend the rest of her life sitting around worrying about the other one.

She had three possibilities, Carol said later, as she tried to ratio-nalize what happened next. Doug could marry her so that she would not be able to testify against him. He could kill her or have her and the boys killed through his Mafia hit-group connections. Or, she told herself, she could cooperate in order to save her own life and the lives of her children. She chose to cooperate.

On June 12, the day after Cindy and Gina died, she had found a $400-a-month two-bedroom apartment on Verdugo Avenue in Burbank, a five-minute walk to the Jergens factory for Doug. If he approved of it, Doug was going to move out of Lydia Crouch's. By the first of July, at the very latest, they'd be living together again.

But before that, something would happen. Carol Bundy would decide that murder was fun.

Helen Kidder still thought that Betsy/Claudia was full of hot air. But a friend of hers from her pre-Homicide days in the Bombing Division was a Rand Institute specialist in terrorist threats. Five days after the Chandler and Marano bodies were found, he ana-lyzed a tape of the informant's phone call. He thought the woman was telling the truth, he reported. Kidder still didn't buy it. The story about swooshing blood out of the car just seemed too prepos-terous to her.

Still, two days later, she and Peggy York met with the *Los Angeles Times*, the *Valley News*, and a local television station. Without using the name "Betsy" or "Claudia," they appealed for their mysterious source to call back. The phone did not ring.

A bullet from one of the girls had been compared with a bullet from the San Bernardino .25-caliber murder victim. The comparison was negative. There had been a similar case in Redondo Beach. But that turned out to be over a drug deal, and suspects were in jail.

Tests had shown sperm in Cindy Chandler's vagina but none in her throat, and none at all in Gina, although there were still more slides to do. The detectives asked for a comparison between the grease on Cindy's clothing and on her heel. And they began checking out the origin of her pink jumpsuit.

The day that Andy identified Cindy and Gina, the Marano family had left the Huntington Beach house to move in with Janet's mother. They huddled in her family room, the four children in sleeping bags, the television going all night. They slept fitfully, awakened by Janet's screams.

The girls' bodies were released to the funeral parlor. Beside the coffin, Janet said to Cindy, who was rouged and powdered, "Where are you? Where *are* you?" At the moment that it happened, she wondered, did Cindy cry out for her? For all their bravado and surface worldliness, the girls had been babies.

As they had lain out in the June heat, their bodies had become swollen, and Cindy's mouth was still puffed up in a pout. It reminded Janet of when her daughter was little and had teased her in mock defiance, sticking out her lower lip.

If she could have got in the coffin to lie with Cindy, Janet Marano would have. One of her tears dropped, making Cindy's makeup run, making her look as if she were crying.

The funeral was held in Huntington Beach. Under a gray, June beach sky, ninety friends and members of the Marano family gathered at the grave side.

"We live in a world filled with violence, crime, pain . . . and death," intoned Bill Dobrener, the girls' bearded youth minister. "Cindy and Gina made some wrong choices. They listened to some wrong voices. Maybe it was through their two deaths that you could have life today."

The only way that Pastor Bill could justify the killings was to tell himself that God had taken Cindy and Gina home before their lives could become worse. He knew his God and knew that He always worked for the best. But as he remembered Cindy and Gina the year before at a church outing to Magic Mountain amusement park, so happy and alive taking care of the smaller children, he couldn't help crying, even though he knew his God was in control.

After the funeral, Janet spoke to the local paper, blaming lax authorities and the "scum hole" of Huntington Beach for the girls' incorrigibility.

"A whipping doesn't help at this age," she said.

Another mother came up to her. Her own daughter had ditched school with the girls, she explained eagerly, but since the murders she had rededicated her life to Christ and seen the error of her ways.

"Your daughters died so that mine could live," the woman said. She seemed to expect Janet to rejoice with her. Instead Janet walked away wondering how anyone could be so insensitive.

You lose friends, she thought. It was happening already. She could sense people judging her, shoring themselves up on her hurt to distance themselves from the possibility that something like this could happen to them.

The morning after the funeral, Janet left her mother's house at dawn and continued her hunt for the girls. The bodies in those coffins had not been Cindy and Gina, so they must be out there somewhere still. She drove up and down the familiar leafy streets of Huntington Beach and stopped her car outside the houses of Cindy and Gina's friends. Janet walked on the beach and she looked and looked, but all she could see were the waves.

11

CAROL AND DOUG TALKED OF NOTHING NOW BUT MURDER AND death. And Doug was rubbing her nose in it with the sex. Not actually having sex in front of her—only a few times with prostitutes in the car—but he brought women around and paraded them. The sweet talk and the compliments had stopped a long time ago. Now she could do nothing right.

"I don't know how you keep a job, you're so incompetent," he kept telling her. And the more he told her that, the more incompetent Carol felt.

In a way, though, there was a comfortable familiarity to it. It was what Carol had always been used to. She viewed herself as a warm, giving person. A gentle woman who sacrificed everything for her men. Seemingly unaware of how controlling and enraging another's victimhood could be, she became puzzled and hurt when the recipients of her generosity turned on her. When things began to go bad, as they inevitably did, Carol felt she worked twice as hard to try and get half of what most women would feel they were entitled to to start with.

Jack and Doug, she decided, were both selfish, self-centered, and violent men. The difference was, Jack beat people and Douglas killed them. He had told her that by the time he murdered Cindy and Gina, he had killed nearly fifty people. His goal was to kill a hundred. As far as Carol could see, he had absolutely no sense of shame, guilt, or remorse.

"You're a sociopath," she said to him one day, wondering if she would be alive herself by the end of summer. She did not think then to apply the word to herself.

It was a softer-sounding word to her than psychopath. But apparently not to Douglas. He looked offended. Swift to offer criticism, he did not like to be on the receiving end.

One psychiatrist would say later that the fragile structure that held Carol Bundy's life together began to collapse with the breakup of her marriage, eroded further with Jack Murray's betrayal, then collapsed completely with the departure of the boys. Carol herself would claim that she had been an ordinary woman, Mrs. Average America under pressure, when the Cathy episode occurred on the twentieth of June.

Doug kept calling into the darkness, "Miss? Miss?"

The girl ignored him. She was wearing cowboy boots, a little maroon dress, and a bolero jacket with red hearts on it, and she was standing near Hughes Market on Highland Avenue in Hollywood in the dark hours of early morning.

Doug tried again. "My wife doesn't like to give blow jobs and I really could use one. Would you mind?"

Finally the girl nodded an okay and walked over to get in the driver's side of the Buick while Doug relieved himself at the front of the car. She could have been as young as seventeen. Or twenty at the most. A dumb, sweet little blond kid who said her name was Cathy.

Doug got in on the passenger side. Carol, in the back seat with the shiny chrome .25-caliber Raven in her purse, said, "My name's Barbara."

"Pleased to meet you," Cathy said, gentle and obliging.

They had planned it. Carol's first hit. But if she didn't want to do it, she didn't have to. If she did want to do it, her code phrase would be, "Boy, am I having a blast." At the very worst, Doug would get a blow job out of it.

Cathy had agreed on a price of thirty dollars. In the parking lot behind the corner gas station at Franklin Avenue and Highland, she took Doug in her mouth. But she wasn't good enough, which may have been another way of saying that Doug did not become aroused. All the while Cathy tried, Doug and Carol exchanged eye

103

signals, Doug knowing that the gun had one under the hammer, cocked and ready to go.

Did he want her to kill Cathy? Or didn't he? Carol couldn't tell.

He shook his head, No. But his own gun was on the driver's side between the seat and the door and he couldn't get to it. Cathy was in the way.

Doug reached his left hand back and waved his fingers at Carol. She slapped the gun in his hand, catching hell for it later, because stupid Carol, inexperienced Carol, gave him the gun pointing in the wrong direction, thinking he just wanted to get it away from her in case she was going to shoot.

He tried to maneuver the Raven around. Cathy, worried suddenly, tried to sit up. Immediately Doug shot her left-handed, but she didn't die right away. She continued to breathe, and her breathing was hard.

Doug yelled at Carol: "All right. All right. I know you're nervous. But be cool. Be cool."

If she had screamed or panicked, he was ready to shoot Carol, too. He had told her that beforehand, worrying that she would freak out on her first actual kill.

"I'm all right," Carol said.

Doug looked back at her. She was all right. Not turned on and not turned off. Simply interested intellectually in the outcome.

He told her to get up front, and Carol jumped out of the car and got in on the passenger side.

Cathy's legs lay across the seat. Her head lay on Carol and she bled all over Carol's striped blouse while the nurse in Carol kept thinking that if they got her to a hospital she could be saved. Doug had paper towels in the car. He handed them to Carol and he said. "Strip her. Strip her."

So Carol began to strip off Cathy's clothes and jewelry. Doug's denim jacket was on the floor and Carol used it to cover up what was going on from other drivers. Under it, she wrestled with the dying girl as they drove away from the crime scene up Highland Avenue, past the Hollywood Bowl and under the bridge into the fast lane of the Hollywood Freeway, then as far as they could go north into the open country.

It was a bitch, Carol thought, trying to get a dress off a dead girl who wasn't cooperating.

By the time they were near Magic Mountain amusement park, turning off onto a country road, with Doug freaking out still and forgetting to signal when he changed lanes, Cathy's pulse was still

104

strong and steady and good, but she was death-rattling, and Carol kept trying to open the glove compartment so she could get a tissue and wipe Cathy's nose, which was bubbling with liquid.

Cathy had a pretty little body with blond pubic hair, Carol observed. But the stupid broad had her cigarettes and her makeup and her pick hair-comb tucked into her cowboy boot on top of her buck knife. What good was that going to do her? Not that she had a chance anyway.

They drove on through the darkness until they arrived at a dirt road with a little stream running by it. Then about a mile along the gravel they came to what looked like a pond across their path. Doug didn't want to drive any further in case the car got stuck in the mud. There they pulled Cathy out of the car and dragged her about twenty feet, where they left her lying in some bushes, probably dead by now.

It was about five in the morning before they got back to the Valley, and Carol would remember the freeway's orange lights shining, eerie, in the first light of dawn. This wasn't something that happened in real life, she thought. This was something that happened in a bizarre movie.

The next day was Saturday, June 21. Doug, taking eleven-year-old Kevin Crouch with him, drove the Buick from Lydia Crouch's apartment to pick up Carol at Lemona Avenue. From there, the three of them went to a coin-operated car wash on Van Nuys Boulevard where they washed out the wagon. The blood, Doug told Kevin, was from a cat he had hit the night before. The poor creature had died as Doug, the Good Samaritan, was rushing it to the vet.

Lydia Crouch, not knowing the real nature of the car wash, became angry for a more mundane reason—because Doug had taken Kevin out with his old girlfriend, Carol Bundy. Doug chose to tell her that night as they sat at a drive-in in a car that smelled to Lydia of raw meat. There was an argument, which led to Doug's packing up his belongings the next day and moving out.

The same day, Carol paid a deposit on the apartment at 240 West Verdugo Avenue in Burbank. Doug was to move in before Carol. But that night he went out hunting, later telling Carol what happened.

The Buick rolled to a stop. Doug opened the passenger window. His usual line, delivered with rueful, boyish charm, was, "My wife doesn't like to give blow jobs."

Three of them were tricking together, a black girl, a thin blonde in a pink dress, and another blonde, soft and plump. He didn't want the black girl, but then he couldn't get either one of the blondes into the car alone and so he had no choice but to drive on. When he returned, the thin one dressed in hot pink was standing by herself.

He tried again.

She hesitated. Then she got in and he drove, looking for a safe, empty parking lot.

She nestled her head in his crotch. Her shoulders were pale and freckled, one of her upper arms tattooed with a heart. There was something vulgar about her. Something belligerent. Something about her strange, hooded brown eyes. Down the side of the car seat he felt for the gun. As her mouth worked on him, he shot her in the back of the head. But with the beginning of death she bit him, and the bite made him angry.

The Studio City Sizzler restaurant was closed. Toward the back of the lot, they were shielded by a wooden fence. Even in daylight no one walked along nearby Ventura Boulevard, and after midnight on Sunday night only an occasional car took the curve near where they were parked.

He was prepared, as usual, with his buck knife hidden in the visor, and he had what he and Carol now called the "kill bag." It was a brown supermarket bag with another knife, paper towels, liquid cleanser, and rubber gloves. Carol was useful for something. It was Carol, in fact, who had suggested that he make each killing progressively more gruesome so the cops would be looking for a psycho and not someone sane like him. Carol, too, would come up with the phrase "bitches, botches, or butches" to describe the women he chose to kill.

He dragged this one out of the car and stripped her, ripping a green ring from her right ring finger. Getting her head off was hard work. He cut and sawed with his buck knife, not enjoying it particularly. With the cutting and the spreading pool of blood, the anger over her snottiness left him. He hadn't wanted to decapitate anyone. But she was dead already, so what difference did it make?

Carefully, he removed a plastic bag from the kill kit and put the head inside. Then he placed it in the back of the Buick. As he drove off, her torso was a pale blotch in the dark of the parking lot.

But then he thought about it. The other women had seen him and maybe could identify him. He circled around. By a stroke of extraordinary good luck, the tubby one was still on the street. This time she got in the car, nicely dressed in a black velvet jacket and a two-piece red-and-black dress. If there was blood from her friend, she didn't see it.

He didn't want sex with her. Never had. She was too fat and every bit as snotty as the other one. Shooting her would be strictly for fun, as well as insurance. Already it was fun. Laughable as hell. He had her poor dead friend's head in a plastic bag in the back of the Buick and Tubby oblivious in the front seat.

Near the Burbank Studios, he pulled the car to a stop. When he took out the gun, she saw it and screamed a loud, shrill scream. At a nearby house, dogs barked, excited, poking their noses through some bushes near the fence as they tried to get out.

He had to hurry.

As usual, he shot her in the left temple, the gun making its little popping sound. And then she died.

He ripped out her earrings, yanking the right one, which made her earlobe bleed. She was wearing a dainty Tinkerbell necklace and he left that but stole cash from her to give Carol for rent money. Then he opened the car door and pushed the body out into the street, where she landed twisted, her head against the curb and her arm flung up over her head as if, in death, she were trying too late to protect herself.

Less than three miles away, at the new Burbank apartment, he parked the Buick and carried the head upstairs with him. At 3:08 A.M., three minutes after a Burbank police detective pronounced the second victim dead in the gutter near the Burbank Studios, Douglas Clark picked up the phone and, from Verdugo Avenue, called Carol Bundy.

Worrying suddenly about the black prostitute's being a witness, he once more got into the Buick and doubled back to try to kill her, too. When he couldn't find her, he drove to Lemona. There, as Carol awoke briefly, he tossed cash on the bed, stolen from the shoe of his last, plump victim.

When they talked about it all, everything that was going on, she felt an extraordinary psychological intimacy. It was their moment of deepest rapport, stronger even than the sexual bond she had felt in the beginning. Doug talked to her about blending in with the crowd, about being careful not to leave any evidence. Suddenly she realized the reason for his anger when she scraped the side of the Buick. What had been an innocuous-looking station wagon suddenly had an identifying mark.

But Doug was not as careful himself as he wanted her to be. Carol had blown up at him when he called her at work to tell her that, posing as a policeman, he had phoned a woman to talk about the Chandler-Marano murders. He had given his real name, and it struck Carol that perhaps he wanted to be caught.

Now they worried that the Buick was too hot to keep, and Doug talked to a coworker at the Jergens factory about buying it. Pleased with his bargain, the man agreed to a price of five hundred dollars. If they were caught, Doug promised to take the rap and Carol would get off. Her defense would be that she was that Los Angeles stereotype: the dumb, station-wagon-driving Valley housewife. A housewife mesmerized by Douglas Clark's charm.

Although Carol idealized herself, never before had she considered quite how wholesome and housewifey she was until Douglas pointed it out to her. Then she began thinking, Yes. That's what I really am. Mrs. Average America.

She hadn't moved into the Verdugo apartment yet and was dropping some things off when Doug opened the freezer and she saw a round plastic bag. Immediately she knew what it was. She wanted to look inside.

"It's too gross," Doug told her.

"Look, I work around dead people," Carol said. "It won't freak me out."

But he wouldn't let her see it that day.

The next time she went over, carrying bits and pieces of kitchen things, the head sat on the side of the kitchen sink. Doug, showing off, picked it up and swung it by its frosted blond hair. He laughed. He said he'd taken it in the shower to play and, fantasizing that the woman was alive, had stuffed his penis in the mouth that was as open now as it had been when she died.

Carol thought he was just trying to be shocking. He thought it was funny as hell, a great trick to play on the police, making them think there was a freako out there.

They'd seen news reports of what the press was calling the Sunset Strip Slayings. Doug followed the stories carefully, clipping them from the paper, keeping them for a while, then throwing them away. Her name, they knew now, was Exxie Wilson, and she was from Little Rock, Arkansas. Because she had an upper plate, their code name for her was Toothless. The fat one was still Tubby; the one up in the north Valley that he killed the night of the Datsun test drive was Foothill or Bush Bunny; and Cindy and Gina were still the Twins.

After a couple of days with the head in the freezer, Doug became nervous.

Jittery, they joked about leaving their spoils gift wrapped on a bus bench. But as Carol wandered around Newberry's on Sherman Way she spotted it. It was a box. A treasure chest made of rough wood, measuring about eleven by thirteen inches, with brass rings and corners. It was so perfect that she returned to buy it, looking above reproach on the hot June day. Mrs. Average America, homely in her Bermudas, tank top, and glasses. The assistant manager, a woman named Shirley, noted absently a comically sinister touch: a pair of black gloves Carol had thought to pull over her dainty hands and wrists.

Preparing Exxie for the drop-off was Carol's turn to have fun. Doug wanted her to look nice, so they got cosmetics and Carol sat at the kitchen table making her up like a big Barbie doll. As usual, though, Carol's work was unsatisfactory to Doug. He bitched at her about the way she'd done one eye, which, still frozen, kept drooping. After a while, though, it occurred to him that they might be leaving fingerprints in the makeup. It then became Carol's job to scrub Exxie down with detergent in the kitchen sink. All that work for nothing.

That early-summer week the heat dragged into the evenings. It was almost seven by the time they finished loading the box at the Verdugo apartment. After it was filled they double-wrapped it in a pair of plastic bags, set it carefully in the back of the Buick, then drove west through the Valley.

The drop had to be in the perfect place. Not long before, a body had been discovered in a small shopping center in Tarzana. Doug was toying with the idea of leaving their box in the same spot. The cops would have fun with that one. But the shopping center turned out to be at an intersection busy with traffic. They would be too visible. Something didn't feel right.

They headed south on Reseda to Ventura Boulevard. Traffic was still heavy. At an In-N-Out Burger drive-in they ordered hamburgers and Carol asked for a diet soda. She hadn't been to In-N-Out before. The kids preferred McDonald's, and anyway she was persnickety about eating in the car. In what felt to her like the periodically altered state of mind she had been in since this all began, Carol sipped her drink and forgot for one brief moment why they were out. Then she freaked.

A cop car had pulled next to them. A black and white just feet away and that box in the back seat containing what the entire Los

Angeles Police Department must have been hunting for nearly a week.

Doug said, in his well-modulated, educated purr, "It's all right. Be cool. They don't know she's here." Even in what should have been a moment of panic, he carried with him that air of upper-middle-class entitlement.

Carol said, "Okay. Shut *up*." But to her amazement now she was cool, just as she had been with Cathy. Ten times as cool as he was, even though she didn't have half the experience. And why shouldn't she be cool? Why should the cops suspect anything of a chubby thirty-seven-year-old woman sitting with her thirty-two-year-old boyfriend in a blue station wagon?

The cops didn't even glance their way. So they drove back through the Valley still hunting for the perfect drop-off place, Doug being as picky as usual. Carol could tell that he was getting nervous now. But maybe because they'd had such a good time with what was in the box, in spite of his nerves he didn't really want to let it go.

They drew closer to the Studio City Sizzler where he had done poor Exxie in the first place. About a mile west, they found an alley behind Hoffman Street a block from the busy intersection at Laurel Canyon Boulevard near the Stop 'n' Shop market, and far from discreet.

Carol had brought the black gloves with her, so she pulled them on. Then she removed the outer plastic bag from the wooden box. When Doug slowed the Buick and told her to throw the box out, she slipped off the second plastic bag, got the car door partly open, and heaved the box as far as she could. But he didn't bring the wagon to a complete stop and she must not have heaved far enough. They heard the horrible sound of shattering wood. Then, as they pulled away, the Buick's door still open, a car turned into the alley from the other end. Its headlights met theirs. The car drew alongside them, then it passed, allowing him to turn on her in anger.

She should have seen the other car. She had taken at least eight seconds to get that box out, when she should have done it in three.

"How am I going to turn you into a murderer when you're clumsy and not observant?" he said.

After that he wouldn't let up. As they drove back to Burbank, he told her again and again that she was stupid and incompetent.

Carol sat there and listened. It was a little after nine on the twenty-sixth of June and it looked as if it would be a long evening.

The box lay there for hours, splintered in the corner where the rear tire had run over it. It was about one o'clock in the morning of June 27 by the time Jonathan Caravello turned in to the alley behind his Hoffman Street apartment. As he began to ease into his parking space, Caravello realized that something was blocking his way. In the glow of his headlights he picked up the outline of what appeared to be a large wooden treasure chest. Caravello put on his parking brake and got out of the car to move his find directly under the headlights. Intrigued, he lifted the lid of the box and saw what appeared to be some clothes. As he looked more closely, he realized to his horror that the box contained the head of a woman. Her mouth was slightly open and she was wrapped in some jeans and a pink T-shirt.

Jonathan Caravello abandoned his find. He ran past the parking garage and down a path next to some bushes. He galloped up the stairs to his apartment. Then he phoned the police.

12

THE DRIVE FROM LITTLE ROCK TO MORRILTON SEEMED TO TAKE FOR-ever, the cop car not air-conditioned and each county hotter than the last. Detective Leroy Orozco's shirt stuck to him. When he and John Helvin wanted to stop for a beer, their driver, a Little Rock policeman, told them there weren't any bars and they couldn't drink in the car because some counties were dry. If they were caught, they could all go to jail. So much for Arkansas.

Humidity had turned the foliage brilliant green, yet to Orozco the landscape was desolate. Past a combination general store and post office they followed directions to the mobile home of Zelma Ammons, Exxie Wilson's mother. Left at the big elm, another turn near a rock, and then Zelma Ammons and Exxie's sister, Minnie, were waiting for them. As they got out of the car, mosquitoes buzzed, sensing fresh meat. Leroy Orozco slapped at them.

The women seemed like plain country folk and he felt like a city slicker. Understandably, they were having trouble comprehending what had happened to Exxie. But as well as they could, Zelma and Minnie told the detectives all they knew.

Exxie's father had died when she was nine. She had graduated from high school barely able to spell, worked as a waitress and in a motel. Then, two years before her death, she had met Little Rock pimp Derek Albright, fallen in love, and turned to prostitution. In

May, Exxie had made the long journey from Little Rock by bus to visit her mother in Morrilton.

Exxie had been having trouble with the local police. Business had dried up and Derek wanted to take his stable to Los Angeles, where Exxie did not want to go. On the twelfth of June, she had phoned Zelma four times to talk about her problems. At the end of the fourth call, Derek got on the line and warned Zelma to quit bothering them. Those who knew Exxie thought, though, that she really loved Derek, which was one reason she ended up in his Cadillac driving west.

Leroy told Zelma what he knew about Exxie's last days, sparing her details of the decapitation. In Los Angeles, he had learned that a group had left Little Rock on the fifteenth of June: Exxie, two girls named Sharon, another called Willie, and Karen Jones, the Sunset Murderer's other Little Rock victim, had crammed into Derek Albright's blue-and-white Cadillac with their bits of baggage. Karen, pregnant, had dropped out of college, where she had been on a scholarship. Later she had spent time in a shelter for battered women, then had turned to prostitution to support her little boy.

Albright and his party had taken about four days to travel beyond the green humidity of Arkansas, through parched farmlands and the deep pink of the desert that led into Las Vegas. They had driven on into the smog of San Bernardino before arriving at Derek's mother's house in south Los Angeles. On Thursday, the women hit the Sunset Strip in Derek's father's car. Almost immediately Willie got busted, but she was out by Friday afternoon. On Saturday night, all Derek's girls were back working the Strip again while Derek played pool near Fifth and Manchester. It was about three in the morning by the time they all got home. It had been a rough but profitable week.

On Sunday they slept in, then rose at about two to go into Hollywood. Derek drove a borrowed Ford; the girls went in the Cadillac. They ogled the sights, then went to see Robert Redford in *Brubaker*, Exxie enjoying a hot dog and popcorn during the show. At about eleven, when the movie let out, they drove west down Sunset and stopped at Carneys railroad car restaurant for hamburgers. Exxie wasn't hungry. The others watched her walk away, wearing her pink dress and new black shoes with four-inch heels that she'd bought for herself on Friday. She was looking for a trick.

After they had eaten, the rest of the women scattered and Derek headed for the pool hall again, stopping optimistically to price a

113

new Cadillac at a Wilshire Boulevard car agency. Between one-thirty and two-thirty on Sunday morning one of the Sharons had spotted Exxie walking alone on the south side of the street a few blocks west of the Body Shop strip joint. A little after two o'clock, Karen Jones had called Derek. She had been hassled by a sheriff outside Ben Frank's coffee shop and was going to move to the city limits.

A few minutes later, still on the Sunset Strip, Karen had been seen standing alone on a corner as she waited for a date. But at some time, the women must have regrouped.

Derek Albright had done time for second-degree murder. On June 9, Exxie had signed a felony warrant against him accusing him of compelling her by force and intimidation to engage in prostitution. But, Orozco and Helvin learned, Derek had come on the line during Exxie's June 12 phone call to her mother, which placed him in Little Rock the day Cindy and Gina's bodies were found. He had also been given an alibi by one of the Sharons for the night of Exxie's death. Their business done in Morrilton, the detectives thanked Zelma and went to eat lunch in a café where fans droned overhead and everything came with peas, gravy, and potatoes.

In the marble-pillared courthouse they spoke to the local sheriff, who told them that in his opinion, by the time she was out of high school Exxie had been destined for a life of crime. There had been little discipline in her family and her four brothers were either in prison or recently released.

Most interesting to Orozco was that Exxie's friends and the police agreed that her attitude could be offensive to dates. She was known to curse at them and steal their money. Maybe, Orozco thought, this had been the reason for her decapitation.

Orozco and Helvin's trip had brought the detectives no closer to finding the Sunset killer than they had been before, but it was basic work that had to be done. In Little Rock, they finally got their beer in a place called the Larceny Lounge, a gated liquor store in a black neighborhood where locals and cops bought six-packs at a counter, then took them into a back room. There was a couch, tables, seats made of crates, and the inevitable fan, underneath which a sweating man kept an eye on everyone.

On their way out of town, Orozco and Helvin took a detour to look at Central High School, the scene of violence and protests during the 1950s desegregation crisis. They walked around the building, the heat choking them, and looked at the steps up which black children had walked, booed by mobs. Today all looked peaceful.

But it was godforsaken country, Leroy thought. He couldn't understand why anyone would stay there. On the other hand, if Exxie Wilson had stayed, she would still be alive.

Back at Parker Center, Orozco reviewed the evidence that had accumulated in his absence and learned about a nineteen-year-old Beverly Hills woman named Mindy Cohen, an acquaintance of Cindy Chandler and Gina Marano. Cohen had received a suspicious phone call and had told this story:

On the first of June, she had pointed her silver Corvette away from her parents' house toward Bel-Air and the home of her lawyer boyfriend, Mark, who was giving a party.

Mindy liked to think of herself as a party animal. At the Melrose Avenue boutique where she worked, she smoked dope with the other salespeople. At night she hung out on the Sunset Strip at the celebrity-studded Rainbow Bar and Grill. This was standard, 1980-style rich-girl behavior. What was not so standard was Mindy's affair with Mark. He was thirty-eight and she had not told her father about him. She had always been Leo Cohen's good little girl and Mindy didn't want him to learn otherwise. She had been underage when the affair began.

Mindy had expected to be the first person at the party. But Mark pulled her over and introduced her to a dark-haired teenager named Gina who looked young and lost. Richie, a neighbor of Mark's who claimed vague movie- and music-industry connections, had sent his chauffeur, Dudley, to the Sunset Strip to look for pretty girls. Dudley, twenty-two and always dressed in a white suit, rarely came back empty-handed. Today he had returned in Richie's hearselike limousine with Gina and her older stepsister Cindy.

Soon about a hundred people milled around Mark's house and garden. Judges and lawyers mingled with young, beautiful, and expensively dressed women. Mindy, in a new Kenzo outfit, her dark curly hair long and wild, was pleased with the way she looked. She found herself judging Cindy and Gina, who were unusually pretty but out of place, dressed like little surfers in loincloth-size cutoff jeans and tiny tops, their feet bare and their hair tangled. They said their parents were mean to them, so they had run away from home and were living with an older girl while they worked at a Taco Bell in Huntington Beach.

After the girls swam, Mindy invited them for a drive, piling them

into the Corvette and heading deeper into Bel-Air to the house of
singer Rod Stewart and actress Britt Ekland. Mindy had gone to
school with Ekland's daughter, Victoria Sellers, and the four girls
sat around in Victoria's bedroom talking and listening to music.

Cindy and Gina had a vulnerable look about them, Mindy
thought, as if they didn't know where their next meal was coming
from. They seemed as if all they had in a world they didn't understand was each other. When they mentioned that they hitchhiked,
Mindy was alarmed and told Gina to call her at any time if she
needed help or a ride, even if it were three in the morning.

Gratefully, Gina wrote Mindy's phone number in a red phone
book, but she didn't call and neither did Cindy. Later Mindy
thought about them and decided that they weren't bad girls; they
were sweet girls whose desperation made her feel grateful for her
own life. Mindy knew that she was not a particularly good girl.
She was simply a privileged girl who, because of that privilege,
could get away with being just a little bit bad.

On the morning of June 22, Mindy had been at home with her
younger sisters when the phone rang. On the line was a man who
said he was an LAPD detective. He had informed Mindy about the
murders of Cindy and Gina. As she had not known that the girls
were dead, Mindy began to cry. The man then became compassionate and apologized for upsetting her. He was going down blind
alleys, he explained, and needed all the help he could get. A
shaken Mindy had told him about meeting the girls at the party.
When the man had asked her if the girls had been prostitutes,
Mindy had told him that she knew nothing about that.

"They were ships that passed in the night," she said. She had
hardly known them.

Only after she got off the phone did Mindy Cohen become nervous. The man had given her too many details. It seemed unprofessional that he had mentioned that Cindy and Gina had been
discovered partially nude and that officers had found a business
card of a man who the caller said admitted having sex with them
for money. When he had said that he would have to come to her
house to interview her, Mindy had told the man that her parents
were away and she was alone with her sisters. He had agreed to
wait until her father got home. Quickly Mindy had written on an
envelope everything she remembered about the call, then she
phoned the Hollywood police. Someone was playing a prank, they
told her. Mindy had then phoned Mark, who called Downtown
Robbery-Homicide.

Now Mindy Cohen was in a panic. If the man had her phone number, did he also know her address? Obviously he was an imposter, and he might well be the killer. He had given his name, Detective something, but all Mindy could remember about the name was that it had two syllables. He had promised to phone again that week to set up an interview. The detectives put a trap on her phone.

On the sixteenth of June, two days after the girls died, a woman named Laurie Brigges, taking phone messages for her husband's moving company, had also received a phone call from a man claiming to be an LAPD detective. He had told her that a business card belonging to her brother-in-law, Henry Brigges, had been discovered on the body of one of two girls who had been killed.

A frightened Laurie Brigges had said quickly that Henry would not have anything to do with any murders. The "detective" reassured her. Henry was not a suspect. They just had to check out all leads.

As the conversation continued, it became more informal. The two girls had been doing what they shouldn't have been doing and they were dumped the way they should have been, the detective said.

"What was that? Was it hitchhiking?" Laurie Brigges wondered.

No. They were prostitutes, the detective said.

Concerned, Laurie Brigges had asked if Henry should contact the police station. The caller told her that it wouldn't be necessary. They would contact him.

Before he hung up, he had a final question. Was Henry tall, and did he have light hair? No, Laurie told him. He was short, with dark hair and a beard.

Laurie Brigges told Henry that she thought the man's name was Detective Clark. But then she had decided that she might be wrong. She told detectives she thought it began with an "H."

When the task force interviewed a worried Henry Brigges, he told them about his encounter with Cindy Chandler and Gina Marano.

With his helper, Charlie Holliday, Brigges had just delivered a load of furniture to Bel-Air when the men spotted the two young, beautiful girls hitchhiking at the isolated Mulholland entrance to the San Diego Freeway in Bel-Air. It was the tenth of June. They had stopped. The girls scrambled into the truck and accompanied Charlie and Henry to the moving-company warehouse in Culver City. The girls said they had been staying with a producer and they were going south to get some money. It was about two o'clock in the afternoon.

While Brigges and Holliday picked up their next load, the girls had waited on a bus bench. Then, a few miles away, the men dropped them under a bridge just before the Braddock on ramp to the freeway. Henry gave the blond girl, whose name was Cindy, his business card with his phone number and that of his brother, George, with whom he worked, and Cindy gave Henry the number of the producer.

Brigges had not heard from the girls again and was not considered a suspect. The calls to Laurie Brigges and Mindy Cohen were an indication that the killer was playing a game, flirting with capture. They also indicated that he had hoped to set Henry Brigges up for the murder—if Brigges had been blond, as the anonymous woman caller had indicated her killer boyfriend was.

On June 25, firearms expert Arleigh McCree had notified Downtown that the bullet in Karen Jones's head matched the bullets found in Cindy Chandler and Exxie Wilson. The latest body, found by the snake hunters in the ravine, turned out to be that of Marnett Comer, a seventeen-year-old Sacramento runaway and prostitute who had last been seen by her pimp around the first of June when he put her out to work the Sunset Strip. The three bullets removed from her body had been fired from the same gun used in the other Sunset murders. There were now five known killings.

Detective Rick Jacques, in his forties, with a Zapata mustache, had been named lead investigator. The plan was for him to see the case through trial, making sure it was airtight against the killer. In court, he would sit next to the prosecutor.

If they found the killer, that was. He was leaving clues at some discovery sites—the bullets were the best evidence—but he seemed not careless so much as taunting. Yet even the lack of some evidence was helpful. It showed them that he was keeping souvenirs. When they had a suspect and filed a search warrant, they would know to look for the victims' jewelry and underpants.

Rick Jacques's partner was thirty-four-year-old Mike Stallcup, a cowboy detective whose blue jeans and boots stood out among the Rolexes and shiny suits of department veterans. As insurance, Gary Broda, Homicide's six-foot blond sophisticate, and his partner, ladies' man Frank Garcia, would go over the work Kidder and York had already done. The men did not trust the women in spite of their Northeast's lieutenant's endorsement.

Early in July, Stallcup and Jacques traveled to Sacramento, where

Marnett Comer had lived. Her pimp was in hiding, and the detectives checked out a nationwide organization of pimps as the possible source of her murder. At her funeral, attended by a handful of family and friends, a hot dry wind rustled the eucalyptus trees, and Mike Stallcup, feeling intrusive, reimagined the cemetery as a golf course in an attempt to detach himself.

Marnett had been hooking since she was thirteen, and began running away from home at fourteen. In January of 1980, her mother had picked her up at a juvenile detention home to take her to the dentist and shopping. That was when Marnett ran away for the last time. A few days after Mother's Day, she had phoned home to say that she had sent flowers. On May 21, she had phoned again and her younger sister had begged her to return. Marnett had refused and her family had not heard from her again.

On a blindingly hot day the entire task force drove to the ravine off Foothill Boulevard where Marnett's body had been found. The men brought six-packs, Fritos, and the inevitable fried pig rinds in brown paper bags. Everyone except Gary Broda snickered under their breath at Helen Kidder's elegant wicker picnic basket filled with French cheeses, salami, and chilled white wine. All that was missing, Leroy noted before tucking into the salami, was a linen tablecloth.

They laid out a grid like a giant fifty-foot-square sieve and began sifting the earth. Snakes rattled in the underbrush. With every move they expected to be bitten. The detectives, accompanied by firearms expert Arleigh McCree, turned over the soil as if they were panning for gold, feeling ill from the stench of fluids that had settled as the body lay in the summer sun. This time they found no evidence beyond a few shell casings that did not match the bullets in Marnett Comer's body.

When he had learned about the trip to Sacramento, Leroy Orozco thought Rick Jacques was wasting his time following up the pimps organization. He'd jumped on it too soon instead of sitting back and letting the case tell him which way to go. Orozco believed in patience and formulating a goal.

He and Helvin were running computer checks on owners of Raven .25-caliber automatics. Following up could take months, but eventually it could lead to the killer. Orozco also thought that if they could determine the origin of the pine box in which Exxie Wilson's head had been discovered, that would also lead them to their man. The box looked homemade. But at the downtown Newberry's, the detectives found a similar treasure chest that had been manufactured in Juarez, Mexico. When the store sent an address list of the thirteen branches that carried the item, the detectives first checked the Reseda Newberry's on Sherman Way in the Valley. There the manager remembered one purchaser as a fortyish white woman wearing shorts, a black tank top, and black driving gloves. All of the Newberry's stores had sold only seven boxes, three of them to women and the others to unknown parties.

The task force was not looking for a woman. The detectives wanted a middle-class white man: hookers would not get into a car with anyone else. They had received a character profile from Helen Kidder's Rand think-tank expert. But Leroy noted with irritation that a bunch of good old cops did not need anybody else's fancy footwork to tell them the guy hated his mother and his gun was an extension of his penis. They could have told the expert that.

The male detectives were ignoring Helen Kidder and Peggy York. They had nicknamed them "the Crack Squad" and thought the women were playing Nancy Drew as they chased down the label on Cindy Chandler's pink jumpsuit.

Affirmative action was getting up everybody's ass. When a cop slipped and called somebody "hon," a critical phone call or memo fluttered down from the upper offices where the administrative pukes lived, their sole purpose in life to make things difficult for those who did the real work.

If Kidder and York were made part of the team, the other detectives reasoned, the women would be bound eventually to complain about something. The telephone would ring and the damned memos would flutter. But if no one talked to them, the women would have nothing specific to complain about.

Too, the *Los Angeles Times* had just printed an interview with Kidder and York. It had been conducted before they moved downtown, but Lieutenant Ron Lewis had confronted them, his fine skin pink with annoyance, to say he thought they had compromised the investigation.

York figured it was the men's problem. But Kidder, who thought Little Ronnie Homicide was a horse's ass, had wept in the Parker Center third-floor ladies room. The real problem with the *Times* story, she suspected, had nothing to do with the investigation. She and Peggy had made the mistake of being honest in it about the department's sexist shop talk and lack of opportunities for women.

"Can't you control these cunts? They're yours!" someone from Downtown had yelled into the phone to their boss at Northeast.

Symbolically, the women had been given the key to the men's

room and the men didn't like it, Kidder thought. In public, she continued to behave like a perfect little lady, never acknowledging her humiliation. But to Kidder, the police department was like a large, neurotic family for women and minorities. They smiled and appeased and thought deep down that even if terrible things were being done to them, it must be their own fault. As in any unhealthy family, in the LAPD everyone was supposed to maintain the illusion of affectionate harmony. She and Peggy had given away the family secrets, and Kidder felt they were being punished.

The investigation continued. Frozen and bagged body parts of two men who had been shot in the head were discovered in the Northeast Division but were unconnected to the Sunset killings. Marnett's pimp still had not surfaced. But Terry, a steady trick from Anaheim, was eliminated as a suspect. He was a big, quiet, shy man with no guns and no record. Devastated by Marnett's murder, he planned to hire a psychic to try to find the killer. His relationship with Marnett had been platonic, Terry insisted. They had talked for hours and he had been trying to get her away from street life.

About ten days before her death, at her last meeting with her older sister, Sabra, Marnett had confided that she was thinking of leaving her pimp. Sabra, also a prostitute, had recognized the pink "Daddy's Girl" T-shirt that the killer had used to wrap Exxie Wilson's head. So had a friend of Marnett's. Blood on the T-shirt and holes apparently made by a knife were being tested. According to Sabra Comer, Marnett had always been careful, either teaming with a friend or using a motel for a trick pad instead of doing car dates like other girls. She had always said that she knew she could fight like hell, if it came to it.

Telephone-company operator 453, a Mrs. Leach, received a call from a man who stated, "I am the guy decapitating the ladies. I want three thousand dollars or I'll do it again." The call was traced to a man who wanted attention but was not the killer. Prints of two other men who owned .25-caliber automatics were checked against palm prints found at the Exxie Wilson crime scene and on a beer can where Cindy Chandler and Gina Marano had been dumped. The prints did not check out.

On the Sunset Strip, streetwalkers claimed that there had been no drastic change in activity in the area and they weren't afraid. But Carol Bundy and Douglas Clark were finding it harder to get potential victims into the cars.

121

13

Doug WAS OUT ALL THE TIME NOW LOOKING FOR HOOKERS. SOMEtimes Carol went with him, her gun in a cosmetics bag in her purse. She was an unlikely target for a police search, Doug reasoned, in the event they were stopped. He had given up his Burbank rental garage and Carol had helped him clean it.

They batted at dust and cobwebs, scrubbed at bloodstains on the floor, and threw out a rusty bedframe. Doug kept the mattress, and later Carol would say that she had not noticed blood on it.

She was still moving into the Verdugo Avenue apartment and was putting away kitchen things when Doug called to her from the living room. She looked up. He had hammered a nail into the wall and was trying to catch the picture wire of a painting he held in both arms. He laughed and turned the painting around. It had spots on the back.

"These bloodstains, these clots, are from Gina Marano," he said, remarking later how well the painting—a rather dreary ski-lift scene—went with Carol's furniture.

Lemona Avenue had been an improvement over Valerio Gardens. Verdugo left them both in the dust. Pretentiously, Doug began referring to it as "the condominium." A string of multicolored flags flapped a welcome in front. Elaborately carved double wooden doors at the top of a flight of steps led to a courtyard carpeted with artificial grass upon which a stone fountain and a couple of planters helped distract from the distinctly prisonlike two-story design. Inside, burnt-orange wall-to-wall carpeting blended with Carol's tweedy sofa and wing chairs.

Fastidiously, she moved in her own side-by-side Harvest Gold refrigerator-freezer to hold the typical foods of any plump woman: frozen chicken, green beans, Weight Watchers dinners, Certi-Fresh Sea Bass in Lemon Butter, plus the makings for Doug's favorites. When it came to food, the American in him had overpowered the cosmopolitan. Out, he ordered steak and salad. For home, he asked Carol to buy creamed corn, macaroni and cheese, and hamburger. As carefully as she prepared the kill bag when he went to do what he referred to as "taking care of business," Carol fixed lunch to deliver to him at Jergens on her days off.

The refrigerator belonging to the apartment, an upper-lower arrangement also in Harvest Gold, was destined, after the departure of Exxie Wilson's head, to remain empty except for a couple of ice trays.

In what must have been her most extreme fit of blind optimism to date, Carol had felt hopeful about the move, believing that she and Doug would be able to make a comfortable and warm home together.

No one but Carol could have been surprised that their murderous adventures would prove the basis for a disappointing relationship. At the new place, even though he slept with Carol, Doug had his own room containing his file cabinet, a narrow cot, and a tangle of clothes, both male and female, some of which were souvenirs from victims, others which he claimed to have bought at the swap meets he frequented.

Life had actually been more domestic at Lemona Avenue. Technically, Doug had been living with Lydia Crouch toward the end, but Carol had seen him nearly every night, the kids had been there, and she had cooked regularly. At Verdugo, Doug was out constantly and he still brought other women around, asking to borrow her bed for their lovemaking.

Doug's treatment of Carol after the murders was a measure of the confidence he had in his ability to control her. But, not for the last time, Doug's arrogance would prove self-destructive. Before the summer was over, Carol would betray him.

Earlier that spring, at the Lemona Avenue apartment, Doug had lifted Theresa onto the bathroom sink and kissed her in the place she called her private spot.

In the beginning, she had felt like Doug's little toy. She slept over sometimes and he tucked her into bed with his teddy bear, Mozart, who was fuzzy and soft to cuddle. Doug handed her his favorite cartoon from a magazine. It showed a little girl in bed with a teddy bear, the blanket bulging where the bear's erect penis would have been if teddy bears had penises.

In the fun times that they had together, they talked about Theresa's friends at school, about hookers, and about Doug's life as a child. He didn't sound as if he had been very happy, Theresa thought. The family maid had seduced him when he was sixteen, and it was her fault, he said. One weird thing. Doug had a crush on Theresa's mom, Jacqueline, and he always asked Theresa to get him some of her underpants. But Theresa wouldn't do it. She thought the idea was gross.

When Doug had started with, "How does it feel if I touch you here?" and had said, "Don't tell Carol," Theresa had thought, Oh, no, here we go again. So that's why you were being nice to me.

She hadn't told. So it was a secret. A secret from Carol. And a secret from her mom, because Theresa was mad at her. Jacqueline had been in the hospital and was distracted by problems with a new boyfriend. Besides, secrets from Jacqueline were nothing new. Since before Theresa could remember, a family friend had been fiddling around with her, and still was. Theresa had long ago decided, this must be something adults did that for some reason had to be kept secret from other adults.

Theresa had been a colicky baby and in her own opinion a smart-mouthed, spoiled-rotten preschooler who had grown into a dippy kid. Now everyone joked to her, "You're eleven going on forty."

When she was younger, she had refused to eat and had so many accidents—falling off her bicycle, tripping over things—that she had her very own pediatric plastic surgeon who had called the police to question Jacqueline about child abuse. Jacqueline, by her own admission a rotten mother but no abuser, had been investigated and cleared. Still, Theresa hadn't told her mother that she was being molested. Maybe because no one had asked her the right questions.

She hadn't lived with her real dad since she was a baby. Her second dad she had really loved, and she had kept seeing him after he and her mom split up. One day, as her second dad disappeared around the back of his house, a strange woman came out.

"Go away. You're not his little girl anymore. He has another little girl now, so don't come around," the woman said. Theresa had run away, her feelings hurt.

Now she didn't think of herself as lonely, but just as a kid who, with Carol and Doug, had latched on to a couple of grown-ups who were nice to her. When she had seen Carol moving some things into the apartment on Lemona and heard her pop off a dirty joke, it made Theresa laugh, so she had popped one off herself.

If Jacqueline, still in her twenties, looked on Carol as Mom and apple pie—a wholesome companion for Theresa if she was out for the evening—Theresa saw Carol as a grown-up buddy and not a mother substitute. In Theresa's opinion, Carol was flaky from the start and not exactly the Donna Reed ideal parent Theresa had seen on TV reruns. She had met a couple of teenage mothers, and Carol actually reminded her of them, treating her kids like little adults and letting them cuss up a storm.

"If you know what it means, you can say it," Carol always said. Which inevitably launched Chris into an explanation: "Fucking is sexual intercourse between two people. . . ."

Sometimes Carol cooked hamburgers and spaghetti and invited Theresa over to eat and play. She was homey and domestic, and she taught Theresa how to crochet and how to cook rabbit, which Theresa had never eaten before. Then one day Carol had introduced her to her friend Doug, who was moving into the apartment. Soon after that, it had started.

It was still a secret from Carol. But Theresa felt Carol sensed something and sensed herself that Carol was becoming jealous. She looked at Theresa as if she were measuring her with her eyes.

One day Carol said about Doug, "That's the man I love," just as if Theresa were grown-up.

But it was a warning. One woman to another. And Theresa thought that Carol looked at Doug the way Doug looked at her, Theresa. Kind of like a spaniel. Carol let Doug totally dominate her. Probably would have washed Doug's feet, if he'd asked her. Doug, on the other hand, put Theresa on such a pedestal that she thought he must really love her, and it began to send her on a major power trip.

Doug would say, "Let's go to McDonald's."

"I want chicken."

"They have chicken at McDonald's."

"I want Pioneer chicken."

They'd arrive at Pioneer and Theresa would say, "This doesn't sound very appealing anymore. Let's go to H. Salt for fish."

Doug would take her to H. Salt.

Being with him, Theresa reflected, was like having one of those clowns on a stick. You knew it was going to jump around, but you didn't know how. She showed off for her friends, becoming, she thought, Doug's little whore who, because of sex, was able to scam money from him to go to the store. In front of her friends one day, he peeled off a twenty-dollar bill and she bought snap-caps to throw at the landlord's window.

Another time she invited a friend over and Doug tried to get the girl to join them, but she wouldn't.

"That's really gross and you're a gross person," she said to Theresa. Then she ran home, crying, and didn't speak to Theresa for two whole weeks.

Sometimes Doug and Carol drove her into Hollywood, and sometimes when Carol was at work, Doug and Theresa went alone. It was a game they played where she sat in the back seat of the Buick as they drove past hookers. Theresa would pick out a potential consort for Doug, and he would ask the woman to suck his penis.

One night a homely young woman sat on a bus bench.

"What do you think of her?" Doug asked. He always let her choose his porno magazines, too.

"She's ugly. But she must do something right to stay in business," said Theresa, helpful.

Doug drove on. "What about that one?" he said.

"She's wearing 'come fuck me' shoes."

They decided to pick up a hitchhiker instead.

"Say something provocative. Make a pass at her," Doug said before the woman got in the back with Theresa and smiled at her in that way grown-ups do with children, falsely and a little too hard. They drove and soon the woman wanted to get out.

"Nice jugs, babe," Theresa said. Timing was everything.

The woman stared at her as if she couldn't have heard right, then she bolted from the Buick. Theresa and Doug had some major giggles after that.

The night she saw Doug scratched up and covered with blood, Theresa had thought, Hooker rough you up, Doug? But she didn't say it. He had come over to get aspirin. Said he was in a motorcycle accident, but she knew better. Her real dad rode a bike, too, and those weren't like any road burns Theresa had ever seen. Doug had tracks down both his cheeks. They were scratch marks that made him look, to Theresa, as if he were crying tears of blood.

* * *

At Valley Medical Center, where she had begun LVN duties in January, Carol's three-month review had been glowing. Her work was deemed good and she was given an outstanding score for her ability to get along with coworkers. By June, things had changed. People were starting to avoid her, particularly nurse LeAnn Lane, who got the creeps whenever Nurse Bundy appeared.

The two women were in the third floor nurses' lounge on a break. LeAnn was an R.N., a tall, slim woman of thirty-seven with bangs, glasses, and a pale, no-nonsense countenance. When she was a little girl she used to put together her own nursing kit with Band-Aids and travel-size bottles of iodine. At fourteen she was a candy striper. Now that she'd achieved her fantasy, she took her work seriously and became irritated when Carol tried to distract her with conversation. If she was on a break, LeAnn Lane wanted a break. If she was working, she wanted to work and not have Bundy staring at her. As well as she could stare with her brown eyes going different ways behind those thick glasses. Today she was trying to engage LeAnn yet again in the sordid details of her sex life, for which LeAnn simply did not have the time or the interest.

In June, LeAnn had shifted from night shift to days, which was when she had begun working with Nurse Bundy. Three-month review aside, in Lane's opinion Bundy was a borderline employee who would have been fired had she, LeAnn Lane, been head nurse. The odd thing was that LeAnn Lane had nothing specific to complain about. Carol bustled around looking efficient, but LeAnn thought she was putting on a big show. If she said she was worried about a patient, LeAnn would go and check and there would be nothing wrong. In spite of her irritation at Carol, LeAnn Lane felt sorry for her because of her diabetes and her bad sight, out of which, to be sure, Carol got more than enough sympathy. The woman seemed to enjoy martyring herself by volunteering for the most demeaning tasks, then basking in the glow of victimhood as people said, "Oh, poor Carol. How many bedpans did you empty today?"

She was talking now. Another one of her depressing sagas that reminded LeAnn, admittedly a bit of a prude, that Carol would do absolutely anything to get and keep the attention of a man.

Apparently Carol had gone to a costume shop and rented medieval costumes for herself and that boyfriend, Doug. The night before, with Carol dressed in panniers and Doug in doublet and hose, they had performed an elaborate play which led to absolutely nothing. Just when Carol thought the boyfriend was getting all worked up sexually, he had changed out of his tights and left to hunt for another woman with whom to quench his passion. He had rejected Carol—and who could blame him—and Carol was furious.

But it seemed to LeAnn Lane that Carol was also rather enjoying the effect she was having as she told the story. She was enjoying being shocking. It was like that time one of the nurses got something stuck between her teeth and Carol suggested the woman use a pubic hair as dental floss. Everyone talked about it afterwards. Or the time when LeAnn was disposing of leftover narcotics after medicating a patient.

"Save it for your kids," Carol had said slyly.

She had a sadistic streak, LeAnn thought, although clearly she loved her own children. She talked about them all the time.

LeAnn Lane abandoned her cup of coffee, gave Carol Bundy a long, hard look, and left the room. She made a mental note to have yet another word with the head nurse, a burly football-playerish man named Howard Wanhoff. If Bundy didn't go, then LeAnn Lane would.

"We're going to get twenty years for this," Doug said to Theresa. They giggled about it, the three of them now. Shortly before Chris and Spike left, Carol had started joining in without the boys' knowledge.

"Let's all take a shower together," Doug had said. And he had told Theresa to approach Carol for sex, which she did.

Theresa thought Carol seemed nervous and awkward, as if she felt guilty. And when Carol told Doug it was wrong, he accused her of being jealous. When she heard that, Carol would stop and think carefully, as if she were questioning herself, wondering was this wrong, or did she just want it to stop because she was jealous of a child? She seemed to listen to everything Doug said and, Theresa observed, she always believed him.

They were both nice about the sex. They said, "If you don't want to do it, it's fine, but we'd really like you to."

Theresa would say, "I'd rather go to a movie."

"Okay, we'll go to a movie first and do it afterwards."

Doug had moved to the Burbank apartment before Carol, and they had taken Theresa to the new place when he was still sleeping on blankets on the floor before Carol's furniture was moved in.

The apartment had a big window in the living room, but the curtains were always drawn. To Theresa it felt like a dark house with dark vibrations. Into adulthood, she would feel afraid of dim places. Still, then, she didn't tell anybody what was going on.

Doug had given her a small, gold-colored music-box key chain that played "Greensleeves." She hung it from her belt. She loved the music box and the song and would not wonder for some time whether it was a souvenir from a girl that she had picked out for Doug when they were driving.

By the middle of July, the women on the streets were getting almost impossible to coax into the car. Doug and Carol read in the newspaper that they were moving to Anaheim out of fear of the Sunset killer. They decided to drive there to troll along Katella Avenue. Carol had her gun in her purse, but the streetwalkers were wary there, too, and they didn't have any luck.

It was dark. On an impulse they continued to Long Beach, driving through the surrealistic industrial landscape across the Long Beach-San Pedro bridge, then up and down Pacific Coast Highway, squabbling over the radio station, Carol as usual giving in to Doug's preference for soft rock. She preferred country music and was always listening for Crystal Gayle singing, "Don't It Make Your Brown Eyes Blue."

No girls were out that night, and they didn't get home until four or five in the morning.

One weekend they went hunting through the streets of Venice, where Carol had lived with Dick Geis as a young woman. They took the guns but again didn't find any prostitutes.

In the late afternoon an orange sun was still up as they passed through Malibu. Sea gulls wheeled and the ocean gleamed on their left. Only a few people were scattered on the beaches, and they had the highway almost to themselves. They were on their way to Oxnard to find teenage hitchhikers to kill.

As they headed north, Doug pointed to the Santa Monica Mountains to their right. He'd dropped a "package" off there, he told Carol. That had become their code word for a dead body.

They did not stop to see it but drove on.

In Oxnard, they had dinner at Denny's, then went to a Big 5 sporting-goods store in a nearby shopping center to look at guns and ammunition. They had found no prostitutes, no hitchhikers. Deflated, they circled around onto the Ventura Freeway and drove home.

Doug had a plan to kill everyone in a Mexican bar on Magnolia Boulevard. He was supposed to go inside with one of the Ravens and a newly purchased shotgun while Carol played lookout outside, her own gun ready as she communicated with Doug over a walkie-talkie. The first walkie-talkie set he bought didn't work, so he sent Carol back to the Golden Mall Radio Shack. She picked up a second set, but nothing came of the plan and Carol decided it was another one of his fantasies, like picking people off on the freeway with a shotgun. Fun, but too risky. It was late July and Carol would say later that there was just too much emphasis on killing.

She was still always after Doug for sex. He had almost entirely lost interest in her unless another woman or the child were involved, and she knew by now that after a kill he was completely unapproachable. It was not that he seemed sexually satisfied, but rather that there was an edginess about him. An elation, as if he were pleased that the murder had actually happened. Whatever his mood afterward, he was withdrawn from her. In that way Carol had of minimizing disaster, she told herself that their "rapport" was breaking down. All they had in common now was murder and Theresa. In spite of their bickering—Doug found Carol too clingy, jealous, and possessive—they still went out as friends and one night went to see *Caligula* at a theater on Hollywood Boulevard. Carol could not understand why Malcolm McDowell was starring in a porn film with scenes of necrophilia, castration, decapitation, and sadism. Doug, who had seen the movie before, seemed jaded to her. He had shown more animation when they saw John Belushi in *The Blues Brothers*.

After *Caligula* she wanted him to make love to her, but he wouldn't.

Their quarrels became more frequent. Doug threatened to leave, fed up, Carol sensed, with her mood swings, even though he himself could switch within seconds from being funny and charming to being full of venom and insult. Still, Carol liked to think that her entire life was wrapped up in him. When she was in his presence, she was his. When she was at work or shopping, she felt free of his control.

Doug wanted to set a false trail for the Sunset killings. Carol called an Orange County rape hot line and told a counselor that she was a prostitute whose black pimp was the murderer. When she got off the phone, Doug yelled at her, furious over what he thought was a stinking acting job.

His next plan was to plant a red herring at a murder scene. Then it came to him. What he really needed was a black pubic hair. Carol helped by asking a pretty young black woman at Valley Medical Center for one of hers.

"Don't think I'm crazy," said Carol.

The woman was horrified and work was not the same for Carol after that. Everyone avoided her in the nurses' lounge. And when LeAnn Lane gave a party and asked to borrow her large salad bowl but did not invite her to attend, Carol's feelings were hurt.

During the summer, Carol phoned her former lover Dick Geis in Oregon to tell him about her relationship with Doug. She said she was frightened of him, that he had killed people. When Geis suggested she leave, Carol made excuses about why she couldn't. She even sounded proud, Geis thought. Within minutes of the first call, Carol phoned back to say that it had been a hoax. She had been writing a story and was testing Geis to see how believable it was. Because he knew that Carol had sold at least one short story, Geis accepted her explanation. He did not hear from her again for weeks.

On the twenty-first of July, Nancy Smith, an exotic dancer friend of Doug's, moved into the Verdugo apartment after a fight with her roommate.

Nancy, who had a little training in psychology, told Doug and Carol she thought they were both weird. They didn't have many friends and seemed mired in their own problems. When they invited Nancy to go with them again to *Caligula*, she chickened out a couple of blocks from home and had them turn the car around. She knew there were scenes showing sex with corpses.

When they got back to the apartment, Doug sat next to Nancy on the sofa and told her that he wanted to experience necrophilia. Carol asked Nancy if she were interested, whereupon Nancy turned around and threw the question back at her. Carol said she was curious herself about the experience.

The phone was ringing. Mindy Cohen, just back from a cruise to Alaska, rolled over in bed and glanced at her digital clock. It was 7:09 in the morning on July 24. No one phoned Mindy that early. She fumbled for the receiver and immediately recognized the voice. It was the man who had phoned on June 22. He was asking if she remembered his call about Cindy and Gina.

"I killed them," he said. ". . . I shot them and then I made love to them and it felt so good."

The voice droned on as Mindy Cohen listened, frozen in fear. The man said he had seen her at Mark's party.

"Now I want you, Mindy . . . I'm going to do it to you, Mindy . . . you're next."

There was a hesitation in his voice. Something about his breathing. The man was masturbating, Mindy Cohen realized. Terrified, she hung up the phone and asked her father to call the police.

At first the task force had worked day and night, turned on by the hunt. But since Marnett Comer had been found in the ravine at the end of June, no more bodies had turned up. Now they felt weary, almost begging for the Sunset Murderer to kill again so that they would have something more to go on. The second Mindy Cohen phone call was the only current sign that the killer was still in the area. But when the bogus policeman had not phoned back after his first call, and when Mindy took her trip, the telephone company had removed the trap from her bedroom phone.

Gallows humor was part of being a cop. To distance themselves from the tension of the chase, the horror of the crimes, they developed their own nicknames for the victims. Exxie was Sexy Exxie or the Headless Wonder. Leroy Orozco left the Newberry's treasure chest in the office at Parker Center. Visitors who walked in said, "Oh, is this the famous box?" They opened it and blanched, seeing what turned out to be a doll's head.

Orozco waited, knowing that another call would come in that would break the case. It could be from a prostitute on the street. Or from the woman who called herself Claudia.

For about a month, Carol had been threatening suicide, even asking Doug to kill her. He told her to go ahead without involving him—unless she wanted to hang herself while he was having intercourse with her as she died.

One night Carol sat in the Datsun outside the closed Baskin-Robbins ice-cream store in Burbank with her gun in her mouth. She was unable to pull the trigger.

But on July 27 she hand-wrote a will in which she left her furniture to Douglas. Then on July 29 at 12:30 A.M., she wrote him a letter in which she explained that she could no longer handle her life, which she saw as a series of manic-depressive ups and downs.

> I keep screwing up everything. The man I love can't stand me anymore. He wants to split. I can't let go and he won't let me hold on.

What's wrong with me? I screw up everyone I love or who ever cared for me. He says he's not my lover he's only a room-mate. He hasn't touched me in months. I just can't stand it anymore[. . .] I deliberately keep him angry. Or I seem to. I'm really just a clutz.

After cataloging her problems with Doug, and blaming herself for them, Carol outlined Jack Murray's swindling selfishness and her own record as "a piss-poor mother" whose kids were the real losers in life.

"Douglas, I love you," she then wrote.

I don't ever wish you harm. If this hurts, I'm sorry[. . .] This is your way out! Honey, I just wanted to love you. I didn't expect it back. Nor did I ever intend to 'own' you, and since you know I can't lie, you know what I was saying was straight-up front[. . .]
    It hurts to be in love alone. In the morning call the police. I'll be in the car parked by the Gristmill. No point in spending money on a room. This isn't your fault. There really isn't even enough of me to bother with anyway[. . .]

If Doug awoke and read the letter, Carol wrote, he could find her in the garage, where she would wait for him for ten minutes. She then phoned Valley Medical Center to tell them that she would not be at work the next day because she was about to kill herself. In the Datsun in the Verdugo apartment's underground parking lot, Carol injected her veins with 1,250 units of insulin and 100 milligrams of Librium before swallowing 100 milligrams of Librium tablets. Although Carol waited, Doug did not come to save her. Beginning to get drowsy, she drove two blocks to the windmill-shaped Gristmill restaurant, where she parked and lost consciousness, awakening momentarily to flashing red lights and a flurry of activity. Valley Medical Center had called Doug and he had called paramedics. Carol remembered nothing more until she awoke the next day at St. Joseph's Hospital in Burbank, where she told nurses that she was in love with a maniac. From her hospital bed, Carol placed several calls to Jack Murray, who came to pick her up and take her home. He brought with him Nancy Smith, Doug's dancer friend, telling Jeannette that he was taking her to keep Carol at a distance. On the way to the Verdugo apartment, the trio stopped for hamburgers and soft drinks and sat eating and talking under a tree, Nancy sensing a wall between Carol and Jack. When Jack stopped again to buy cigarettes, Carol, still groggy, left him and Nancy and walked home in the summer heat.

The next day was the first of August. Carol picked Theresa up in Van Nuys and took her to Burbank, where she was to stay overnight. As Carol had arranged to meet Jack, she left the child at the apartment. Then, when Doug came home from work, he took her trolling with him in the Datsun. They weren't far from home when Theresa spotted a blond girl dressed in a brief black-and-lavender outfit. She was waiting by a bus stop, and although Doug swore she was a hooker, Theresa didn't believe him.

They stopped and the girl asked for fifty dollars for a blow job. When Doug didn't want to pay that much, they compromised. He would give her thirty dollars and a ride to a bar in Hollywood.

With the girl in the car, they found a dark spot near a fence. Doug handed the girl her money and Theresa watched as she unzipped his pants and put her mouth on his penis. In Theresa's opinion, the girl didn't seem very interested in what she was doing. When it was over, Doug dropped Theresa at the apartment and drove off with the girl, later phoning to ask Theresa to give a message to Carol saying he had met a girl at a bar.

Carol got home at about ten and Doug later. The three of them went to bed, where they had mutual oral sex, Theresa and Doug naked and Carol in a nightgown.

The next day was August 2, a Saturday. In the morning, Carol went to a family-counseling center in Burbank. While Theresa sat on her lap feeling, with Carol's arms wrapped around her, like Carol's child, Carol told the male counselor that she, her boyfriend, and Theresa were sexually involved.

The counselor asked Theresa if she were bothered.

"Not really," Theresa said.

If the situation was not bothering her, said the counselor, then it was not his job to moralize.

Sometimes Theresa really believed that she wasn't bothered. She thought Doug and Carol were her friends. When they got out the fancy underwear that Doug had given her, she thought, Oh, dress-up time. Then when Carol took the Polaroid photographs of her in garter belt and bustier, with one spike heel planted firmly on Doug's neck and Doug naked except for a dog collar, they'd given her wine to make it easier. On the night they had decided it was

134

time for Theresa to lose her virginity, they had given her six little pills to make her sleepy. Even through the druggy haze Doug's penis had hurt like hell. It had felt enormous to the little girl, and she had screamed, "Stop! You're hurting me!"

It had been a hot summer night, and the bedroom window was open. So were the windows in the apartment house across the way. Theresa knew her scream had sounded like that of a little girl in pain. A long, loud, child's wail. After she heard it ring out, she waited, but no one came. It would have been a relief if they had, because it would have put an end to it without Theresa having to do anything.

Doug had stopped then, which was the part that Theresa had thought was kind. He had given her a hug and told her to wait until later. But Theresa never could understand why none of the neighbors called the police.

Since that night, whenever Doug had suggested trying again, Theresa had given him her mournful puppy-dog eyes and he'd stopped pressing her.

Perhaps given license by the counselor and Theresa's apparent lack of resistance, Carol planned an assignation with Jack Murray on the same day as the counseling session. Carol had been after Jack for sex, too. But like Doug, he now refused to have anything to do with her unless another woman was involved. They had talked about the possibility of Nancy Smith, but Nancy was not enthusiastic. Carol, who did not know anyone else willing, suggested the child. Jack told her to bring Theresa to the van. There he fondled her, nervous, his hands shaking.

"Oh, what a nice little snatch you have," Jack said.

He wanted to sleep with the girl, he told Carol.

"She's for Doug," said Carol.

Afterward, as Carol took her into the bright lights and noise of Farrell's to buy an ice-cream cone, Theresa thought how much alike the two men seemed. But Carol thought how dirty the episode had been. The sex between Doug and Theresa had been sweet and wholesome and something that Theresa wanted, Carol told herself. With Jack, it had been sordid and disgusting.

"Doug mustn't find this out," Carol said. "He hates Jack. He'll kill him."

14

On August 3, when Jack Murray prepared to leave for Little Nashville by splashing on his Pierre Cardin cologne, Jeannette did not complain beyond her ritual "Who are you trying to impress?"

It was Sunday night. She knew he had to get away. Temperatures in the Valley had reached 101 degrees that week. Predictably, Valerio Gardens' residents had broken more bottles in the driveway than usual, and Jack and the assistant manager had been called more often to pull husbands off their wives and parents off their children. Jack had kept things under control, once by calling police, then watching his people scatter like Vietcong beneath the bright lights of an LAPD helicopter.

By nine-thirty, Jack was draped over a table near the entrance to the Nashville Club, sipping a Chivas on the rocks and talking to Avril, a twenty-seven-year-old Australian woman with red hair, wire-rim glasses, and a pale, narrow face.

They danced, and Jack rolled dice with his friends for drinks, usually a raucous occasion. Because he invariably won, everyone tried to beat him.

At about ten o'clock, Carol Bundy appeared and ordered her usual vodka and 7Up at the bar. She sat staring at Jack and Avril and after her second drink walked over to them.

"You have to talk to me outside," she said to Jack, her little-girl voice reedy and urgent.

There was a quiet, melancholy, city-in-summer sound to the traffic on Sherman Way. Laughter and upbeat country music wafted from Little Nashville and the Playtime club next door. Carol opened the trunk of the Datsun and showed Jack the kill bag. She had told him about the guns but this was the first time he had seen them. Before, he had teased her when she tried to tell him what was going on.

"Are you still running around town with those heads?" he had said.

Carol had done the same thing she had with Dick Geis. She had pretended she had made it up.

Now Jack looked pale in the darkness.

"We're going out almost every night hunting," Carol said. She was scared. Things were escalating and she wanted Jack to help her. There was a storage room at Valerio Gardens and he could hide her there.

Jack didn't want to do that.

"Give me some more details," he said. They made an arrangement to meet after the club closed. To be sure that Jack would be there, before having some drinks in the club then going to wait in the car, Carol slipped him a note offering him sex.

His distinctive brand of Australian "Hello, you old bastard" bonhomie was dampened as he returned to Little Nashville. To his friends Danny and Dwane he looked terrified as he called them out to the parking lot, where they sat on a car fender and talked.

Carol was crazy, Jack told them. She had opened the trunk of her Datsun and shown him some guns. She said she and Doug had killed someone, and he didn't know how to handle it.

"Call the cops," said Dwane.

But Jack did an about-face and tried to make light of it, making Dwane think that he would try to pacify her with sex.

Back in Little Nashville again, Jack got up to sing "The Green, Green Grass of Home." In the middle, he flubbed a few words and went off key, something he never did.

"I may be in trouble," he said afterward to Thumper, the waitress. "Oh, women, women, women."

I've blown it, Carol thought, as she sat in the Datsun. I've told Jack too much. If he goes to the police, Doug will link it to me and there'll be hell to pay. Doug was right. She was a motor mouth.

At about one-thirty, Avril and Jack left the club for Sambo's coffee shop a few blocks down Sherman Way. When they returned to the club parking lot an hour later, Carol was there looking agitated. Jack sighed and said the evening was over. As Avril drove off, she saw Carol on the passenger side of the Chevy van, half in and half out of the door. She had already made the decision that Jack should die because he knew too much.

Doug wanted Jack dead. They had talked about killing him. But Doug had told Carol to stay away from it.

"Don't do anything on your own. You're an amateur. You'll get caught right off the bat," he had said.

Carol's explanation for what happened next would change from telling to telling, perhaps to justify what she had done. But whatever the version, one thing was clear. She was going to have to kill Jack herself.

Jack drove south of Sherman Way and turned right onto Barbara Ann Street where all the neat little blue-collar houses were dark for the night and the children long tucked into bed. He parked. The van was black inside, its shades pulled down.

Carol, in the passenger seat, was rattling on about dead bodies. Jack didn't listen. His mind on sex, he climbed in the back and arranged himself on one of the red-upholstered bench seats. Outside, crickets chirped in the almost tropical August air. In a nearby elm tree a mockingbird started a raucous song.

"I'm freaking out," Carol said.

Jack unbuttoned his shirt, tuning her out. He unzipped his pants and dropped them around his ankles, leaving his cowboy boots on. It was late. He didn't want this to take any longer than necessary.

Carol climbed into the back of the van. From the kill bag in the Datsun, she had taken a pair of rubber gloves and a cleaning rag, which she had stuffed in the pockets of her Levi's Bendovers. A boning knife was tucked in her purse and she had her Raven hidden in the waistband of her pants.

Roughly, Jack began to push her head down toward his penis. She was still trying to tell him about Doug.

"You crazy, Carol. You'll get that guy into trouble," Jack said. Then he said something that she heard a second after it lay suspended in the air as if it had a life of its own. He asked her to bring Theresa over again. He wanted to sleep with Theresa.

Carol would say that was the moment when she knew for sure that Jack had to die. She made him turn over so that she could play with his anus. He liked that, and that was what she had promised him in her note. She had just started to get him excited but she still wasn't sure. Then she thought, No, there can't be any choice. There's absolutely no choice.

She pulled the gun out, held it up to the back of Jack's head, and pulled the trigger.

The gun went boom, and Jack went "ahh" very softly. She felt his pulse to see if he was dead. It was steady. Surprised that his heart was still beating, she shot him again in the other side of the head, feeling a surge of her own power. Killing someone really was fun. It was sort of like being on a roller coaster. Nearby a fire engine thundered past, its siren screaming, startling her. She took the knife and stabbed Jack half a dozen times in the back.

The Seiko watch he was wearing was one of her gifts. She considered taking his jewelry to make it look as if robbery were a motive. But the watch and chains would be too dangerous to keep around, she decided. Instead she stabbed him again, then slashed at his buttocks and anus to make it look like another psycho murder.

"If you want a piece of ass, here's a piece of ass," she said, angry as she did it.

Then she thought, Oh, no. Stupid me. The bullets. They'll be able to identify the bullets in his head.

After that, Carol decided that it was lucky she had been blind for a while. Otherwise she wouldn't have been able to do what she had to do in the darkness. Cutting Jack's head off certainly wasn't any thrill.

When she was finished, she took the rag and cleaned up as many fingerprints as she could. A few didn't matter, because everyone knew she was Jack's friend and had been in the van.

It was about three in the morning, just as dew was beginning to rise on the small lawns nearby. Carol carried the plastic bag containing Jack's head, holding it away from her heavy body. The air and the streets were still dark gray as she hurried a short half block, turned left, and started to cross the street. Under a lamp that was bright as day, she would swear, she dropped Jack's head, then scooped it up as best she could, wondering if she were going to be sick.

At the Datsun, she put the bag in the well on the passenger side, then called Doug from a pay phone in the Little Nashville parking lot.

"I've got Jack," Carol said. "I've got Jack's head in the car. I killed him."

"What are you going to do?"

"What do you want me to do?" Carol asked.

"Come home."

Doug had told her that she could never kill anything. That she didn't have the guts. She wanted Doug to look in the bag and see what she had done.

Paramedics were at the apartment when Carol arrived. Doug had called them to report that Nancy Smith, an epileptic, had had a seizure. But Carol would always suspect that Nancy, who fled to Illinois the following day, had picked up the extension phone, heard the conversation about Jack, and begun screaming.

In the doorway, Carol watched silently as the paramedics gathered their equipment. When one of them saw her, she said, "I'm a nurse. What's wrong? Is there anything I can do?" They refused her offer and left.

Doug noticed the small spatterings of blood on her glasses and wristwatch. She was wearing a blue blouse and there were tiny droplets on that too.

Nancy, doped, went back to bed.

"Where's the head?" Doug asked.

"It's in the car."

They took a roll of paper towels from the kitchen and Carol stuck it in a paper bag with a pair of rubber gloves. Downstairs in the parking lot, Doug walked around the side of the Datsun and looked in. A trash bag covered a bundle in the front passenger well. Doug couldn't tell it was Jack but he saw flesh and the severed part of the neck.

"Wrap it up," he said.

Carol pulled on her gloves and put Jack's head in a fresh plastic trash bag, then wrapped it in a blanket.

On the freeway, Carol began to laugh. As usual, Doug was driving.

"Well, what are we going to do with it?" he asked.

She suggested sticking the head on a fence post. Then she had another thought. "It's got three holes. We could go to a bowling alley and bowl it down the lane."

Doug got off the freeway and drove around for a while through the back streets of Atwater near Griffith Park. The sun still wasn't up, but there was a pink band on the horizon to the east and he had to be at work by five-thirty. On one side of them was industry, on the other side were houses and little outcroppings of trees.

140

Trash cans were lined up along the street. It was garbage pickup day.

He stopped the car. Backing it up to a big green bin, he said, "Roll your window down . . . throw it in there."

Quickly, Carol threw Jack's head in. After the fuss Doug had made over her disposal of Exxie's head in the alley, she wasn't about to waste any time or have any regrets.

Quite simply, that was the end of Jack Murray.

PART
THREE

15

THEY TALKED ABOUT GETTING CAUGHT.

Even if he beat the rap, said Doug, he'd be watched for the rest of his life. He was a registered Republican who had voted in 1978 to restore the death penalty in California. Now he was beginning to regret it. He knew this would be a death-penalty case, and he didn't want to die.

Not missing an opportunity for an inappropriately self-righteous comment, Carol said, "I don't think the girls wanted to die, either."

"That's doesn't matter, they're disposable," said Doug.

He had nicknamed the last victim Water Tower, after the tall water tanks near where he had dumped her body in the Antelope Valley. As usual, he had told Carol, he had shot the woman in the head while she had his penis in her mouth. After she was dead, he kept driving around with her, the jiggling of the Datsun so exciting him that he orgasmed twice. Near the water towers in the dark mountains that smelled sweetly of sagebrush, he propped her body against the hood of the still-running car, pressed his hand on her belly to release her urine, then let the car's movements help him simulate intercourse with a live woman.

Afterwards he gave Water Tower's maroon satin handbag to Carol and kept her red underpants for himself.

Carol was still on sick leave following her suicide attempt, about which Doug had been as unsympathetic as had the Murrays and Linda when they learned about it. They all thought she wanted attention, reasoning that if she had really wanted to kill herself, she was a nurse and damn well knew how.

Now Doug was even less sympathetic than before. Carol had blown it, he kept telling her. She'd fucked it up. All well and good that she cut off Jack's head to get rid of the bullets. But what about the shell casings? He never would have left those in the van.

"Whatever you do, don't get me hung for Jack," he said. "I didn't do Jack and I don't want to take the rap."

But Carol told herself that she wouldn't have killed Jack Murray at all if she hadn't had a good teacher. She was not really and truly a murderer, she rationalized. That was why she had forgotten to remove the shell casings.

On Tuesday, August 5, the day after Jack died, Doug did not go to work. He did a great deal of moaning over the phone to a supervisor and claimed to be passing a kidney stone.

On Wednesday, Carol returned to Valley Medical Center to work a double shift. But she felt as if she were not on top of the job. If the phone rang, she jumped, and she was popping four or five ten-milligram capsules of Librium a day to stay calm.

By Friday night, after another eight-hour shift at work, Carol felt well enough to go out to dinner with Doug at Leon's Steak House in North Hollywood. He still wasn't making love to her, and she hoped that if she introduced him to Tammy Spangler, a former girlfriend of Jack's, they could have three-way sex. Tammy was a raw-boned security guard of twenty-two, 190 pounds and six feet tall in her suntan-colored panty hose. She and Doug took to each other immediately. Neither of them, however, wanted sex with Carol, who reluctantly gave them her bed and went to sleep on Doug's cot in his messy room. After all they had been through together, she could not understand why Doug did not feel closer to her.

The week before, when she went with Theresa, Carol had made a follow-up appointment for herself at the family-counseling center. She failed to keep it. On Saturday evening, she went to Little Nashville.

Jack had been gone six days. On Monday, the day after he left for the bar, Jeannette had thought, He's off playing hanky-panky again somewhere. On Tuesday she filed a missing person's report with the police. On Wednesday she learned of his breakfast with the Australian woman. With her friend Lola along for support, Jeannette took to the streets to search for the van.

Twice that week Carol had phoned Linda, the assistant manager's wife. First she called to express concern that Jack was missing. In a follow-up call, she wanted to know if he had turned up. When Linda told her, Jeannette was irritated. Since Carol had left Valerio Gardens, life had improved, and she did not want to be reminded now of her husband's most blatant episode of infidelity.

By Thursday, Jeannette had begun to suspect that he was dead, and she prepared the children.

Still, though, she tried to hope. On Saturday, reasoning that if he were going to surface it would be on a weekend, she left for Little Nashville flanked by Thumper, who was not waitressing that night, and Lola.

It was about ten-thirty by the time she settled at the bar. A few minutes later, when Carol Bundy walked in, Jeannette made a point of ignoring her.

Briefly, Carol paced back and forth. Then, just as pointedly ignoring Jeannette as Jeannette had ignored her, she walked behind Thumper and leaned over the bar to order a vodka and 7Up. Sitting between Thumper and the waitress's station, she kept taking dainty sips. Then she put her glass down and walked to the door, where she peered out before walking back again.

A couple was about to go on the dance floor and Carol intruded, as she often did at the club. Considering her lack of self-confidence—which, nastily, everyone felt was thoroughly justified—her sexual boldness had always caused comment. Tonight, she grabbed the man's hand and turned to the woman.

"You don't mind, do you?" she said. Then she two-stepped off.

Groups of neighbors stood on the sidewalk while Detective Roger Pida, called away from a barbecue, methodically made his way from one end of the van to the other. Residents of Barbara Ann Street had called the Van Nuys Police Department to report an odor wafting from the vehicle, but Pida didn't wear a mask. It wasn't that he liked the smell, but it didn't bother him the way it did other cops. In his opinion, you didn't go into homicide if you were squeamish about smells.

Pida, compact and Slavic-looking, had an 89 percent solve rate, and he liked to think that if a cop stood quietly at the center of a crime scene, the scene itself could tell him who his murderer was.

He surveyed the plush red interior of the Chevy through his narrow eyes, then he began to write, describing the curtained windows, the blood spatters on the upholstery, the positioning of the body, which lay on the van floor in the back between the seats.

The man still had his cowboy boots on. His trousers and racy red European-style underwear were around his ankles. Blisters had erupted on his body, which was bloated and blackened from the heat. The first detectives on the scene had not been able to tell from outside the van if the corpse had a head or not. Now Pida could see. Where the man's head had been was a blood-soaked pillow. He was a murder victim and not, as they had speculated, a suicide.

The body had numerous stab wounds on its back, the buttocks had been sliced like somebody's Easter ham, and the victim had been cut around his anus. An expended .25-caliber shell casing lay on the floor of the van near the rear on the driver's side. There were no bullet holes in the body. Either the victim was shot in the head before it was hacked off, or the bullet casing was unrelated to the killing. Within fifteen minutes, Pida knew he wasn't going to find the head. The killer either took it away to play with it or had some kind of statement to make.

A number of questions ran through Pida's mind as he left the van. Other questions, though, had already been answered by regulars from the Little Nashville bar up the street. The man's name was John Robert Murray, nicknamed Jack. The Chevy was parked near where he drank. He was a womanizer. And Pida could tell from his state of undress that he had been preparing for or engaged in sex at the time of his death. His suspect, Pida knew, was a woman.

Tammy Spangler was at Little Nashville with Doug. It was near midnight when she noticed flashing police lights and, accompanied by a friend, followed them a block south to Barbara Ann Street, where she saw Jack Murray's van surrounded by floodlights, policemen, and the coroner's van.

So Jack was dead. He had been an asshole, Tammy thought, nice to his women one moment and mean to them the next. But she had liked him. She'd slept with him on and off for four years, had cooked him dinner, and was one of those who had helped pass on the news that singing was not Jack's only accomplishment.

She walked back up Varna Street to Little Nashville feeling glum. Word was still spreading through the club, but some patrons, oblivious, were dancing as usual. Tammy spotted Doug and told him the news, worrying aloud about how to tell Carol.

"Not now. She's having a good time," Doug said. Almost instantly he changed his mind and told her himself.

Jeannette had tried to get to the van, but no one at the club would let her leave. As she pulled out of the Little Nashville parking lot to drive to the Van Nuys Police Department, she heard the high-pitched scream of Carol Bundy, who had just been told the news.

As the night of the discovery of Jack Murray's body wore on, Van Nuys Division detectives continued their interviews with Jeannette Murray and the Little Nashville regulars. They told of Jack's fear after Carol Bundy showed him the guns in her car, and they mentioned Avril, the Australian woman with whom Jack had last been seen. Avril, a film editor who carried a knife, seemed a likely suspect. But no one knew her last name or where she lived. Jeannette, at the police station until 4:00 A.M., kept asking questions. Was Jack dressed? How did he die? Was he stabbed or shot? Did he have a heart attack?

She received no answers. At that time, Jeannette was a suspect herself. In vain she watched television, hoping for clues. But the news was full of the Democratic convention and Jimmy Carter's possible renomination.

Inside the club, Carol had clutched elaborately at Tammy and said what she thought someone would say under the circumstances: "No. It's not true. He can't be dead." Then she lapsed into what appeared to be a state of shock. Doug put her in the Datsun and drove her home with Tammy following, concerned, in her own car.

At Verdugo Avenue, Carol continued to act for Tammy Spangler, carrying on as if she were distraught over Jack's death. It made her jittery. She and Doug couldn't talk freely and he showed no signs of getting Tammy out of the apartment. As soon as she could, Carol pulled Doug aside and spoke in an urgent undertone.

"Get rid of the toys, now."

The Ravens were hidden in a small opening underneath the dashboard of the Datsun. A couple of times before, when they thought things might be getting hot, they had ditched them. Carol had even hidden them in her locker at work a couple of times. But now those guns really had to go.

She watched Doug walk around the balcony outside the apartment and get into the elevator. Within fifteen minutes he was back. It was a little after two o'clock in the morning.

On Sunday afternoon, after a restless night, Carol padded across the carpet in her bare feet, dripping water as she went. She had been in the shower when the doorbell rang. In his own bathroom, Doug was showering with Tammy Spangler. Now whoever had rung the bell gave up and began thumping on the door. Carol opened it and saw two men in suits. Detectives.

"Excuse me. I'm stark naked. Can you wait while I put some clothes on?" she said. She shut the door quickly and wondered what to do. All she could do was let them in. She pulled on a housecoat, then hurried through the apartment and spoke to Doug through the steam.

"I've got a house full of cops," she said.

"Oh c'mon," he said. "This is no time to be lying to me."

He emerged smiling into the living room, pulling on a bathrobe, trying to disarm the poker-faced policemen. Arrogance, curiosity, and the need to be in control sent him after Carol, who was escorted politely to the Van Nuys Police Department. Light streamed through the west-facing window of the interview room where Doug sat, volunteering information to Roger Pida. The sun was high in the sky, and outside the heat had reached ninety-eight degrees. That still didn't explain the dark patches on Doug's orange T-shirt, Pida thought. The room was air-conditioned, but he was sweating like a can of Coors fresh out of the refrigerator. The guy was dirty.

Doug gave Carol the alibi that they had agreed upon: on August 3, the date that Jack disappeared, he and Carol had spent the entire night together in the same bed.

In another office, Carol chattered freely to Howard Landgren, a detective with large, mournful features, telling him about her relationship with Jack and the money he had taken from her. She contradicted Doug, admitting that she had seen Jack briefly on August 3; she also admitted that she had once owned two .25-caliber automatics. She had sold them for one hundred dollars late in May, she said.

Landgren asked her if she could describe the man to whom she had sold them.

Of course Carol could, in all too vivid detail. He was a white male, aged thirty-five to forty, with blue-gray eyes, a potbelly, a mustache, and a large pockmark on his cheek. He was about six feet tall, weighed over two hundred pounds and—oh, yes—he had driven a white pickup truck with New York plates.

Tammy Spangler, wearing an orange T-shirt that matched Doug's, had her own story to tell. On Jack's last night at Little Nashville, she had noticed him talking to an Australian woman. Tammy had seen

Douglas Clark's booking photo. He was charged with child molestation until detectives could link him to the Sunset Murders.

Doug poses for the press in Los Angeles County Jail more than a year after his arrest. He's wearing the pin-striped suit Tammy Spangler bought for him.
Photograph by Michael LeRoy

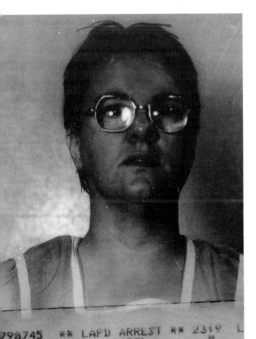

Carol Bundy in Los Angeles, booked on first-degree murder charges.

Carol Bundy waits to have an
identification photo shot the day
after her arrest.

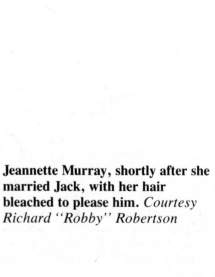

Jack Murray in his Tom Jones
look-alike days.

Jeannette Murray, shortly after she
married Jack, with her hair
bleached to please him. *Courtesy
Richard "Robby" Robertson*

her before and, she claimed, Avril was an unsociable misfit with an "I'm bad" attitude and a buck knife always on her right hip.

Pida and Landgren knew something was wrong. Clark and Bundy's stories had conflicted, and they seemed such an unlikely couple. Carol was so unattractive, while Doug was intelligent, articulate, nice-looking, and held down a decent job. But there was nothing on which to hold them. They let them go.

For the moment, the Australian woman with the buck knife seemed like the best bet. That day, after a tip-off that she was at Little Nashville, Avril was handcuffed and arrested. She wept over Jack's death, and seeming believably grief-stricken, said that the last person she had seen talking to Jack was Carol Bundy, who earlier had frightened him by showing him some guns in her car.

All the way back to Verdugo in the Datsun, Carol had to listen to Doug being angry because he thought she had talked too much.

"Motor mouth," he said.

Ever since Jack died, Doug had been telling her that they were both going to be arrested and she was going to know what the bite of metal would feel like on her wrists. Now Doug threatened to move out of the apartment on the first of the month.

He and Tammy hadn't actually had sex in front of Carol, but they might as well have. Doug was rubbing her nose in it again, proving to Carol how little she meant to him. When she killed Jack, Carol had expected him to be impressed. But instead of drawing them together, it seemed to distance them even more.

Maybe, unconsciously, she had expected them to get caught over Jack, Carol thought. Maybe it had to come to an end. Both of them were falling apart.

They had not been back at the apartment long before Doug and Tammy went out without telling her where they were going.

It was 5:45 on Sunday when Carol picked up the phone and dialed long distance to her mother-in-law, Carmeletta Bundy's harsh midwestern voice sounding bad-tempered across the line to California.

"The boys are raisin' Cain," she said.

"Well, tell them Mom's on the phone and they'll stop raising Cain," said Carol, who was taping the call. She had been doing that more lately. It helped her feel more in control.

Carmeletta was planning to fly to California on the twentieth of August to bring Chris and Spike home, but Carol warned her that it was a dangerous plan.

"Mom," she said. "Right now, the way things are with my life, I cannot have the boys."

Maybe in a couple of months, she promised, she would be able to work things out.

Spike's husky baby voice was full of excitement over a fishing trip with his granddad.

"I miss you," he said.

Chris sounded more subdued. "Where you living now?" he asked, insisting on writing the Verdugo phone number down for himself even though Carol told him his grandmother had it.

Carmeletta's voice spoke again, accusing. "Carol, why didn't you finish talkin' to Spike before you let Chris interrupt?"

Instantly Carol became defensive and childlike. "Apparently Chris stole the phone away from Spikie. I didn't have anything to do with it."

She was breaking Spike's heart, Carmeletta told Carol with more prescience than she could have realized.

Both boys got on extension phones now to talk more about fishing, Chris excited that he'd caught a dogfish and sad that he had to throw the little ones back, until Carol became worried about the cost of the call.

"I love you both. You boys be good, okay? Bye-bye, darlings . . . bye, Spikie . . . bye, Chrissie. Love you, honey."

It would be years before the boys saw their mother again.

At twelve minutes past six, Carol picked up the phone again to call Dick Geis in Portland. This time she told him about her part in the murders and said she was afraid for herself and the children. Geis, still convinced that Carol was concocting reasons to phone him, did not take her seriously. He told her not to come to Portland. The call lasted only two minutes.

Carol was still taking as many as half a dozen ten-milligram Librium tablets a day. At bedtime, she popped another handful in her mouth. This was the end of her supply.

She slept. But in the morning she had nothing left with which to calm herself. After dropping Doug at Jergens—he bitched for the entire two blocks—she proceeded to Valley Medical Center, where she arrived late for her 7:00 A.M. shift.

LeAnn Lane had been wondering where Nurse Bundy was when she spotted her in her yellow shirt sidling in toward the end of report. It was a pain. Everyone's charts would have to be explained again for Carol, which would hold the night shift up from leaving, which would mean medications would be late and get in the way of breakfast service.

Twice during the previous week, LeAnn had not been able to avoid eating lunch with Carol, who had seemed depressed and nervous. As much as she disliked the woman, it was difficult not to feel sorry for her. Her main problem, LeAnn thought for the umpteenth time, was that she'd do anything for attention, anything for approval. Which she certainly was not going to get for arriving late today.

LeAnn sighed. Next Carol was going to have to go to her locker to change into her uniform. And she's a diabetic, she thought, so then she'll have to eat. She watched Carol lumber out of the room, her bottom wide and flat in the stretch pants she always wore.

At 8:45, charging the call to her home number, Carol again called Dick Geis to ask once more if she could come to Portland. The time had come to be blunt. Geis told her that he did not want a relationship with her ever again.

"I guess it's all over between us," Carol said. Then she hung up.

For LeAnn Lane, burdened with work in general, and at this particular moment trying to take photographs of a patient's bedsores, this was the breaking point. It was about nine-thirty. Carol had materialized and was hovering around looking upset behind her enormous glasses and asking for help with a patient.

LeAnn went in to help her, and there, right over the bed of old Mrs. Schneider, luckily too far gone to absorb any of it, was Carol saying something about her boyfriend being found dead in a van.

I don't have time to listen to this shit, LeAnn thought angrily, sick once more over Carol's lack of professionalism in dragging her personal life to work. She ignored Carol, finished the job, and walked out of the patient's room. It was nearly ten-thirty. Time for her break. She went to join head nurse Howard Wanhoff for a cup of coffee in the third-floor nurses' lounge.

They had been there only a few minutes when LeAnn Lane groaned inwardly. There was Carol standing in the doorway. She came in and sat down, then she began talking in her clear, girlish voice.

Soon LeAnn Lane began to tremble. The tiny hairs on the back of her arms stood on end. This was too outlandish, and yet she believed every word. Carol was saying that her boyfriend Doug had killed two girls he had left near the freeway, and another girl that he had cut as if he were going to do exploratory surgery.

Why is she dumping this on me? LeAnn Lane thought. As she and Howard Wanhoff stared, completely immobilized by shock and fear, Carol, standing by the door now, told them that she was in the back seat when Doug shot another prostitute, whose body she had helped him drop in some bushes near a creek. Her other boyfriend hadn't simply died as Carol had claimed earlier. Now Carol was saying that she had killed him because she had told him too much about Doug's murders.

"LeAnn," Carol said, talking even more rapidly than usual. "You'll have trouble stomaching this. I cut off his head, but I made a mistake. I forgot about the shells that ejected."

She could imagine, Carol said, what his body must have looked like after six days in heat that must have reached 135 degrees inside the van.

As Carol talked, her hand hovered around the pocket of her uniform. LeAnn was sure that she had a gun and that at any minute she, LeAnn Lane, was going to be dead like the boyfriend who had been told too much. But Carol backed out of the room, saying that she couldn't take it anymore and was walking off the job. She was going home to turn herself in to authorities.

LeAnn Lane and Howard Wanhoff rushed to the administrator's office. Within minutes police sealed off the upper floors and fanned out, guns drawn, around the hospital. But as they went up in the elevators, Carol rode down to her basement locker, where she changed out of her uniform and slipped from the building. On her way to the Verdugo apartment, she stopped at the Jergens factory to tell Doug that she had left her job and wanted him to take what was left of her money and leave town.

"I'm not going anywhere, and I don't want your money," Doug said, annoyed that she had called him out of work.

At the apartment, Carol began gathering evidence of the murders: a bullet that Doug claimed to have shot through the head of Gina Marano; a pair of Gina's bikini underpants; and a pair of fuchsia-and-black panties that Doug had said were Marnett Comer's. She also had a pair of red high heels as well as a little blouse with hearts on it that had belonged to Cathy.

The scenario that followed was worthy of the Keystone Kops.

After calling information to get phone numbers for three homicide divisions ("I'm busy, aren't I?" she said to the operator, as if hoping for a shocked response. "Yes, ma'am," the operator replied blandly), Carol dialed Northeast and couldn't get through. She tried again. The number was still busy. She dialed Van Nuys. They were busy too. Finally, when the Burbank Division answered and she asked to speak to Homicide, she was placed on hold before being given a different number and asked to call them directly.

The new number was busy.

Finally, Carol called the "O" operator to ask for an emergency break-in. The operator refused but did try the number. It rang and Carol was hooked up to a Detective Kilgore at Northeast.

With an important sound to her voice, she reminded him of the series of Sunset murders—he knew about them—then asked if he had heard of the Betsy-Claudia code name.

When Kilgore said he wasn't sure and would have to look it up, Carol became more dramatic.

"Would you like to have your man today?" she asked.

"Uh, yeah."

Kilgore sounded taken aback at the B-movie turn in the conversation.

"I can give you your man today if you would also like to join Van Nuys and Burbank police departments," said Carol.

Kilgore wondered what this man was supposed to have done.

"All right," Carol said. "Are you well versed in the details of these murders?"

"Am I—am I—what?"

"Are you well versed in the details of the murders?" Obviously deciding that he wasn't, Carol changed her approach. "I'll give you some of the details."

"Okay. Go ahead." There was a beat, then Kilgore, trying to regain his dignity, added, "Because I have so many of them."

Carol had been treated like a crackpot last time and she wasn't about to let it happen again. As she gave a quick rundown of the Marnett Comer, Cindy Chandler, and Gina Marano homicides, she sounded like a nervous military commander.

"Foothill Boulevard. . . . she was cut down her belly. Check? . . . Second sister. Chest wound right through her heart. . . . Check?"

"Yeah."

Carol sighed and explained that "the next one up the line" was with a different gun. She was talking about Cathy.

"We dropped her in some bushes up near the Saugus-Newhall area by a stream. I don't know if you found her."

"Okay."

"You found her?"

Kilgore fudged. "We might. We have a lot."

155

Carol was not stupid even when stressed. "Okay. So you don't know about that one," she said, quickly moving on to Victor Weiss, the Mafia hit victim that Doug had told her about on the Saturday following Cindy and Gina's murders.

"My man did not stuff him in the trunk, by the way."

Kilgore was curious. "How come all of a sudden you want to roll over on him?" he asked.

Carol thought for a minute. "Because—" She thought again. "Oh, for quite a hell of a long time he's been treating me like shit. It's been worse and worse and worse. And now I've done one on my own. Done one completely on my own and he's falling apart over it and I'm just plain sick of it."

She told Kilgore about Jack Murray and the decapitation. Then she began explaining about Doug.

"The point is, he wants to continue this and continue and continue and continue. And I can't handle it. I'm falling apart."

Did she feel bad? Kilgore wondered.

"The honest truth is," said Carol, "it's fun to kill people and if I was allowed to run loose I'd probably do it again. I have to say— I know it's going to sound sick, it's going to sound psycho, and I really don't think I'm that psycho—but it's kind of fun. Like riding a roller coaster." She began to back off. "Not the killing. Not the action that somebody died, because we didn't kill them in a way that hurt them . . ."

"Now, is this your boyfriend or your husband?" Kilgore wanted to know.

"He's a boyfriend," Carol said. She sounded resigned, as if her actions might have been more understandable had she been the killer's wife. She would not give Kilgore his name. "Let him have a chance to get off his job."

Carol's plan now was to call the Van Nuys and Burbank police departments and have them meet her at the Gristmill for a two o'clock lunch. She invited Kilgore to join them, saying she expected they would all be squabbling over who would get to arrest her.

"I don't give a damn," she said. "I know I'm facing the gas chamber and it doesn't particularly freak me out, okay? I just—I've had thirty-eight years of just one pile of shit on top of another and I'm tired of it. I want out. . . . If it isn't this, then I will blow myself away. But what is imperative to me . . . he, Doug, will arrange to hit [my] kids. He will try to get back at me, he . . ."

Kilgore promised to protect the boys, then he asked Carol how he would recognize her.

She described her yellow terry top and gray slacks, and her voice got smaller as she described herself. "I've got short brown hair and glasses, and I stumble a lot. I've got a vision problem. I—I—I'm awkward-looking, in other words."

Kilgore double-checked Carol's address.

"Please don't come and arrest me," Carol said. She sounded panicked. "Please let me play this my way."

Presumably anticipating some glory, Kilgore tried to talk her out of calling Van Nuys and Burbank and meeting him alone. "See, if you call all of them, there's gonna be problems."

"How soon can you get to me?"

"Um. . . . well, I'm not too sure because I don't have a car right now and I've got to find my partner and that's how soon it will be." Kilgore then began to sound as he were making a real luncheon date. "Two o'clock sounds like a good time to me. Unless you want to make it earlier?"

It was not yet noon, and Orozco, listening to the tape later, would think, Couldn't Kilgore have borrowed a car? Didn't they have taxis in Northeast Division?

Poor Kilgore was to miss out on any kudos for arresting one of the Sunset killers. He and Carol settled on two o'clock for their meeting, but Carol was still on the phone when four plainclothes Van Nuys Division detectives, accompanied by a uniformed officer with gun drawn, converged on her apartment and banged loudly on the door.

As the call had come in from an officer in the field reporting Carol's confession at Valley Medical Center, Pida and Landgren had been discussing a search warrant for the Clark-Bundy apartment. They had rushed to the hospital, but when they found out that Carol Bundy had left, Landgren headed to Verdugo and Pida to Doug Clark's factory, where he had been planning to go anyway.

That morning Doug had phoned Pida several times before reaching him to retract the alibi he had given Carol the day before. He had been mistaken, Doug now said. Carol could have left the apartment on the night Jack Murray died but definitely was there when paramedics arrived to tend to their other roommate, Nancy Smith. One thing he did want Pida to know: Carol was weird.

Pida had gone on alert but kept his voice calm. "I'm glad you made the phone call," he said. "But we shouldn't talk on the phone. I'm going to come down."

It was now eleven-thirty. The American flag hung limply on the Jergens roof with barely a breeze to stir it. Roger Pida, standing outside the factory, felt his holster hot against his chest. He was packing a gun, because he didn't know what Doug Clark might do.

The eleven-thirty whistle blew to let employees know it was time for lunch. Men in work clothes began filing out of the plant past bubbling vats of tallow and citric acid. Suddenly Doug Clark emerged, heading for the lunch truck, and Roger Pida had time to think that he looked preppy in his slacks and crisp shirt.

As the detective moved toward him, with two other officers nearby as backup, Doug walked across the yard into the guard shack where he and Pida met. They smiled at each other. All seemed perfectly gentlemanly. Except that when Doug reached out to shake the detective's hand, Pida took it and didn't let go.

Doug saw the cuffs in Pida's other hand. "Are those necessary?" he said.

"I believe so."

Pida was enjoying the moment.

They drove in an unmarked squad car for two blocks. Then the car pulled to the curb a hundred feet east of the boxy beige stucco apartment building at 240 West Verdugo. Cop cars filled the street. Pida and another detective jumped from the squad car, leaving Doug and a uniformed officer inside with the engine running.

From inside the car, Doug could hear nothing. But he watched the lips of the detectives move as they conferred in undertones, and he seemed to become more and more agitated.

He leaned forward and cried out to the uniformed driver, his voice dramatic. "Carol's got a twelve-gauge shotgun. There could be a massacre at the front door."

Inside the apartment, Howard Landgren was trying to read Carol her Miranda rights. Instead of brandishing a shotgun, she had opened the door clutching several pairs of victims' underpants. Now that she'd started, she couldn't stop talking, miffed that her plans for a tasty Gristmill lunch had been aborted by the arrival of a platoon of detectives. As she gathered up more evidence, she led Landgren and another detective around, pressing on them a bullet that she said could be linked to the Chandler-Marano murders.

In Doug's bedroom, she unlocked a file cabinet.

"Here. This will give you an idea of what Doug is like," she said, handing Landgren a photo album containing pictures of Doug and Theresa simulating sex.

"I killed Jack all by myself because he was a real asshole and deserved to die," Carol said.

16

P_IDA PUT DOUG IN A SMALL HOLDING TANK. WHILE HE WAITED FOR task-force members to arrive from downtown, he read Carol her Miranda rights. She said she had given them enough to work with and she wanted to remain silent. But she began to put out feelers about whether it would be to her benefit to talk. He had never seen a case where cooperating hurt anybody, said Pida, nevertheless refusing to advise Carol about how to proceed. She would remain silent, said Carol, talk it over with an attorney, then reconsider if it turned out to be in her best interests.

But, of course, Carol could not keep quiet. While task-force members Leroy Orozco, Rick Jacques, Mike Stallcup, and Gary Broda helicoptered to Van Nuys from Downtown, she talked about Doug, who, she said, did not make her do anything against her will, and Jack Murray, who panicked when she tried to get him to help her. She had been unable, she said, to handle Jack's problems as well as her own.

On the way to Van Nuys, the task force had decided that Mike Stallcup would race back downtown to Ballistics taking Carol's bullet with him to be analyzed. As the helicopter took off again from the Van Nuys courthouse roof next door, Broda and Jacques began to question Carol while Orozco monitored the conversation from outside.

She began by asking them a question.

"Mr. Clark is incarcerated?"

It was a prissy turn of phrase, surely intended to impress the officers with her gentility and lack of criminal credentials. But as she began talking about the murders, Carol dropped most of this genteel pose, even as she was telling them the truth about her intended defense of being simply a middle-class Valley housewife.

Her story tumbled out. "I don't know if you guys have ever in your entire life shot anybody, but it's really fun to do," she said, repeating what she had said earlier to Kilgore. She spoke of her involvement with Jack, "the clinker who spoiled it all," and about the guns and Doug's necrophiliac fantasies. She told them of Theresa, a "plump little darling." She talked about victims that the cops knew about and others besides, the details forcing these hardened homicide veterans to pretend they were not close to tossing their cookies.

"You know something, Broda? Do you know what's wrong?" Carol said suddenly.

"You can call me Gary." Broda, sitting there impeccably groomed in his imported tailor-made suit, suspected nothing.

"Gary."

"Yeah."

"Do you know what's wrong?"

"What?"

"You look incredibly like Doug, and you smile just like him. And I hate to tell you this, but I'm having—what's the way to say this?—clitoral spasms. . . . And you know it's going to be a long time before I get to a man again."

Orozco, monitoring the interview from outside the room, waited with a grin on his face for Gary Broda to emerge.

"You've still got the touch," Orozco said.

Gary Broda smiled.

But he and Rick Jacques had been left reeling. None of the cops had ever met a woman like Carol. No one thought women did this kind of thing.

"You know what's really sad?" Carol had said at the end.

"What?"

"Now that I've done it, it was really kind of interesting. . . . It's sure as hell not like going to the beach or barbecuing."

Doug Clark came out of the Van Nuys holding tank.

"You're under arrest," Leroy Orozco said.

160

It was around six in the evening as they left for downtown in the unmarked green Plymouth. Leroy drove, fighting the August heat and the evening traffic south along the Hollywood Freeway to Parker Center. In the back with Mike Stallcup, Clark yattered away in some self-serving monologue that Leroy tried to tune out by concentrating on the blast from the air conditioner.

Already he didn't like him. The guy was handcuffed, but all six feet and two hundred pounds of him exuded blond, WASP attitude. He'd emerged from the tank with a smirk on his face. Clark was cocky, that was his problem, acting as if he were doing them a favor by helping them out with their little investigation. He thought he was better than they were. Clearly he thought he could outsmart them.

Heat burned through the windows of the Plymouth and bounced off the dashboard. Orozco wanted to loosen his tie but wouldn't. A DA had pointed at a lawyer once in court who loosened his tie in front of a jury. "Looks weak," the DA had said. The lawyer had lost his case. Ever since then Orozco had kept his tie up to his Adam's apple.

Clark's annoying air of noblesse oblige did not add up. He was wearing work boots and a pair of tan pants and he worked in a factory. But nothing ever added up at this stage. The public's perception was that a case ended with an arrest. But that was when everything began. They were just now beginning to know Douglas Daniel Clark.

By Alvarado Street his soothing, hypnotic voice began to get on Orozco's nerves. He was complaining about the weather. About wanting something to eat.

To shut him up, Orozco said, "We don't want to talk. We're going downtown."

He did want Clark to talk. But he wanted him on tape.

Just south of Olvera Street they got off the freeway and drove past the Immigration and Naturalization building. By the time they pulled into the Parker Center underground parking lot, a gloomy trap for the heat still radiating from empty evening pavements, Clark had taken Orozco's advice and shut his mouth. Silent and grim, they rode the back freight elevator up to Robbery-Homicide on the third floor, where they put him in interrogation room B, ironically nicknamed "the Free and Voluntary Room" after the question, "Are you making this statement freely and voluntarily?"

Carol, in the captain's office across the hall, had asked them not to tell Doug that she was feeding them information, and they had agreed. They wanted her as happy as she could be under the circumstances. She was their key to Doug Clark and the evidence.

"I'm going to need some smokes."

He was still cocky and smiling, out of his cuffs and wanting to talk. Best to let him go, say what he wanted to say, and talk himself into a corner, Leroy thought.

Someone went to find him some Marlboros and they Mirandized him. Told him he was charged with murder, had the right to remain silent, and could have an attorney even if he couldn't afford one. Clark said he'd like to try to get one, but he'd talk "in the interim."

A microphone was hidden in the thermostat in the acoustic-tile wall. In the harsh yellow light Orozco, Stallcup, and Helvin sat around the table, not yet fixing Clark with their stares, wanting him to feel as if he were in control.

He began and kept talking for three and a half hours, lying to them in the very beginning when he told them that his relationship with Carol had been "platonic" since February. To ease him into it, they asked him about his background and he told them about being chief engineer at Jergens and his marriage.

"She's still a good friend of mine."

This part was true.

"Do you have any idea what we're all talking about?" Orozco asked him.

"I'm pretty sure. Jack Murray, right?"

They said there was something else.

"We'll start with Jack Murray," Orozco said.

So Doug told the story of the night Jack died. How he fell asleep and thought Carol was there all night. How he awoke to Nancy Smith having a seizure and called paramedics.

"And then Carol was there. But Carol was fully dressed."

He rambled and seemed nervous. He's lying, Orozco thought.

See, said Doug, Carol had a motive to kill Jack, because Jack had taken her money. But he didn't think she had actually done it. While they were on the subject, he owed Carol six or seven hundred bucks himself.

"You see, I drink, number one. I make more money but I drink a lot, and I—and I gamble. And I—I—I manage to fuckin' blow money like crazy."

He didn't mean to depreciate Carol, but he was trying to break the habit of having her handy to do the dishes and the shopping. The woman would do anything to get in the sack with him.

"I'm not bragging. I'm no he-man. I'm not even hung."

He didn't know what they knew, so to cover himself, to make himself look honest in case they had heard, he told them about the bad blood between him and Jack.

"He is a pussy. If I wanted to mess with him, I'd throw a head-lock on him and bust his skull."

And when they asked him, he told them about the guns. Carol's guns. He knew her guns were Ravens, because he had tried to clean them once.

Orozco wondered if Doug ever drank in the city, and when he said yes, at the Ski Room on Sunset Boulevard, Orozco thought, Aha. He'd put himself in the area of the murders.

"Ever been a time when you picked up a prostitute?"

"I'd pick up hookers, yeah."

It must have been a slip.

"This isn't going to be held against me, is it?"

Mike Stallcup allowed himself a small smile. "I'm not going to arrest you for prostitution," he said.

Talking about prostitutes must have reminded Doug of an incident when he worked for the Department of Water and Power in Sun Valley. He told them that a Mexican hooker's old man stabbed him and stole his eight-hundred-dollar IRS refund check. He was covering up for an earlier murder, the cops sensed.

"I reported it, 'cause I got the scars to prove it."

He was still dying for a smoke. Which meant they were getting to him and it was time to lighten up for a while. Relax him in case he tightened, thinking he'd given away too much.

Somebody gave him his cigarettes.

"You're a lifesaver."

He lit one and the smoke curled around everyone's heads, all of them breathing in smoke that had come from Douglas Clark's lungs. Orozco, who didn't usually, smoked to keep him company. If he could have given him a beer, he would have, and he'd have had one with him.

They kept it light, nonthreatening, with biographical questions. Father? Franklyn. Mother? Blanch. Ex-wife? Beverly.

Beverly's phone number?

Doug had to think. They weren't going to call her, were they?

Well, they wanted to get this thing cleared up. Did he have brothers and sisters?

Was this really essential? Why all this shit about Sunset?

LOUISE FARR

But they didn't answer him. They backed off again and asked if he belonged to a union.

He tried joking. He wished he did belong to a union, he said. Maybe then he'd get some time off once in a while.

Still on the subject of work, he told them he'd been accepted at the police academy and they all felt a chill. Never took his physical, he said. The pay was pretty low.

It was a jab at them to try to make himself seem superior. He must still be smarting from having to tell them he hadn't gone to college, Orozco thought.

"I'm well read," Doug said defensively. Then he referred to the prosecutor-author from the notorious Manson family murders. ". . . I've read everything Bugliosi ever wrote."

They returned to the Sunset murders. Not able to shut up, let them ask questions, think before he spoke, he volunteered that all the girls on the Sunset Strip were terrified of someone he called "the ax man."

Orozco leaned forward.

The lights in the room emphasized Clark's pallor beneath the sandy blond hair. In repose his soft, full mouth was almost petulant, and his eyes revealed nothing.

Las moviras, Orozco called them. People's moves. He could pick up a lot from someone's body language. A brief intake of breath, a blink, a tapping fingernail. But this Doug Clark was cool. His *moviras* gave little away.

"Do you know any of these girls?" Orozco asked. "The ones that have been killed? Have you ever dated them?"

"There's one I think. Yeah." He smiled. "And it's in the wallet. Where in the hell's that wallet?" He made a show of patting at himself as if he were looking for the wallet even though he knew Van Nuys detectives had taken it from him and given it to Downtown. "I got her phone number . . . I think it was Cindy or Cynthia. Something like that . . :"

They showed him a picture of Cindy Chandler, and he said he had been down at Malibu girl-watching when he met her. He'd had lunch, was getting a little blasted because he usually carried a pint of Kessler's whiskey or Crown Royal if he was in the chips. After that they had dated half a dozen times.

"She had on a crocheted one-piece that just had the tits and the crotch covered and a tan and a body. She's something else."

When he looked at photos of the other victims, he pretended he

164

didn't know they were dead. Christ, he wouldn't date most of them, he said.

Stallcup pushed the murder book with the victims' photos closer to him and Orozco pointed and spoke.

"Do you recall picking up these two girls . . . giving them a ride?"

"Uh-uh." He spoke, worried, of getting into trouble because Cindy Chandler was underage.

That was when Stallcup told him they were talking about bigger trouble than that. They were talking about five murders.

"And that's what you're under arrest for," Orozco said.

"I'm under arrest for this, not Jack Murray? Hmm. That's really goofy."

It was time to tell him they'd connected him to the murders. At Ballistics, Stallcup had paced the floor until Arleigh McCree came out and said, "It's a make."

Now they told Doug Clark that Stallcup had the link to the murders in his pocket.

"Jesus. What is it?"

No need to tell him it was a bullet. Let him sweat.

"I'm curious. I'd like to know."

"Are you familiar with the term 'necrophilia'?" Stallcup asked.

Yes. He'd heard of necrophilia, he said, but it was not his cup of tea.

The wooden box, asked Orozco. Had he seen it in the paper?

"No . . . Must have missed it."

"We're aware of the fact that you shot Cindy Chandler and her half sister—"

"I haven't shot—"

"—in a car that you sold—listen to me just a second. In a car you sold to an employee where you work. . . ."

"Hon-honest to God. Don't know a damn thing about it. Keep going, though."

In the old days, Orozco thought wistfully, in George Raft's day, it would have been a great interview. They could have beaten the shit out of him. Nowadays that was considered unprofessional.

"Let me ask you a question," Stallcup said.

"Shoot," said Clark. He paused, then laughed, still trying to disarm them. "Wrong term for this discussion."

Orozco asked the question. "You ever heard the name Exxie?"

"Just know the name 'cause I saw it in the paper."

The look was sincere, and Orozco thought that he was used to

LOUISE FARR

having women hang on his every bullshit word. But now he was
bullshitting the prize bullshitters, who knew his game but couldn't
do much about it yet.

They changed the subject and asked about sex again. Liked it
all, he said. Oral, vaginal, with young or old women. "As long as
they're clean and got their head screwed on straight." Black, white,
Oriental. "I just have never been able to, you know, get it on with
a Mexican girl."

And what was the youngest girl he'd had sex with since he'd
been an adult?

He paused. He hung his head. "That's something I'm ashamed
of, but it's nothing to do with any of this."

When he heard they had the photo album with the pictures of
Theresa and they weren't going to let it drop, he turned white and
lost his composure.

"That was a case of fucking seduction you wouldn't believe . . .
we were resisting it completely."

They had him. He admitted he knew Cindy Chandler. Now this.

"She was grab-assing on me and Carol constantly."

They talked some more about the murders but he got back to
the child, sexually well-adjusted but trapped in a twelve-year-old
body, he said.

"But this kid's no loud-mouthed little kid. She's a conniving little
bitch. . . . She's got that sense, you know, when you can tell somebody's kind of kinky."

Then he made the connection. Carol had given them the book.

"Somebody is trying to lynch my ass. And I have a hunch I
know who it is. . . ."

Probably with his mama, Orozco thought, he got away with
blaming other kids.

They sent somebody up to Phillippe's restaurant to get him a
couple of beef-dip sandwiches and they spoke to him about the
guns and his knives.

"This thing with this kid is going to kill my mom," he had said.

It was 10:20 P.M. when he signed a consent to search his apartment and storage garage. He had admitted helping Carol dispose
of Jack Murray's head, but he hadn't admitted the murders.

A little before midnight, criminalists and detectives converged on
the Verdugo Avenue apartment accompanied by Douglas Clark. As
they walked up the steps to the front door, Doug stopped and

166

asked if Carol was there. Then he backed up in another affected display of fear.

They emptied a pair of handcuffs and twenty-nine live rounds of .25-caliber ammunition from Carol's bedside drawer. As well as stained clothing and carpet fibers, they took four pairs of Doug's boots, two shotguns, and piles of pornography and bondage magazines that sat along with *Playboy* and *Good Housekeeping* in the living room.

In his bedroom, Doug stood watching with his ever-present smirk as Orozco searched his file cabinet.

"Don't you have anything better to do?" Doug asked.

Orozco ignored him. In the file cabinet, he found the *Valley News* folded and open to a story about Exxie Wilson and the wooden treasure chest. He also discovered a hardcover textbook that included a photograph of a severed penis in the mouth of a head. The head was impaled upon a stick. A second pair of handcuffs was in the cabinet. Orozco got out his police-handcuff key and was able to unlock them.

Detective Helen Kidder, long since back at Northeast Division, missed out on the arrest and interrogation. That night, the night it all came down, she was on the Sunset Strip, three sheets to the wind from knocking back imported champagne. She and Peggy York had just signed a contract with Jack Webb Productions, which wanted to produce a televison series about a pair of female detectives. Nothing would come of it, but Helen Kidder would always suspect that the series "Cagney and Lacey" had been sparked by their story.

Somebody contacted Kidder and York at the restaurant and they rushed downtown in time to get a glimpse of Clark.

He was good-looking, Helen Kidder decided, but there was something wrong.

Leroy Orozco booked Clark into county jail on felony child-molestation charges. Then he looked through his wallet. As Orozco studied the contents, he realized that the wallet contained startling and valuable evidence. Inside was a card about six inches long, and on the card was a list of typed phone numbers. Penciled in below was, "Cindy . . . Blonde hooker. $30," and "Mindi C. . . . Not working. Friend of Cindi's. Pretty."

17

It kept coming back. The image of Cindy and Gina being brought up from the side of the freeway in body bags. Janet Marano had never seen a body bag before and to her they looked like trash bags. You have kids and you raise them, she had thought, and they end up being hauled up a hill like somebody's old garbage.

The Marano-Chandler family had moved to a new house in Irvine, the surviving children terrified and sad and Janet and Andy cold, guilty, at each other's throats and swift to blame.

In the night, Janet still awakened to her own screams, and the children were out of control. They knew that she and Andy were scared to death to get tough with them.

Now she stared at the first pictures of Douglas Clark and Carol Bundy on the television news—accompanied by the clip of the body bags—and she tried to get clues from what she saw.

There were none. Clark was good-looking. Normal-looking. If she could have tortured him to death, she would have, which made her feel guilty. Then she decided not to. She might be Christian, she told herself, but she also was human, with normal, evil impulses.

She watched the news over and over again until the time they showed Cindy and Gina's school pictures. That was when they had to bring an ambulance for Janet Marano, who was screaming, "I'm sorry. I'm sorry."

At the hospital her doctor was a Christian from their church. He wanted to pray for the murderer, and so they all prayed, she and Andy too far gone to question. Only afterward did Janet Marano ask why she should pray. Let other people forgive him, while she and Andy dreamed of torture.

Janet got out of the hospital. News of the crimes had traveled inland with the family, and strangers wanted to meet her, not to offer comfort but to learn gory details. Other mothers, smug in the certain knowledge that their own children would never rebel, worked into conversations glowing accounts of their parenthood. One night the phone rang and a voice said, "Dead girls. Dead girls." Then whoever it was hung up.

Every day Janet Marano looked at the plants in her new garden. Every day she made them promises out loud.

"I'll give you some water tomorrow," she said. But she never did. And as she watched, the flowers died.

The task force fanned across the city, interviewing witnesses and gathering evidence. In spite of Cindy Chandler's phone number in Doug Clark's wallet, they found nothing to indicate that he knew or had met her before the day of her murder. There was also no indication that she had been a prostitute. The phone number in Doug's wallet belonged to a pay phone at a hooker motel on Sunset Boulevard. The manager did not know Cindy.

Carol had been booked into Sybil Brand Institute for Women. The next day Orozco, Broda, and Jacques took her out to re-create the murder-site tour she had taken with Doug and to inspect a wash near the Jergens factory where she thought he might have stashed the guns. They found nothing. A police search of the plant, conducted the day before, during Carol's interrogation at Van Nuys, had also failed to turn them up. It was possible that Doug might have tried to melt the Ravens down in one of the boilers, but Jergens was resisting the expense of shutting them down. The task force told the company they had until the weekend to find the guns themselves without a court order.

In the afternoon, detectives took Carol to visit Theresa at the apartment in the north Valley where she and her mother had moved. The little girl waited for them alone, planning how she was going to pack a bag and hide up in the hills when she saw her mother, who was on her way from work.

Carol sat next to her on the sofa in the living room.

"Doug's been arrested for murder," she said. "I turned him in. I want you to cooperate as much as possible."

Theresa gave them jeans, tops, and jewelry that Doug had given her. Reluctantly, because she loved the tinkling melody, she turned over her "Greensleeves" music-box key chain. Theresa thought Greensleeves was a prostitute.

Greensleeves was all my joy,
Greensleeves was my delight;
Greensleeves was my heart of gold,
And who but Lady Greensleeves.

They took her to the hospital for her first pelvic and a VD test, which made her bleed all over her white satin shorts.

Her mother cried, and Theresa said, "Mom. Calm down."

After it was done, they went into a special room, where Mike Stallcup and Peggy York interviewed her.

She told it all to them, about trolling with Doug for prostitutes, once with Carol along, and about going with Carol to Jack's van. She mentioned the times Doug had put handcuffs on her, and about how when he asked her to spank him, she had said no. And she remembered once lying on the couch and discovering a big gun underneath it.

"How big?"

"*Very* big."

Another day he had shown her an army bag full of guns and told her they were for protection. He wanted to pick up a rowdy prostitute, he said, and shoot her if she pulled a knife on him.

They asked if she had ever seen Doug or Carol with blood on them. In the excitement of that day, and because Doug had not actually been bleeding, she forgot the time she saw him with scratches on his cheeks, the track marks that she had thought looked like tears of blood.

After the interview, because of the blood on her own white shorts, she and her mother couldn't go to McDonald's, which was disappointing. Jacqueline drove her straight home and Theresa cried and cried until she thought she would never stop. She didn't want her mother to know all the sordid details. And she didn't want the police to know her fear that the girl she and Doug had picked up on August 1 might have been one of his victims.

* * *

170

That night Leroy Orozco accompanied Frank Garcia, Little Ronnie Homicide, and two criminalists to Doug's rental garage off Alameda Avenue. They raised the rickety wooden door and Garcia was first to enter, aware as always of the creepiness of being at a murder scene. He looked around in the eerie glow of a police floodlight. He glanced at the floor. That was when he saw brownish marks that could have been bloodstains. They were about two and a half feet wide and six to eight feet long, and they looked as if they had been made by an object being dragged. They ended at a clean, square outline, as if a bed or mattress had been on the floor.

Quickly, one of the criminalists collected samples from the area to take to the lab. Later they would make a schematic of the garage detailing every blood spot. But now Garcia noticed droplets and other bloody smudges nearby and the outline of what appeared to be a bloodied work boot with a patterned sole.

Everyone stood around trying to decide what to do. If they could link the pattern to Clark's boots, it could be crucial. But in order to perform a positive test for human blood, the criminalists would have to remove a sample of the print. This meant losing some of its identifying details. Rather than risk that, they sprayed the print with a chemical called Orthotolidine. It turned bright green, indicating blood. But it was impossible to say conclusively that the blood was human. At least, though, the details of the sole were preserved and could be photographed for comparison.

Near midnight, they left the garage, taking with them hair samples and a number of their own red-stained cloth squares for further testing.

The next morning Carol, being held without bail, was charged with one count of murder and her Datson was impounded for tests. The bloody drag marks in the garage had corroborated part of her story, and a search of the car confirmed more of the details she had given of the Marnett Comer murder. The car's gearshift knob was fractured, and there were three holes in the door panel on the passenger side. From behind the panel, criminalists retrieved one .25-caliber bullet. The seat cover and cushion on the passenger side were saturated with what appeared to be dried blood. In the trunk, a paper bag—the kill bag—contained paper towels, a large Ginso brand kitchen knife, and plastic garbage bags.

The task force had interviewed a frightened Lydia Crouch, as well as Doug's former live-in girlfriend, Bretta Jo Lamphier, known as Joey. Lamphier was tall, rangily attractive, and intensely loyal to Doug. Still, she turned over a buck knife that Doug had given her, and the detectives were preparing a search warrant for a trunk of clothes that she was storing for him. They also wanted telephone records for the Verdugo and Lemona apartments and for the Jergens factory, as well as for Lydia Crouch and Joey Lamphier's phones.

Three days after Carol's confession, Doug was formally charged with three counts of child molestation and one charge of accessory after the fact in the Murray case. He had been brought up to Parker Center to get a blood sample drawn. Afterward, he sat in the Robbery-Homicide office, as cocky as usual, one leg crossed casually over the other.

Orozco was studying him. Suddenly he nudged Frank Garcia and pointed.

"Fuck," Garcia said.

None of the boots that the task force had confiscated from the Verdugo apartment matched the sole print from the garage floor. But they could tell. The sole on the black leather work boots Doug had been wearing when he was arrested and was wearing now looked like the bloody boot print in the garage.

Leroy called out, "Let me see those boots."

Quickly Doug uncrossed his legs. He was too late. Orozco directed Mike Stallcup to confiscate the boots.

On the Friday after the arrests, the task force gathered at the Code Seven bar near Parker Center to hash over developments in the case. They were paged there in the early evening.

Carlos Ramos, a Jergens factory boiler operator, had walked up three flights of metal stairs to make his hourly check of the boiler. He was climbing down when he stumbled and almost fell. As he put out his hand to save himself, he discovered a soft, multicolored cosmetics bag hidden underneath some pieces of brick and lumber. Ramos opened the bag. In it were two .25-caliber Raven automatics, one chrome and one nickel.

Ballistics tests later linked the nickel gun to all the known victims except Jack Murray.

The day after the guns were found, accompanied by a criminalist and a local police officer, Leroy Orozco examined the Buick in Youngstown, Ohio, where its buyer had moved. There were bullet holes through the driver's-seat cushion; another hole through the back seat indicated, Orozco thought, where Gina Marano had been shot. Under the front seat lay two .25-caliber bullets, and a .25-caliber casing rested in the crevice between the driver's-seat cushion and back. On the front passenger-seat floor lay a pair of women's black vinyl gloves.

The carpet on the front passenger side, the right rear seat, and the right rear floor mat were dry but had been saturated with what appeared to be blood. Later the blood from the front would be linked to Karen Jones. The blood from the back would turn out to be type O, as was Gina Marano's.

Jack Murray was cremated and the funeral was held at Forest Lawn on another scorching day. As she sat in the little white clapboard imitation New England chapel, not unlike the chapel in which she and Jack had been married in Las Vegas, Jeannette Murray was in a trancelike state of shock.

She had heard that Douglas Clark was claiming innocence and blaming Jack for the Sunset murders. The police had taken a 9-mm gun and Jack's boots and sneakers from the Valerio apartment. But his feet were smaller than Doug Clark's—and Jeannette had been able to alibi him for two of the murder nights. When Exxie Wilson and Karen Jones were killed, Jack had been on a fishing trip with Little Nashville friends. And on June 11, the night of the Chandler-Marano murders, Jack had been playing poker. His host, a lawyer named Bob Connors, had lost heavily and had written Jack a series of checks. One of them, for $250 and dated June 11, had been returned by Connors's bank and he had turned it over to police.

Still, Jeannette could not shake the idea that Clark and Bundy might be released from jail.

On August 26, sheriff's deputies, alerted by an informant, made their way down a graded road near a hilltop in Canyon Country, north of the San Fernando Valley. The hill was covered with heavy brush and was strewn with discarded and broken machine parts. Near a large, rusting cylinder-shaped tank the investigators noticed the strong odor of decomposing flesh accompanied by a dark oily spot in the brush. Several hundred strands of light-colored hair glinted in the noontime sun. So did four teeth and a yellow metal earring.

Looking north, the investigators noticed bones: a skull, a rib cage, a complete left leg, and a right femur with a pelvis attached. A further search turned up a larger clump of hair, a scapula, and a faded red sweatshirt. Two days later the coroner removed an expended .25-caliber bullet from the base of the skull.

The coroner's office tagged her Jane Doe no. 18, but this was the victim that Doug and Carol had called Water Tower. The bullet from her skull was linked to Douglas Clark's nickel Raven.

Two days later, the Los Angeles County Sheriff's Department

received a report that more human remains had been spotted in the Malibu mountains three miles from the intersection of Tuna Canyon and Saddle Peak Road. When a deputy proceeded to the area, he found the mummified body of a young woman wrapped around a bush down a leafy embankment. Her black tank top and skirt were around her waist. Her jewelry consisted of a gold ankle chain, an earring stud, and an Egyptian-style ring. The only other evidence at the scene was a clump of hair beneath the young woman's body. It was blond, as was the hair on her head.

Later the coroner's office determined that the woman, about twenty years old, had been killed by a .25-caliber bullet wound to the left forehead. The bullet fragments shared the same characteristics as the bullet found in the skull of Jane Doe no. 18, and the rest of the Sunset murders victims. But a firearms expert said that although it was possible the bullet had been fired from the same gun, he could not say for certain. There simply was not enough left of the bullet jacket retrieved from the young woman now named Jane Doe no. 99, the "package" that Douglas Clark had pointed out to Carol Bundy on their July drive up to Oxnard.

To Leroy Orozco, Carol Bundy was a nothing girl sitting in a bar who'd give it up to anybody. He felt sorry for her; she'd do anything for a man. On a court order, a group of cops checked Carol out of Sybil Brand Institute a second time to take care of her banking and the Verdugo apartment. On the day of her arrest she had said proudly that she was being treated like a choice piece of property. She still was, because she was still their connection to Douglas Clark.

"I feel bad about doing this to Doug," Carol said in the car on the way to Verdugo Avenue.

"You're doing it for society," said Frank Garcia, who still thought of her more as an ally than a murderer.

Carol also felt bad that a presidential election was coming up. For the first time since she came of age, she reflected, she would not be able to vote. Unlike Doug, who considered himself a law-and-order Republican against "revolving door justice that put assholes back on the street," Carol had retained the liberal Democratic sensibilities of her Peace and Freedom Party days. She was not a Ronald Reagan fan and would have voted for Jimmy Carter. Anyway, what did it matter? Their votes would have canceled each other out.

At the Verdugo apartment, Orozco gave Carol permission to

change clothes and told her she'd have to leave the bedroom door open.

"Why don't you come in?"

"*No.* C'mon, Carol. Get your clothes. What do you want?"

She picked out an assortment of pants and tops and skirts.

"Am I going back to jail?"

"We'll finish at the bank and then we'll get something to eat."

Carol had a look in her eye. The look was becoming familiar to any policeman who had spent time around her.

"Close the door," she said. "Let's have dessert. . . . It's the last time I'm going to be with a man. I won't tell anyone."

The cops shouted in a chorus, "*No*, Carol."

"Maybe one of us ought to do it for history," Gary Broda joked to Orozco later. "One for the Gipper."

In September, Carol sat down in her cell to write a five-page letter to Broda. It was in pencil on yellow lined paper and it illustrated again Carol's uncanny knack for being self-effacing and demanding almost in the same breath. It also showed her ability to pounce on the smallest positive gesture and out of it manufacture romance.

First she apologized to Broda for being nervous and loud during an interview that day at Sybil Brand Institute. That out of the way, she reminded him that he had reached out to her in friendship, which carried with it responsibility. She wanted him to write to her or to give her his phone number so that she could call him.

> Of course you may not be interested in knowing the lady behind the scared face.[. . .] I really don't want to cause you to be involved if you don't want to be. I genuinely want to get to know you. Who am I[. . .]?
>
> I'm a gentle, usually quiet woman. Sometimes I get boisterous and I am subject to mood changes.[. . .]
>
> Let me see, for that dinner you promised when I get out . . . rack of lamb, rice pilaf, tossed salad, ice tea . . . you.

Signing the letter with "Affection and Lotsa good stuff, Carol B.," and suggesting that Broda disguise his identity when writing to her, Carol also asked him to let her know if she were pipe-dreaming.

Broda, thinking he was on safe ground as Carol was not getting out of jail, had jokingly promised her a meal. But he was appalled.

"That fucking bitch," he said to Garcia. "How could she think I'd be interested in her?"

175

But like the rest of the task force, Broda felt sorry for Carol. He wrote back, lightening the blow by enclosing a copy of *Shogun*, to tell her that she had mistaken professional courtesy for personal interest.

In turn, Carol let him know that his message had come through.

I guess I miss-read signals again. I really believed (perhaps my need is so intense) your offer of friendship.[. . .] I guess it just isn't in the cards for the lady to be genuine friends with the man who arrests her.

Carol's brother, Gene, had changed his phone number. They had not been close, and Carol thought him a prude. But still she was hurt. Grant Bundy was disbelieving and in shock. When she phoned him to tell him about her arrest, he had broken down and told her that he had developed lung cancer.

"I always thought one of us would be around to take care of the boys," Grant had said.

His mother, Carmeletta, was as supportive as she could be to Carol from two thousand miles away. But then Carol hadn't actually told Carmeletta all the details of what was going on.

To her mother-in-law and to other friends and acquaintances, Carol was trying, in letters, to justify her situation. First she had lost her sight, then she had split up with Grant, then Jack had taken her money, Carol wrote, her attitude indicating that under similar circumstances anyone would have fallen in with a serial killer and become his accomplice.

Carol's preliminary hearing was on September 18. Samuel Mayerson, a fifty-seven-year-old Texas-born sole practitioner and former Los Angeles chief deputy district attorney, had been appointed to represent her.

At his request, the court was cleared. Carol, dressed in a matronly aqua-and-white print dress and black sandals, sat next to Mayerson listening to LeAnn Lane; Avril, the Australian woman; Jeannette Murray; detectives Roger Pida and Howard Landgren; and, of course, the coroner.

Jack Murray had died from multiple stab wounds, Dr. Eugene Carpenter told the court, some of them inflicted before and some of them after death. Murray's head had not been found to verify Carol's claim that she had shot him. But that would not be inconsistent with his findings, said Carpenter. "It is a rule that people live for quite some time with head wounds."

The stab wounds on Jack Murray's body were made, he thought, with a large kitchen knife. But in Carpenter's opinion, for the decapitation, a little larger instrument would have been "more efficient."

On the basis that Van Nuys detectives had not read Carol her Miranda rights at the Verdugo apartment, Sam Mayerson tried to exclude Carol's first admissions to Detective Howard Landgren regarding Jack Murray and the Sunset killings. When Landgren testified that he had been unable to shut Carol up for long enough to speak, Mayerson's objection was overruled. So was his motion maintaining that there was insufficient evidence with which to charge Carol.

A second motion then became crucial. The California penal code contained a series of special circumstances that could lead to the death penalty. They included multiple murder, the killing of a law-enforcement officer or prosecutor, and eliminating a witness to a crime. The district attorney's office considered Jack Murray a witness. If found guilty at trial, Carol could face death.

Samuel Mayerson felt the penal code made it clear that a witness should observe a crime rather than simply hear about it as Jack Murray heard about the Sunset murders from Carol.

Again the court disagreed. Carol's arraignment was set for October 3 at 8:30 A.M. The special circumstances would stand.

Carol was not enjoying jail. She hated the wrinkled pink smocks, which reminded her of 1950s housedresses. She despised eating off a paper plate with a spoon. She had no desire to spend her life in prison, as she did not consider herself to be a criminal. But she had no visitors, and so, like Doug, she passed the time letter writing.

"Dear Tammie," she wrote to Tammy Spangler on September 26:

> I know you're seeing Doug. I wasn't right for him. I'm too housewifey and motherly. He's bloodthirsty and so are you. There is a term describing his type, your type, and my type of behavior. There are a number of terms, but I'll use the one that's least upsetting: 'sociopath.' But he carries it beyond reasonable limits. He has said he's a psychopathic killer. That does not mean he's insane.
>
> I allowed him to destroy the rest of my life. I did it, but he set it up. Just remember that except for a trick of timing, it could be you sitting in jail and not me. I followed him on his 'spree.' Funny, but I would still follow him. However long I live, he will always influence my life. He is part of me. So is Jack.

Tammie, he needs you now. Stay with him. But be cautious. Be sure it's you he wants and not just a runner to gather his clothes, handle his mail, get him money, etc.

It would be nice if you could visit me here. It gets kind of lonesome.

Best,
Carol

Less than a week later, Carol wrote to Doug to say that she regretted turning him in, but would not have broken down if he had not treated her badly and told her she "wasn't worth dingo shit." They had a "bond," and because of it she could not understand why she was not more important to him. She did not state what the bond was, but the implication was that it was the murders.

Doug was still charging that Carol had framed him and that Jack Murray was the real Sunset killer. She answered his charges.

If I were "sticking" you, why didn't I set you up for Jack? I could have. It would've worked. You can get me out, but I can no longer effectively help you.[. . .] In many ways you and I are alike. We are both users, both honest with each other, both devient, both psychopathic in behavior.

A week later, perhaps expecting Carol to testify against him at his upcoming preliminary hearing—or more likely hoping that his mail was being seized and read by authorities—Doug wrote back. First he sweetened Carol up by introducing a jail mate named Bronte who wanted to correspond. He then launched into a self-righteous display of wounded innocence:

what ever you are doing or why is beyond me. You must really want to see me dead.[. . .] I won't assist the DA to kill you, even though at first I was very mad at you for claiming I did all this shit. Now, I'm just sad for you and wonder "why." You cover for someone at my expense. OK. And a jury may believe. But why is all I can't understand.[. . .] I was just convenient I guess.

If he found out that she had arranged the unforgivable murder of Cindy Chandler, "a gentle, wonderful girl," he would lose sympathy for Carol, he wrote. "I hope you didn't. I doubt you could kill anyone, no matter what you told me. You are not my idea of a murderer."

178

When Bronte wrote Carol a rambling and romantic letter, she replied, thanking him for his sincerity. It did not occur to her that Doug, hoping to learn something that he could use against her, had offered to pay Bronte for every letter that he got back.

Carol wrote:

 I feel like I shit on the dicks of two friends, one is dead and the other may die. I don't want that. I want him to live. I want to go back to what we had. I liked it. But it is over.

Sam Mayerson had cautioned Carol against writing to Doug, and she was trying to take his advice, but in a message through Bronte she warned that there was no point in Doug's trying to con her. She knew the truth and she planned to take the stand for the prosecution—if the district attorney's office would drop all major charges against her—which, as their case was too strong, they were not about to do.

Bronte had written about sex, and Carol replied primly that it was too early to discuss such matters. Still, she went on to do just that. "I will put pussy juice on this," she wrote, drawing a helpful little box and message:

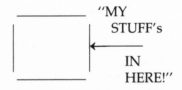

"MY
STUFF's

IN
HERE!"

Not that she wanted Bronte to get the wrong idea. "I could go kinky sex with Doug. He made everything sexual great. But I don't know if I would be willing to try it with a black man."

Carol had a fantasy that she asked Bronte to pass on to Doug. In it, she was about to go to the gas chamber when she asked the warden if Doug could stay with her for her last night. She left to Bronte and Doug's imaginations what the warden replied and what ensued. But she did wonder if Doug would agree.

"I like to read, fish, hunt," she said, in closing, although all Carol had hunted in her life were the prostitutes she and Doug had looked for on Sunset Boulevard. "Stalking game," she added cryptically, "is fun."

By her second letter to Bronte, Carol had spotted Doug on television on the first day of his preliminary hearing and had plunged into a romantic mood worthy of a Little Nashville country and western song.

"My heart aches for want of him, but he was never mine," she wrote. Naturally, this heartache once more aroused in Carol the need to turn herself into a doormat.

Tell him to go for it! Whatever he needs to do for himself is okay. If his attorney can destroy me or my word if they should use me, I understand.[. . .] Do what he must to win the best advantage for himself.

Hillside Strangler Kenneth Bianchi's self-appointed girlfriend, Veronica Lynn Compton, was on Carol's row. There was an empty cell between them, but talking across it through the bars, they had become friends. The flamboyant Compton was twenty-four and about to be extradited to Bellingham, Washington, to be tried for an attempted copycat strangling she had planned to make authorities think that Bianchi was innocent and the real Hillside Strangler was still free.

"She's crazy, but I like her," Carol wrote to Bronte. "Considering Tammy, and Veronica and me, women like us aren't as rare as we thought."

Under a court order, a team of doctors from the University of Southern California's prestigious Institute of Psychiatry and Law visited Carol to talk to her and administer a battery of tests. Bruce Gross, one of the doctors, was instantly put off when Carol mentioned that her case was so spectacular that someone should make a movie about it. He told Dr. Seymour Pollack, the head of the institute, that he did not care to get involved. Pollack and Dr. Ann Cangemi, an institute fellow, continued to evaluate Carol, who wrote to Doug describing the distinguished Dr. Pollack as a nice gray-haired man at whose cock she liked to stare.

After the first psychiatric session, Carol wrote to her old friend Dick Geis to tell him that she had been declared a normal woman under a great deal of strain. (The doctors actually would not file their report for five months, after many more hours of testing and interviews.)

Again, to Geis, Carol mentioned that she was the mildest of women and not a criminal.

Funny, five hours with those doctors, and I gave them much of my life history, and I still didn't open up and reveal my deeper self. Why am I guarded at this late date? Have I finally learned not to trust? Shit. It can't be that. I would trust the devil himself if he smiled at me and his cock was hard.

Funny, Carol also wrote, that she seemed to be the only woman in jail who admitted to doing anything wrong and the only one who suffered any guilt. Finally she understood the reasoning behind gun control.

> Dick, here is one simple truth. It is very easy to kill. We all have the potential. Only social conditioning from childhood prevents each of us from being murderers.[. . .] I have been told that murder is the easiest of crimes to get away with. I believe it. If I hadn't confessed . . . ah well. Too late. Too late.

Carol was beginning to think about legal strategy. The prosecutor assigned to the case was Robert Jorgensen, known for his meticulous—some psychoanalytically minded colleagues felt anal-retentive—preparation. They dreaded the single-spaced twelve-page directives known sarcastically as "Jorgensengrams" that landed with regularity on LAPD desks in the months before a trial.

Not knowing this, Carol was not intimidated. Including Sam Mayerson in the flurry of mail to and from Sybil Brand Institute, she wrote a grandiose letter in which she suggested that this might be Mayerson's "life-case."

She also warned him not to contact Jorgensen about making a deal in exchange for her testimony:

> Let him be the one who feels off balance. Sam, he needs me. He knows it and so do we. If he deals with me too early, the other side will have time to work on discrediting me and that must be prevented. Doug can't scream "DEAL" to the press if one doesn't exist.

It was true, Carol continued, that her honesty made it difficult for Jorgensen to make a deal. Nonetheless, she pointed out, "I'm his star witness, Sam. Watch me shine!"

On the tenth of November, almost three months after her arrest, Carol wrote to Doug complaining about his lousy strategy in blaming Jack Murray for the killings. She also told him to stop writing to her to protest his innocence because she knew better.

"I've been reading up on our modern Tom Sawyer, boy adventurer, Ted Bundy. The parellels, oi vey. Did you know last January he married a woman named Carol?"

Was it, she wondered in yet another letter, the name association of "Bundy" that made Doug pick her for his partner?

It was a comment that would spark in Doug an outlandish idea for his defense that would surface at his trial.

She signed the letter "Tiger" and told Doug that she still loved him.

Seeing Doug on the television news as he appeared at various pretrial court proceedings continued to stir her. Again in one of her slavish moods, she bought a card from the canteen cart at Sybil Brand and addressed it to "Douglas Clark the Magnanimous, Keeper of the Soul, mentor, Noble Leader."

On the front of the card, a large cat said, "Cyclamates are out. Sugar is out. Red dye #2 is out." Inside the card the cat pointed at whoever was reading. Tears trickled down its whiskers. *"You are out*—of my life," it said. "Weep, weep," Carol wrote, signing, "Carol Bundy the Meek."

Before jail, Carol had slept five or six hours a night. Now she took Elavil for depression and slept sixteen hours a day. Long before Christmas, not wanting her children to feel shortchanged, she sent three hundred dollars to a relative to buy presents. The money was "lost," there was nothing under the tree for the boys, and they would not remember receiving any of their mother's letters.

"Dear Chris and Spike," Carol wrote early that winter.

Hi. Well, now you are going to see real snow falling. It is fun to watch. It is very quiet when it falls. My mother (your other grandmother) used to tell me it was the angels shedding their wings.

I miss you boys so much. We always had fun. I miss the dada game and jumping on my bed, and movies and fishing.[. . .]

If I can straighten out my problems, and we can get back together, I think we will move out of the valley and go somewhere else.

There is a small chance things will be okay. But don't hope too hard. I don't want you hurt or disappointed.[. . .]

Mind your manners now. You are my men and I need you to be strong for me. I love you for ever and ever and ever.

Hugs and kisses,
Mom

182

18

TAMMY SPANGLER HAD BEEN VISITING DOUG THREE TIMES A WEEK AT Los Angeles County Jail, taking him fifteen dollars every time. She felt so sorry for him. The poor baby kept telling her he simply couldn't believe what was happening.

"You'd better believe it, 'cause it's going on," Tammy said to him one day, sharp with Doug even though she was furious with Carol for getting him in the jam he was in. Tammy spoke over a jail telephone and stared through a glass window at Doug in his navy-blue inmate's jumpsuit. It was three months since his arrest. His hair was beginning to curl over his ears and he was trying to get a court order to bring a licensed cosmetologist into county jail to give him a decent haircut.

Every day he wrote to Tammy, his "tigress of passion," describing her "moist, quivering thighs" and "clutches of ecstasy." This was interspersed with carefully worded instructions about how to run his errands. As he was not satisfied with his court-appointed lawyer and hoped to represent himself, he had written to Tammy asking her to track down "a diminutive, softly spoken female attorney" to be his cocounsel. This, he thought, would let the women on the jury know that he was not a villain. It would also give the men someone attractive to look at.

Unable to hide his rage at Carol Bundy, he wrote: "Wouldn't

183

you like to slam her in the face, kick her up the ass . . . or we could get some whipped cream and chocolate syrup and party her to death! Just kidding, honey."

The letter that Doug addressed to their mythical future child signed "Love, Dad," really got to Tammy, who knew that as soon as Doug was found not guilty and had written his autobiography, for which he was expecting $100,000, the two of them would disappear into the sunset driving a long-distance rig.

Now Doug stood formally accused of the murders of Marnett Comer, Cindy Chandler, Gina Marano, Exxie Wilson, Karen Jones, and Jane Doe no. 18 (aka Water Tower). He was also accused of three counts of child molestation and accessory after the fact in Jack Murray's murder.

He would not be accused in the murder of Vic Weiss. Weiss had been hit a year almost to the day before Carol watched what had turned out to be an update story about him on the television news. Doug may have pointed it out to her at the time she learned of the Chandler-Marano killings both to impress her and to intimidate her with his alleged mob ties. Even though the driver of the Weiss killing getaway car had been described as blond, Leroy Orozco doubted that it was Doug. He was not cool enough, Orozco thought, to be trusted by the mob.

Doug's preliminary hearing had begun on October 20 and lasted six days, during which the prosecution produced a parade of thirty-four witnesses, including pathologist Dr. Joseph Choi, who gave the gruesome details of how animals had gnawed and carried away the bones of Jane Doe no. 18.

Not surprisingly, at that stage Doug's court-appointed lawyer, Karl Henry, had offered no defense. Doug's arraignment had been set for November 13.

With this court date upon him, Doug was coaching Tammy in the importance of staring boldly into the lights of television cameras while uttering a firm "No comment" in response to reporters. Tammy, in between taking care of his cleaning and laundry, practiced dutifully.

Doug had a fancy for tinted wire-rim glasses like the ones prosecutor Bob Jorgensen wore. He wanted his mother to send a hundred dollars to pay for them. She wouldn't.

"He's not in a position to be picky," Blanch Clark said testily over the phone to Tammy.

Then the cleaners lost Doug's suits, and Tammy had to go to Harris and Frank and plunk down $237.50 of her own money for the Jorgensen-style three-piece navy-blue pinstripe that Doug had requested. A new shirt had set her back another twenty-six dollars and wiped her out financially.

The night before the arraignment, Tammy tossed, waking every few minutes to think, I hope that mother fits.

In the morning, after twenty minutes' sleep, Tammy dragged herself out of bed and into a rust velour dress-and-jacket ensemble with a deeply slit skirt. If Doug wanted to look like an attorney, she wanted to look like an attorney's wife. She fastened a little crystal unicorn around her neck for luck, then she put a new pair of shoes in the car for Doug. In her anxiety she left the shoes behind in the underground parking lot and didn't realize it until it was too late to return for them.

So there was Doug in Department 100, the courtroom of Waspy Judge William B. Keene, dressed in a lawyerly three-piece navy-blue pin-striped suit and a comical pair of county-jail-issue canvas slippers.

The defendant did not look pleased.

An orderly progression through the checks and balances of the legal system was perhaps from the very beginning destined to go awry with the case of the Sunset murders. But no one, at this stage, could have realized that because of Doug's grandiosity, he was doomed to despise any authority figure with whom he came in contact, and doomed to feel that he could do a better job himself.

He claimed to have been angered over Karl Henry's offering no defense at the preliminary hearing. He also said, wrongly, that Henry had refused to read his annoyance into the record. But by the time of the arraignment, Henry had been relieved by the court of the burden of representing such a testy client.

Judge Keene's first act was to appoint well-known criminal attorney Paul Geragos in Henry's place. Prosecutor Jorgensen read aloud the six murder charges; the defense stipulated to the other allegations; Doug pleaded not guilty; and January 19 was selected as a trial date, with Doug waiving the time for a speedy trial. No one thought that the case would actually go to trial in five weeks, but in the meantime, Doug asked to assist Geragos with his defense.

When Judge Keene seemed reluctant, Doug, who had dark circles under his eyes and a jailhouse pallor, made impatient faces and rapped his knuckles on the podium. Geragos motioned him to keep quiet, but Doug did not seem able to.

The problem was not Geragos, he insisted. He could feel a "good rapport" developing between them. It was just that with his court experiences thus far so totally negative . . .

Keene cut him off, probably not wanting to listen to more bad-mouthing of Karl Henry. Work with Geragos as his attorney, he said to Doug, going on to explain that his ruling against Doug's assisting Geragos was "not binding for all time."

Doug's next court appearance would be for a pretrial hearing on December 9. He was escorted from the courtroom, and a deflated Tammy Spangler drove home to the Valley. No one had pointed a camera at her. No one had forced her to say "No comment." No one had shone any lights.

In the attorney room at county jail, shackled to his seat, perhaps influenced by the spate of publicity surrounding Kenneth Bianchi's claim that he possessed multiple personalities, Doug declared Carol to be the victim of the same disorder. When she had attempted suicide in July, Doug postulated, she killed the personality that loved Jack, allowing the one who hated him to emerge. Carol's other personalities, according to Doug, included good and bad mothers, the shrinking Carol who hated blood, and Carol the cold-blooded murderer.

So far, the victims' families and friends had resisted Doug's invitation to visit him and listen to his side of things.

That, though, was not the interesting part. That was not what Doug wanted to get out to the public. In his nonstop monologues, he vented his anger in that smooth, well-modulated drawl that nearly disguised it. He was particularly angry at Detective Gary Broda who, Doug said, had "fabricated" voice identifications: after listening to a tape Broda had played them, Laurie Brigges and Mindy Cohen had identified Doug as the phony detective who had telephoned them.

Mindy, said Doug, was "a hot-pants bitch," and he hoped she got "her tit caught in a wringer," because he had been at his ex-wife Beverly's when Mindy received the 7:09 A.M. phone call. Broda was "a lying son of a bitch," and Doug was going to get him. "I see him as a personal enemy," he said. "This town ain't going to be big enough for both of us."

And while he was on the subject of lying cops, Leroy Orozco had planted the .25-caliber shell casing that had been found between the driver's seat and the backrest in the Buick. Doug didn't want anyone to mention it yet, but he was planning a one-and-a-half-million-dollar false-arrest suit against the LAPD.

Persisting with the story that he had known Cindy Chandler,

THE SUNSET MURDERS

Doug said that he had liked her, but she had liked only his Kawasaki. He spoke of a motorcycle trip up the coast on June 1 (a date when he would later say he was living with Lydia Crouch): he and Cindy had checked into a motel, he claimed. But she was a beach girl who loved the sun as much as Doug hated it. It burned his pale skin. He had wanted to stay indoors all the time, so they had quarreled and returned early.

Doug, it turned out, was making much of a Cindy Chandler link because Jeannette Murray's brother, Warren, had mistakenly identified as Cindy Doug's old girlfriend, Bobbi, with whom he had driven north on Memorial Day weekend. Carol had told Warren that she hoped the bike would crash. If there were a witness to Carol's jealousy of Cindy Chandler, Doug must have thought, it could suggest a motive for Carol's killing Cindy herself with the aid of Jack Murray.

"I helped her out financially, the little bitch," Doug said about Cindy. "Twenty here, fifty there." This made it seem as if he really did know her. But he realized that a flash of anger toward one of his victims was a mistake. "She's good people," he said, smiling and changing the subject to the blood in the Buick on the day he and Kevin Crouch picked up Carol to go to the car wash.

Doug's story (the first of many) originally went that Carol had dropped the bloody car off with him, saying that there had been a "hassle" at the Little Nashville bar and she'd taken someone to the emergency room. For some reason that Doug did not explain, he had "laid on" young Kevin the tale that he had hit a cat.

He couldn't understand why the cops had not investigated John "Jack" Murray more thoroughly, Doug went on.

"Jack," he said, "had access to everything of mine."

And Carol, after all, in her Betsy/Claudia call had told the cops about her lover, John, who drove a Plymouth, and Jack Murray's Plymouth had been stolen.

"How convenient," Doug said, his voice bitter. "How very convenient."

It would have been convenient but for the fact that Jack Murray had never owned a Plymouth, let alone had one stolen.

"I do need help," he said, speaking of Theresa with an earnest look on his face. "I know there's something wrong with a grown man who can't say no." But then again, Carol had instigated the sexual escapades and persuaded him that no harm could come of them. Carol had bought the kid the fancy underwear, and Theresa was a healthy child who enjoyed sex.

187

"There's things she won't do," he said thoughtfully, instantly becoming angered by his memories. "Well, fuck her."

One of Doug's most bitter disappointments seemed to be that he was not receiving as much attention as he had expected as the accused Sunset murderer. But there was competition. The news had been full of the Iranian hostages, while everyone wondered if Carter would get them home before the election. Then there had been the election itself and Reagan's victory.

It didn't help that Doug was in jail with accused Hillside Strangler Angelo Buono, cousin and accomplice of Kenneth Bianchi; with Roy Norris, who had ratted on his partner, torture killer Lawrence Bittaker, "a strange-looking dude . . . crazier-looking even than Manson," according to Doug; with Muharem Kurbegovic, also known as the Alphabet Bomber; with Freeway Killer William Bonin; and with the Skid Row stabber.

"It's not the Rosenbergs or Sam Sheppard," Doug said, gloomy about the Sunset case. "It's just another mass murder."

19

THE PROSECUTOR LIVED ALONE IN A HOUSE THAT LOOKED DOWN over the San Fernando Valley. Robert Jorgensen was a former General Electric executive who at thirty-three, after ten years with the corporation, had come to dislike what he saw as its authoritarianism and vulgar bureaucracy. He resigned from his job. Then, a frugal man long divorced from his first wife and married a second time, he traveled west to pay his own way through Boalt Hall, the school of law at the University of California at Berkeley.

Berkeley in the sixties had been perfect for him. Jorgensen was a liberal who in the 1950s had despised Dwight Eisenhower and felt that the Communist witch-hunts of Senator Joseph McCarthy were a threat to Constitutional liberties. The semester he enrolled at Boalt saw the beginning of the free-speech movement as well as a wave of opposition to the Vietnam War. Lyndon Johnson had replaced Joseph McCarthy as Jorgensen's symbol of evil. He joined the antiwar protests. He grew his hair, not hippie-length, but longer than would have suited his Salt Lake City, Mormon upbringing. When it was time to pay his income taxes, he wrote his check on toilet paper and in a letter to his eleven-year-old son from his first marriage said: "I would go to prison before I would participate in this dreadful war."

In the summer of 1967 Jorgensen had graduated and taken his

bar exams, filled with a fire to help humanity. All cops lied, he thought, and anyone accused of a crime was probably not guilty and needed a defense.

The following year, unable to find a Bay Area position as public defender, he decided to move to Los Angeles, where he would work for the district attorney's office. It was just for a year or two, he told his brothers and his son. Then he would return to Berkeley and private criminal-law practice. In the meantime, he would be a spy for the other side, helping to keep prosecutors honest.

Perhaps because he was more attuned to ideals than the messy realities of life, Jorgensen was now divorced from his second wife. But he found Los Angeles lively and exciting: in short, a pleasant surprise. He joined the California Democratic Council and was hoping to help the drive to produce a write-in vote for Eugene McCarthy in the next election.

As the years passed, Jorgensen deplored Richard Nixon, Spiro Agnew, the mediocrity of the Supreme Court, and the country's passion for law and order, which he saw trampling its concern for individual liberties and justice. He looked forward to a better society founded not on sexual taboos, geography, or piety but on the uniqueness of each human life. In the meantime, he bettered himself by stopping smoking and taking up the guitar.

Everything he did in life, whether it was learning French, Russian, and German; quoting Schiller and Goethe; painting watercolor portraits; or recording thousands of hours of German lieder, Mozart, or Harry James, Jorgensen did with passion.

He was an obsessive who slept only three or four hours a night, filling his extra hours with music, literature, and fanatical exercise: he ran; he did push-ups; he slammed at the ball during intense games of tennis. And he did this not only because of his extra reserves of energy, but because his passion for expensive chocolates could send him through a two-pound box in one sitting. Either that, or he would give them away untouched so as to keep his six foot, two-and-a-half-inch frame down to 165 pounds.

After about four years in the district attorney's office, Jorgensen stopped speaking of innocent defendants and began to channel even more of his passion into prosecution. He no longer regaled his relatives with stories of cops who lied. Justice, he now thought, was served when criminals were put in jail.

As always, he lived in the lonely pursuit of his own standard of perfection as well as that of society. In the nighttime hours he wrote flowery letters to the son he hardly knew about the arrival of spring, the fall of leaves, and the easy relationship they might have someday. Always Jorgensen focused on what might be, realizing sometimes, to his dismay, that he was missing out on the present. And in his diary, he scribbled dark thoughts over his growing sense of impotence to control crime.

He was far from a violent man, but sometimes he stood watch with an air-pump rifle with which he took joy in shooting gophers that popped from their holes after eating his roses. The defendants he saw in court had begun to seem like vermin, he had come to think, and he wanted to see them destroyed too.

A dead elk slung across a pickup truck offended his sensibilities. But the analogy of the hunt fit his approach to prosecution as he spurred detectives on to seek obscure evidentiary details in his quest to corner and trap his prey.

He had become a passionate reactionary of the most extreme kind, a libertarian who—oddly for someone as rigorously intellectual as Jorgensen—embraced with delight every word that came from Ronald Reagan's mouth.

By 1980, the year of the Sunset murders, his notorious cases included a Weather Underground bombing and a Hell's Angels gang rape case with eighteen defendants. Recently he had been assigned to prosecute a particularly unpleasant murder case in which Israeli Mafia types carried dismembered bodies out of Los Angeles' Bonaventure Hotel in suitcases. The last one had tipped him over the edge, so that, in his late forties, he was now a man with a mission. Bob Jorgensen, observed one of his colleagues in the district attorney's office, thought that God was on the side of the prosecution.

It was Los Angeles, Jorgensen had begun to think: the amorphousness of life here; a sort of free-floating hideousness that he became unable to disassociate from the place. Somewhere in the city was a threat that could not be articulated or anticipated, but instead erupted at random from Los Angeles' underside to destroy the beauty of life the way the gophers destroyed his garden.

The Sunset murders made him want to get out. He wanted to go back to Utah, where as a three-year-old boy he had been trotted out, a local celebrity in the tiny town of Nephi, to sit at the side of the interstate highway. There, an obsessive from the start, he had been able to name every car that sped past his grandfather's gas station.

But before he left California, Robert Jorgensen wanted to prosecute Douglas Clark, whom he saw as the personification of evil.

He wanted it to be nothing less than a battle that would end in Douglas Clark's death. The death penalty, Jorgensen thought, could restore order to the land.

On the morning of December 9, the prosecutor had arrived early in the courtroom of Judge Gordon Ringer, where the defense was to make a predictable motion to continue the trial date. In his characteristic pin-striped suit, with pocket watch, Jorgensen idled away the time awaiting the arrival of Clark and the judge by talking with another lawyer, a strikingly attractive dark-haired woman. Jorgensen, who had not been good marriage material, was known to talk only to attractive women. Preferably of twenty-five and under.

"What are you here on?" she asked.

"The Sunset Slayings." Jorgensen chuckled.

"I can't keep 'em straight," said the other lawyer.

"I blame it on the State Supreme Court. It's Rose Bird," Jorgensen said, invoking the name of the controversial first woman chief justice of the California Supreme Court. She aroused in him a fury the depths of which were unknown to most men. Bird had her own political agenda, Jorgensen thought, and was manipulating legal concepts to further her liberal views regarding redistribution of wealth and enhancement of criminals, all of this to the detriment of society. He stopped just short of calling Rose Bird a Communist.

It did no good for family or colleagues in the district attorney's office to argue with him, because he seemed to have memorized every one of the Bird court's decisions to bolster his arguments.

Even to those who did not share Jorgensen's extremist view of Bird, her court had become notorious for its overturned convictions. This irritated police and prosecutors as well as much of the Californian public. The cases were always described disparagingly as having been reversed on technicalities, rather as if due process itself were nothing more than an annoyance that kept criminals out of jail.

"Now that Reagan's in . . . ," Jorgensen trailed off, sounding hopeful. Then he added, "The safest thing is to take the power away from the appellate courts."

"The voters . . . ," the other lawyer began tentatively.

Jorgensen pounced on her. "It's too complex for the public. You try and explain it even to another lawyer . . ." But the defendant and the judge were in the courtroom by now and the discussion ended.

Today something had gone wrong with the delivery of Doug's pin-striped suit, and he was dressed in a baby-blue cowboy-cut polyester leisure suit that undermined his intended image as much as his county-issue slippers had last time. As he complained to Judge Ringer about the case being continued, Doug was testy. But it seemed almost a formality, with his real goal to again request "cocounsel pro per or whatever the hell the status is."

Judge Ringer, a short balding man with a long face, looked at Doug over his glasses and denied his request.

"I won't accept that, Your Honor. I will not accept that."

"I'm afraid you're obliged to accept it."

He did not want to interfere with the legal process, Doug assured Judge Ringer, but his life was on the line. He wanted to understand whether or not he was receiving an adequate defense.

"I cannot understand it with the tools that are available to me in a five-foot-by-seven-foot damn cell in county jail."

Again Judge Ringer denied his request and tentatively reset the trial date for March 30, 1981.

As they left the courtroom, the dark-haired lawyer whispered about Doug to Jorgensen.

"He's very bright," she said.

Jorgensen agreed. It was one of the attributes, he thought, that made him so dangerous.

The prosecutor was nothing but a crook, Doug said back in county jail. "They could show Jorgensen a videotape of Jack committing the murders and he'd still say I did it."

At the beginning of a protracted battle to convince people of his innocence, Doug had worked his way carefully through a copy of Carol Bundy's arrest statement to police. Wherever she said "Doug" and "Buick," he had crossed the words out and written "Jack" and "van." When she said of the guns, "His is nickel, mine is chrome," Doug wrote "Switched. Bitch!" next to the comment before handing the statement out to the press. He had also written that Marnett Comer had been raped at gunpoint in the van.

As part of his game plan, Doug was also corresponding with Veronica Lynn Compton. She was showing "good insight" into Carol, he said. He did not mention anything about Veronica's already proven willingness to try to fool the police on behalf of her former man, Hillside Strangler Kenneth Bianchi. He had spotted the glamorous black-haired Veronica when she was handcuffed and tearstained, awaiting an extradition hearing, Doug claimed.

Handcuffs and tearstains alone should have been enough to

pique the interest of Douglas Clark. That Veronica and Carol had become buddies must have made the whole package irresistible.

"Bianchi's not happy," said Doug. But on the other hand, "Bianchi didn't behave like a gentleman."

"Chill you—cool you, makeup in pale powder *blue*, eyes so deeply sunken with shadows.[. . .] Black licorice dye on tongue," Doug would write later to Veronica, adding in another letter, "Cyanide gas is such a waste—you can't do anything with the remains except over cook them into ashes . . . I'd offer, but what possible value this would be to you my . . . wife?"

After Veronica's play, *Night Symphony*, had flopped in Hollywood, she had lapsed, with the help of unknown quantities of exotic drugs, into an enchantment with guns, murder, and Kenneth Bianchi. But her plot to kill a young woman in Bellingham, Washington, had backfired when the woman escaped.

"Any publicity is good publicity," she said at the time, a dictum with which even Hollywood, in this case, would have been forced to disagree.

Doug was not impressed with Veronica's writing. Or, for that matter, with Hollywood, where, he commented, "Everyone's a producer or a hit man."

He was, though, contemplating a mass wedding ceremony, which he discussed in the attorney room at county jail under the watchful eye of an armed sheriff. His fiancées were Veronica; Bobbi, his former sweetheart from Indiana; Joey Lamphier, with whom he had been living when he met Carol; and Tammy Spangler, who now had disappeared, taking with her, he grumbled, his prized sewing machine from his upholstery-business days and his four-year-old teddy bear, Mozart. This unfortunate occurrence had forced Doug's ex-wife, Beverly, into taking over laundry and dry-cleaning duties.

"I want my goddamn sewing machine and my teddy bear," said Doug, wondering if he'd pushed Tammy too hard.

Although he was wooing Veronica by telling her that he would be out of jail by August 1981, Paul Geragos had told him, "It looks pretty grim."

Yes, he loved Veronica. "I love all women," said Doug.

With one notable exception. Carol Bundy, about whom he was in a white-faced rage.

"She made up a murder. At least we assume she made it up. They never found the body."

He was speaking of Cathy. A helicopter and patrol-car search of

the area Carol had described as the Cathy dump site had not produced the victim, and Doug was pretending that there had been
no crime.

If he were found guilty, he planned to put Carol at the scene of
every murder, he said, neglecting to explain how, if he were innocent, he could do this.

"I'm going to put the gun in her hand. 'Vengeance is mine sayeth
the Lord.' I'll take her down in flames."

20

On March 3, 1981, NEARLY SEVEN MONTHS AFTER THE ARRESTS, Deputy Gerald McCune of the Los Angeles County Sheriff's Department went to investigate a report by a citizen. He drove north past trees and rickety wooden cabins through Bouquet Canyon in the Santa Clarita Valley. At the intersection of a dirt road, McCune turned off and descended for almost a mile until, at a hairpin bend, he was stopped by water running across his path.

McCune got out of the car and began to walk. On the northern side of a creek bed about a hundred feet west of the hairpin turn, he noticed a scattering of rib bones. Further west was a femur, and about thirty feet from that was a lower jawbone. Next to a large tree, lying in the shallow, rippling waters, lay a skull with what appeared to be a bullet hole in its lower right side.

Someone from the coroner's office came and put the bones in a bag. McCune had found no personal belongings nearby. No clothes. No jewelry. On March 9, Dr. Joseph Choi examined the remains of a woman who, for lack of identification, was being called Jane Doe no. 28. The one hole in her skull was about two inches from her right ear and similar in size (although on the opposite side of her head) to the holes in the skulls of Exxie Wilson, Karen Jones, and Jane Doe no. 18. Choi thought number 28 was between seventeen and twenty-three years old. She had been dead,

196

as close as he could tell, between three months and three years. She was Cathy, the "sweet, obliging" little prostitute Doug and Carol had privately nicknamed River Rat.

In April, Drs. Pollack and Cangemi sent their evaluation of Carol to Sam Mayerson. The doctors' primary goal had been to determine whether Carol was mentally impaired at the time of the Jack Murray murder to an extent that would qualify her for a not guilty by reason of insanity (NGI) defense. At the time of the Sunset murders, the test of legal insanity was based on the American Law Institute rule, known as ALI. Under ALI, a defendant was not considered responsible for criminal conduct if at the time of the crime he or she was subjectively incapable of appreciating its criminality or conforming his or her conduct to the law.

Carol had not seemed disoriented or peculiar to the doctors, although they did find her initially condescending and controlling. She also had joked inappropriately about some of the gruesome details of the case.

On the Wechsler Adult Intelligence Scale, Carol's full-scale IQ tested at 109, with her verbal IQ a bright-normal 110 and her performance IQ an average 106. But the doctors emphasized her fund of general knowledge and suggested that her true potential lay in the superior range.

Not surprisingly, her battery of personality tests revealed a woman of poor social judgment unable to profit from experience. Also not surprising was Carol's insecurity and exaggerated need for attention. There was no sign of any organic brain dysfunction and no indication of gross psychopathology.

The doctors' report interpreted her actions on the night of the Murray murder—based on her story of what happened—as an explosion of anger, frustration, and resentment over being used, abused, then rejected by Jack at a moment when she was asking for his help.

Carol projected the blame for her circumstances onto others.

"It appears," the doctors wrote to Mayerson, "as though she wants (and perhaps desperately needs) to see herself in terms of an ideal self, i.e., attractive, sensitive, good, compassionate, naive, unsophisticated, and untouched."

Although there might be mitigating psychiatric factors that could be presented before sentencing should Carol be found guilty as charged, Pollack and Cangemi determined that she did not qualify for an insanity defense or the other mental-impairment defenses of diminished capacity or unconsciousness.

By this time, Samuel Mayerson had been named a municipal court judge. In May, Dwight Stevens, a fifty-seven-year-old Wilshire Division Robbery-Homicide detective turned lawyer, was appointed in his place.

In spite of the Pollack/Cangemi report, Carol and Stevens discussed the possibility of an insanity plea. In a letter to the lawyer she worried that the tape recordings of her calls to the police and her task-force interrogation would work against her. As Carol waffled again about testifying, she made another point: "How can I be used in full credibility against Clark if I'm to be declared insane?"

Regardless, she asked Stevens to get things rolling with a mental-health defense. "I am tired and getting depressed and morbid again. I can't handle it when I get that way."

After giving even more serious thought to pleading insanity, Carol wrote to Stevens about her "flights from reality" that could last for weeks and days. "I am helpless at such times, but I *cannot* see myself as wrong."

She asked Stevens to try to get her placed in the prison hospital both now and as a condition of a plea bargain.

I just don't ever want to be susceptible to a similar situation again. I don't want to unleash uncontrolled, undesirable potentials again. I am *not* either evil or criminal. I do need help.

In jail Carol was snubbed by other prisoners, who saw her as a snitch, and alienated from guards, one of whom would draw a decapitated angel on the dayroom window at Christmas. She had, though, managed to form what appeared to be a warm friendship with a prison volunteer named Beatrice, who was older than Carol, motherly, and a staunch Catholic unaware of the case details.

In between Beatrice's visits, Carol wrote to her new friend, exhibiting her propensity for putting a sheen on her unpleasant and difficult life. In one letter she told Beatrice that she had almost died from whooping cough as a toddler, was seriously injured in a car accident at age nine, at twenty-one had become diabetic, at twenty-eight had suffered from childbed fever, and not long after that had made two serious suicide attempts.

"You can see," she wrote, "that God has cared for me all my life."

In another stickily sentimental letter, Carol asked Beatrice, her "sweet, adopted 'Mother of the Moment,' " what to do about the boys. She wanted them to remember things as they were and "Mommy" as she had been, not as she was now.

All the trips to the zoo, to movies, to the park or lake, fishing and camping, bowls of hot popcorn on the living-room floor, the nagging to put their dirty clothes away, do their homework, clean their room, Christmas and birthdays with big whipped-cream cakes are all gone. I can't give it anymore and I can't put things back as they were [. . .] I'm sorry, but this tears me up so bad.

Perhaps feeling that she had aroused enough sympathy, Carol here changed her tone abruptly. "Mr. Dwight Stevens, my attorney, got my car out of impound but has no place to put it." If Beatrice didn't mind, Carol would take her up on her offer to store it. What a shame there weren't more people as caring as Beatrice. How blessed must be her daughter and husband.

An unsavory sidelight of Beatrice's Datsun storage turned out to be her discovery of a pornographic note about vaginal death spasms. It was signed by "Betsy." Hastily, Carol wrote to Dwight Stevens, assuring him that she had not written the note and that "Betsy" was a "swinging" alias that Doug liked all his girlfriends to use, as he used the alias "Don." "LAPD apparently overlooked a brown parka jacket in the car. Too bad. They could have held it. It was important."

The bloodstained parka had been used in the cars to toss over the bodies of some of the victims.

Carol was beginning, perhaps, to go a little overboard in her wooing of Beatrice. On the envelope of one letter, instead of her more usual Garfield cat cartoons, she wrote:

S
A
C
[CHRIST]
I
F
I
C
E
D

She had been thinking about what to wear in court, Carol told Beatrice in the letter. The charges facing her were severe, and it was crucial that she make a favorable, upper-middle-class impression.

Strong colors must be avoided. Either a neutral gray if a suit, or if a cottony dress is worn, a pale (innocent) pink.[. . .] We could consider a cotton-polyester dress (pink?) with a peter-pan collar.[. . .] I want to appear ladylike and respectable. A middle class housewife type. Stature is important. Avoid sophistication, arrogance or worldliness.

A few weeks later, Carol wrote again to Beatrice, who had been sick.

You always surprise and delight me.[. . .] Why couldn't I have met you *before* I got into trouble?
You are in my prayers and God will have you on your feet in no time.
Enclosed is the order sheet.[. . .]

At the end of the letter, Carol again played her ladylike role. She was doing better, she said, since she had met Beatrice:

What a delight it would be to have you with me when I get a bee in my bonnet to visit a floral garden or museum or go to the beauty shop or shopping.[. . .]

Much love,
Carol

The jury at Veronica Compton's trial in Bellingham, Washington, had not believed her story that her strangulation attempt on a young woman had been a publicity stunt with which the victim was playing along. After less than five hours' deliberation, they had found her guilty.

In the early afternoon on the day after her conviction, a single red rose surrounded by delicate fronds of baby's breath had been delivered to Veronica's cell, a token of consolation from Doug. He hoped that she would be a witness at his trial, and they were working on a plan for Veronica to testify that Carol had confessed to committing all the Sunset murders.

"THIS IS THE TIME OF YEAR IT ALL HAPPENED," Doug wrote to Joey Lamphier a year after the murders. "#1—June 1st. #s2+3, June 11th." The letter ended with: "See the freeway lights from where #70 lay in a ravine for 30 days. Feel the chill and feel the mystery wrap you in a cobweb net."

200

Number 70 referred to Marnett Comer, killed on the first of June, and before she was identified known as Jane Doe no. 70.

The pretrial proceedings dragged on, with Doug's complaints mounting. Pleading a conflict of interest, attorney Paul Geragos asked to be removed from the case. In his place, Judge Gordon Ringer appointed Maxwell Keith, a disarmingly soft-spoken lawyer in his fifties. After a few years in the local district attorney's office, Keith had cut his defense teeth on the notorious 1950s Dr. Bernard Finch murder case. His career had peaked in the seventies, when he had drawn praise from the usually self-reverential prosecutor Vincent Bugliosi for his defense of Charles Manson family member Leslie Van Houten. Keith had pulled off a hung jury during three trials with Van Houten and years later was said to still kick himself over one ill-chosen juror at the trial in which Van Houten was convicted. Immediately, he began filing discovery and suppression-of-evidence motions.

Foreshadowing the trial, a courtroom tone was being set of a morally outraged Douglas Clark, appalled by a criminal-justice system that he insisted was railroading him and that he seemed determined to put on the defensive. He was high-handed and utterly unintimidated by the court's authority.

Judge Ringer, a legal scholar with a master's degree in French literature and a 1976 County Bar Association award for judicial excellence, was for the most part outwardly patient. He had granted changes in Doug's mail delivery, and orders for new glasses and a complete physical examination: Doug had dropped close to fifty pounds from his arrest weight of 210 and claimed this might mean he had cancer. A more likely explanation, Jorgensen and Leroy Orozco felt, was that Doug wanted to thwart eyewitness identifications by changing his appearance.

When Doug grumbled that the sheriffs were watching him with a two-way mirror, Judge Ringer ordered a closed-front cell. Later he canceled that order, saying that it had been based on Doug's misinforming him that "legions of ladies touring the county jail were in a position to see Mr. Clark while he was sitting on his potty."

But Doug still wanted to move, and the sheriffs were claiming they had nowhere to put him. A hearing was held.

"I have been stabbed," said Doug. "I have had fecal material thrown all over my cell and myself. The deputies are aware of it and they haven't done a goddamn thing about it."

Maxwell Keith was unaware of any stabbing, and Judge Ringer,

who did not seem moved, decided that while he didn't want Doug
assassinated, he wasn't going to shuffle him from cell to cell simply
to make him comfortable.

There were snitches on his row, Doug insisted, and he knew
Robert Jorgensen wouldn't hesitate to use one. Judge Ringer was
placing him in a prosecution mill, he went on, and shirking his
duty. In an attempt to shame Judge Ringer into action, Doug then
invoked Nazi Germany.

"[It's] 1946 Nuremberg all over again. 'It wasn't my responsibility. It's not my job. . . .' This is not sufficient. I don't think it's
acceptable."

Even Doug seemed to have sensed that he might have gone too
far.

"If the court will accept it," he said. "I have to accept it."

"I accept it as of now," said Judge Ringer.

"Pardon me?"

And court was adjourned for the day.

Doug had also increased his pressure on Carol, whom he called
"Mouse Mouth" for ratting on him. In one letter he pointed out
none too subtly that he had the boys' and Grant's addresses. In
another, lying that he was cocounsel on his case, he told Carol he
was certain of acquittal on the murder charges. If Paul Geragos had
stayed his attorney, the case would have been easy, except that
Geragos had refused to go along with his plan not only to prove
that he did not commit the murders but to prove that:

Jack
Jack & you
Or Jack/you/and "X" did.[. . .]

hell, carol, a law student would be able to convict you. We have
literally hundreds of supporting points.

Her way out of her own charges, Doug wrote, would be to claim
that the real killer had been Jack, at whose direction she had framed
Doug. Carol then could say that when Jack ordered her to go with
him on her first kill, terrified, she had instead murdered Jack on
an impulse, copying his own description of the Exxie Wilson
decapitation.

I am telling you bluntly I intend to destroy you completely if
you persist.[. . .] You don't have anything left carol. It is over.

You tried, and now for subtle reasons I offer a truce, but the vanquished don't get to name their terms.

"If you are a masochist, you'll love what I have in store for your mind," he signed off.

During the seemingly endless series of pretrial proceedings, Doug became more and more obstreperous. One Monday in December he objected to a witness being called and to motions being held out of order.

"Look," said Judge Ringer, "you're not your own lawyer."

Lieutenant A. L. Durrer from Van Nuys Division had barely spelled his name, "D as in David . . . ," when Doug lit up a Marlboro and was told not to smoke in the courtroom.

"I'm not in this courtroom, Your Honor."

"There is no smoking here." Judge Ringer turned to the bailiff. "Remove the cigarette if you have to."

"Take it by force then," said Doug.

"The record will reflect," said Ringer, "that with the utmost and exquisite gentleness the bailiff of this court has removed the cigarette from Mr. Clark."

"You are gently denying me due process," Doug said. "As long as you do it gently, I suppose the Constitution means nothing in this court."

"I am denying you the same cancer causers that I smoke," Judge Ringer said.

"I see you smoke in this courtroom."

"I choose when I smoke."

Things degenerated until the judge told Doug to shut up and Maxwell Keith told him, "Keep your fucking mouth shut."

And, until court was adjourned, Doug did just that.

"We will resume on Wednesday . . . ," Judge Ringer said, "at which time Mr. Clark will behave himself."

On Thursday, during a defense effort to block her statement to the task force, Carol Bundy was called to the courthouse to testify.

Maxwell Keith's first question was whether she had given police a photograph album taken from Doug's filing cabinet.

"I'm sorry," said Carol. "I can't answer that question on the grounds that it might tend to incriminate me."

She was excused and returned to Sybil Brand.

Letters flew back and forth again as Doug now pressed Carol to agree to a joint defense. His side would impeach any testimony she might give against him at his trial, he threatened. But out of niceness, they would, for the moment, withhold the information they had about her from Jorgensen.

This will encourage asshole of the year to cut you a decent deal, if you want.[. . .] Just let us cook your goose on cross and look like you were false witness. Not verbally per se, but by body English and tone et cetera.[. . .]

The best thing for both of them, Carol began to think, would be for her to testify at Doug's trial, change her story, and blame Jack for the murders.

21

After a December 1981 lunch, Bob Jorgensen walked into his office, glanced at his desk, and spotted a pile of manila envelopes. As he began leafing through them, he became dismayed. Operating under an appellate court ruling of *People v. Manson*, which held that officials in charge of prisoners awaiting trial could open, read, and censor their mail, he had asked the sheriffs to send any Bundy-Clark correspondence to him.

But some of the letters that Jorgensen had in front of him now were from Carol Bundy to her attorney, Dwight Stevens. They were privileged communication, protected from the eyes of the prosecution. Jorgensen prided himself on his integrity. He had been brought up strictly in the Morman faith, and although he had drifted away in adulthood, he was now drifting back.

Tempting as it must have been, he looked at none of the documents. So he assured the court in a letter in which he asked that the correspondence to Stevens be sealed and the rest of the material held pending a decision on the propriety of its being read and offered in evidence.

"Have you any idea what damage was done by that mail fiasco?" Doug wrote to Carol afterward, suggesting that in the future she write to him under the name "Dan Troth" at his post-office box in Glendale to let him know her thoughts on the perjury plan they'd been discussing before their letters were seized. Now calling Carol "Baby" and "Hunny," instead of his earlier "Mouse Mouth," Doug wondered if she could "leer a little, maybe snarl" and plead the Fifth again in court when questioned about her own guilt.

I'm sorry for asking, but I've no choice. I don't want you to incriminate yourself, Carol, but I'm going to point the finger of suspicion at you. Can you deal with it?

To reassure Carol that she would not be incriminating herself for nothing, Doug added a postscript. When it was his turn to sing at Carol's trial, he'd wear lederhosen and yodel.

"They want a circus," he wrote, "so let's not disappoint them! I wanna be a clown! What fun! Lets!"

In an addendum, he expanded on his confusing plan. Carol's trial had to be first. And if he could persuade Tammy Spangler, she would testify, claiming that Detective Roger Pida had given her details of the Jack Murray murder, which she then passed on to Doug. The earlier plan, in which Carol was to have claimed that she killed Jack because he was the Sunset murderer, was changed. She was now to claim that she had made a false confession based on details Tammy had learned from Pida. He too would testify, Doug wrote.

Clark takes stand, wearing jail clothes. He is surly, arrogant, self confident. He tells of basic relationship with Bundy, her inept clumsiness and dependent nature. She hasn't enough savvy to know which fork to use, if 3 are on table (sorry kid).

Doug and Carol had begun referring to her attorney, Dwight Stevens, as Dwit. Stevens was not responding to Carol's request that he arrange a joint strategy conference. It was not in anyone's best interests, Stevens felt, least of all Carol's. Doug Clark had managed to convince her that the DA had nothing on either of them and that neither could be convicted if Carol refused to testify against Doug and instead proceeded swiftly to her own trial. Stevens's own plan was to have Carol's case follow Doug's. Then, in the middle, when Jorgensen realized he desperately needed her testimony, they would make a deal with Carol pleading to second-degree murder instead of the first degree, plus a twenty-five-year sentence the DA's office was now offering. First-degree murder, Stevens thought, was all the DA had on her anyway, in spite of the threats to take her to court facing the death penalty and special circumstances.

In January of 1982, though, the DA upped the pressure, threatening to file a second murder charge against Carol over Jane Doe no. 28, or Cathy. Again Carol refused to deal. Then, in a more than foolish move, she tried to get her friend Beatrice to smuggle a watch out of Sybil Brand. Beatrice had gone to the sheriffs, and although they had not been able to link the watch to anyone, the DA's office now suspected that it belonged to a victim.

Gamely, Stevens proceeded with the plans for an insanity defense. The court appointed a warm, dark-haired psychiatrist named Winifred Meyer, whose first examination of Carol was scheduled for January 27.

The day before, Carol wrote to Doug pondering her best pose for the evaluation. In case he needed a lunatic for his trial, she leaned toward giving the facts, but "grossly exaggerated data to emphasize crazy then, crazy now." But she worried that if she did that, Doug would think she "blew it" when she could have played things straight. She was nuts to trust him still, she wrote:

> But know this, I am your woman. I'll have other men in bed or in my heart, but nowhere else in my life have I ever found a man whose mind parellels my own.

In February, Carol dipped into her savings, producing a $5,000 retainer for an eager thirty-three-year-old criminal lawyer named Joseph Walsh. To Carol's disappointment, like his predecessor Stevens, Walsh refused to set up a meeting between Doug and Carol. But to see what Doug had to say, he met him in a private room at county jail with Maxwell Keith and Doug's investigators. Doug brought a small box containing photos of victims and crime scenes, which he seemed eager to share. Walsh took one look at him and thought, This man's never going to be free.

His Jack Murray-as-the-real-killer defense was a bunch of nonsense, thought Walsh. The fellow was simply trying to reach out and regain control of Carol Bundy through her lawyer. Walsh listened politely, then left, holding Doug off when he called collect from county jail to inquire about progress with his defense plan.

"We're studying it," Walsh told him.

In December of 1980, Robert Jorgensen had sent an eleven-and-a-half-page single-spaced letter to Rick Jacques, the task force lead investigator. He wanted seventy-two points checked out, including interviews with everyone at the Jergens factory who might know about Doug Clark's activities; a reinterview of Doug's dancer friend, Nancy Smith, about the night of Jack Murray's murder; and a discussion with Carol Bundy's children to find out if, as Doug claimed, Carol had been the one who whipped Chris. In order to impeach Doug's predicted explanation that he had run over an animal the night before the Buick car wash with Kevin Crouch and Carol, the prosecutor also had asked Jacques to find an expert who could testify regarding the quantity of blood in a cat.

In January, Jorgensen had followed up with a phone call to Jacques, after which he made a note in his file. Nothing was ready, the detective had said, and he couldn't give it priority. He had, though, promised to get going on it at the end of the week or early the following week.

The Jorgensengrams had continued to arrive, and more than a year later, in February of 1982, Rick Jacques threw the murder book with the lists of evidence and requests on Leroy Orozco's desk.

"Here," he said. "You're doing the trial."

Orozco gave Jacques what his wife called "the Look." It was an Apache look straight from Geronimo on his mother's side, and it made Orozco look like a statue carved from stone. He posed as a grouch, but he was a man of unflagging good nature whose reputation in the department was for being the kind of cop who would always help out when another cop was in a bind.

Jacques had tossed him the book just in time. Orozco could have said no, but he didn't want to. The Sunset murders trial was getting closer. The evidence and story line were complex and needed fancy detective work to tie everything together and eliminate loose ends. There was an enormous amount of work to do, but Orozco felt the department owed it to the case. He wanted to see Clark in the gas chamber, not just because he was a son of a bitch, but because of the victims and their families.

"I'll do the best I can," he always said to them. That was what he had said this time to Janet Marano.

What an ass, he thought about Jacques, everything about Rick annoying him now. Not just his hair and his Zapata mustache, but his cowboy pose that grated so. Shit, Orozco thought, Rick had never ridden a horse in his life.

Orozco began to formulate his plan. Like everyone else, he dreaded the Jorgensengrams, but he'd give the prosecutor what he knew he needed until the guy began to trust him enough to relax and back off a bit.

Orozco sighed. It was February 1982, and the most recent Jorgensengram contained forty-five evidence requests. They included asking if Joey Lamphier had an explanation for Laurie Brigges's phone number showing up on her bill, and if the task force would interview each of the twenty-nine officers from the Chandler-Marano discovery scene to make sure one of them did not find a card with Henry Brigges's number or an address book containing Mindy Cohen's. Jorgensen also wanted Jergens factory logs to verify statements that Jack Murray had never been in the plant. To everyone's relief, the task force had already determined that Doug Clark had been lying when he claimed to have been accepted at the police academy.

Trial would begin in eight months.

Several things happened that spring. A doctor at the USC Medical Center Vivarium Unit let Leroy Orozco know that an eight-pound cat contained only about half a pint of blood. Maxwell Keith brought in a blond, smart former DA named Penelope Watson to be cocounsel on the Clark case; this meant that Doug at last had the attractive (if not soft-spoken) female attorney he had wanted for so long.

Perhaps, though, the most important event that spring as the Sunset murders case lumbered toward trial began with a March phone call from Carol Bundy to Robbery-Homicide. At the time, Carol was angry with Doug for interfering with a plan she had to publish her short stories. Through the Sybil Brand grapevine, she had heard about a woman she knew only as Char who had been the victim of a knife attack. The descripton of her attacker had sounded like Doug. Carol called detective Frank Garcia.

The next day Garcia went to Sybil Brand with a photo lineup.

Char, or Charlene Andermann, was a prostitute who had been picked up on Sunset Boulevard on April 27, 1980, and stabbed twenty-six times before leaping to safety from her attacker's blue station wagon.

Andermann looked at the photos Garcia showed her.

"God," she said. "Those eyes. I'll never forget those eyes. As sure as I can be after the lapse of time, it's number six."

Number six was Douglas Clark.

Doug was brought to a live lineup at county jail.

Under orders from Maxwell Keith, he refused to appear.

"Kiss my ass," he said to Bob Jorgensen, when Jorgensen told him it could be held against him.

After an April 14 preliminary hearing, Doug was held to answer for the Andermann charges of attempted murder and mayhem, and Jorgensen made plans to seek a motion to consolidate the Andermann case with the Sunset murders.

At around the same time, the district attorney's office was following through with its threat to charge Carol with the murder of Cathy.

Jorgensen had handed the Bundy case over to Deputy DA Ronald Coen, a thirty-four-year-old, barrel-chested weight-lifter and legal whiz whose chest expanded even more, Orozco thought, when people told him he looked like actor Christopher Reeve.

"Tell Carol she'd better tell the truth," Coen said to Orozco. "She's going to be dealing with Superman."

As the few bones that were the basis for the Cathy charges might not have stood on their own, Coen approached the grand jury for a superseding indictment to consolidate the case with Murray.

At an April preliminary hearing, Joseph Walsh, flabbergasted by the paucity of evidence, argued that the Cathy bones did not constitute a corpus delicti. But calling it "a very close case," the judge disagreed. Now Carol stood charged with two first-degree murders, plus special circumstances and firearms-use allegations.

As Joseph Walsh left the courtroom, he was surprised to see Bob Jorgensen hovering in the corridor, briefcase in hand.

"This is what we're offering," the prosecutor said. "She'll plead guilty to one count of first-degree murder, get twenty-five years to life, and she'll testify against Clark."

Still Carol refused to deal, so consumed with guilt about turning Doug in, Walsh reasoned, that she was willing to face the gas chamber.

Immediately, Walsh set about filing a 995 motion with the court of appeal. In it he tackled the special circumstances, arguing that Jack Murray had not been a witness to a crime. He also, for the reasons he'd argued at the preliminary hearing, asked the higher court to dismiss the Cathy/Jane Doe no. 28 count.

If the stay were denied and the charges stood, Walsh thought, Carol would need more money to hire her own expert witness to refute the coroner's claim that the hole in Jane Doe's skull had been made by a bullet.

Between January and April, Dr. Winifred Meyer had met Carol several times in order to evaluate her mental state. What had really floored Meyer was Carol's answer to the question of whether she had any role models.

"Eleanor Roosevelt," Carol had said.

Dr. Meyer had just sat there for a moment taking it in. Because Carol wanted to be seen as a lady, she covered up her abnormalities, Meyer decided. Her idea of a lady was Eleanor Roosevelt.

Doug Clark had given Carol an identity when she didn't have one, Meyer thought. When Carol turned herself in to police, she was a burned-out fuse, expecting arrest. As someone who had always been an outsider, Carol's post-arrest high had come from being at last on the inside, feeling like "a choice piece of property," as she had put it during her confession.

Jail structure had glued Carol back together. Whoever she was with for the moment became the controlling element, and it seemed no accident to Dr. Meyer that this formerly out-of-control, now determinedly ladylike Carol Bundy was living in an institution that had been founded by Los Angeles society woman Sybil Brand. Of course Carol would seem stabilized. Jail had returned to her the structure that had disappeared when she lost her eyesight and her marriage, Jack Murray stole her money, and she sent her children away.

Carol had told Winifred Meyer of her growing fascination with Doug's bizarre behavior and of wanting to keep up with him because she was afraid of losing their relationship. But more important, she had also said that shortly before her intense involvement in the murderous episodes, she had begun to fear that she could no longer control herself or disassociate herself from Doug.

In July, Dr. Meyer submitted her confidential report to Joseph Walsh: Carol had been psychotic at the time of the crimes and had shown "grossly psychotic behavior" on the day of her arrest when she made sexual advances to Gary Broda. But her "psychosis was somewhat in check at this point in time."

After telling so many stories and so many details about the crimes, Carol would "forget whether it was fact or fantasy," said Dr. Meyer. Carol, conveniently, had also begun to have trouble remembering which murders she had been involved with and was now claiming innocence in the Jack Murray killing. She had confessed to it, she now said, because Doug had threatened her. In spite of this she had fantasies about joining him again and becoming part of a twosome, she told Meyer, even though she knew this was unrealistic.

Not knowing about the letter in which Carol planned to act

"crazy then, crazy now," Dr. Meyer concluded that while competent to stand trial, Carol had been insane at the time of her crime. She had known right from wrong, but because of psychosis was unable to conform to the law. For her own safety and the safety of others, Meyer advised, Carol Bundy should be confined to a mental institution.

Joseph Walsh did not doubt that Carol had been mentally unbalanced at the time of the crimes. He felt, though, that her comment about Doug threatening her into confessing to Jack's murder was simply Carol's trying to back out and hang Murray on Doug. Her confusion over "fact and fantasy" was likewise an attempt to distance herself from all of the crimes.

There were, of course, other questions that Meyer and Walsh could not pose. If Carol Bundy thought she knew how to act "crazy then, crazy now," did that mean she was really sane? Or was she so crazy that she was unable to realize the extent of her insanity? Confusing matters even further, Carol would say later that she had not followed through on her plan to "act crazy."

In July, the same month that Meyer handed in her report, Joseph Walsh's 995 motion was turned down by the court of appeal, and a hearing on the special circumstances charge, the possible violation of Carol's Miranda rights and Jane Doe no. 28 evidence was denied.

Carol had run out of money and Walsh was now off the case. But he comforted himself with the thought that, by a quirk of California criminal law, the issues in his writ could be taken up again. Carol's next lawyer would be able to ask the trial judge for a full evidentiary hearing, after which the Cathy charges might be dropped.

22

FROM COUNTY JAIL DOUG HAD GRUMBLED LOUDLY ABOUT THE SYStem of court-appointed defense lawyers. They were "nothing but an escort from arrest to execution," he said. He despised Maxwell Keith, whose battered briefcase, unruly shock of gray hair, and rumpled appearance did not fit his client's pretensions. Sarcastically, Doug referred to Keith as Clarence Darrow. Whenever possible, he insulted him and interrupted him in court, trying to take over.

In the nearly two years since his arrest, Doug had turned into a competent jailhouse lawyer. He had also learned well during pretrial hearings the pompous officialese used by witnesses who, finding themselves "unable to recall," had "refreshed" their memories by consulting their notes.

During the arguments for a motion to suppress the album with photographs of Theresa, the key questions had been who at the Verdugo apartment had control of the bedroom where the file cabinet was stored, and was it Carol Bundy's right to unlock that cabinet, which Doug said was his private property?

Even though he had told the task force that he slept in Carol's room, now, testifying on his own behalf, Doug claimed that he had been nothing more than Carol Bundy's roommate, with his own bedroom over which Carol had no jurisdiction. Perhaps in an effort to seem thoughtful while obfuscating, he seemed fond of meandering as much as possible with his answers.

"Where did you spend the night of August 8, 1980, Mr. Clark?" Robert Jorgensen asked.

"Friday, August eighth? Without refreshing my memory with my notes, I would say that was the night I spent in the company of Tammy Spangler. But right now I can't recall if that was the night or Saturday night was the night. The ninth would be the night I spent at a hotel with her. Or at the apartment with her. I don't recall which one was which right now."

Well then, which room, Jorgensen wondered, had Doug occupied on the night he did spend with Tammy Spangler?

"I believe the night that I spent—I recall the night I spent with Tammy Spangler at the Verdugo apartment, I borrowed Carol's room."

Judge Ringer was curious. What was wrong with Doug's room that he had to spend his night with Tammy in Carol's?

"She had a queen-sized bed and the activities of the evening required it."

"I walked into that one," said the judge.

Doug was also claiming that he had been trying to get Carol out of the apartment by using "various slightly coercive tactics."

"Such as?" asked Jorgensen.

"Such as just being an obnoxious person."

"Rather difficult for you to do?"

Maxwell Keith objected.

"Sometimes I can't resist. I'm sorry," Jorgensen said, withdrawing the question.

"Neither can I," said Doug.

And the bickering continued toward trial.

Doug had been granted two hours a day in the county jail law library. Twice he had asked for cocounsel status and been denied. In June, during a pretrial conference, he accused Jorgensen of impeding discovery, complained once more about Maxwell Keith, said he had been trying to "get rid of" Judge Ringer for a long time, then told the judge he wasn't going to listen to his drivel any longer.

"You are in a state this morning," Judge Ringer said, ordering that Doug be removed from court when he refused to be quiet.

"Bullshit," said Doug as he left the courtroom.

In July 1982, two months before the beginning of jury selection, Judge Ringer denied a defense discovery motion. Then, as a routine question in a complicated case, he asked Doug if he would waive time for a speedy trial. Matters were piling up; there was much to attend to.

Doug exploded, furious with Keith about the lost motion. "No, no, Your Honor. Under no circumstances will I waive time. Bring in the goddamn jury panel. This man is dismissed. . . . I'm thoroughly capable of handling this case."

Judge Ringer told Doug to behave himself. "Be silent, Mr. Clark, or you will be damned. Mr. Keith is not relieved. You are entitled to a lawyer. You have got two lawyers. They're both competent."

And so the summer passed in a flurry of pretrial motions and outbursts until Judge Ringer asked that the case be transferred. According to Doug, Ringer told Maxwell Keith that he thought the defendant was trying to kill him by aggravating his ulcer and hiatal hernia.

Before the Sunset murders case was sent to another court, Doug again asked for *pro per* privileges. *Pro per* (short for *in propria persona*) meant representing oneself without the aid of counsel. Judge Ringer told him to take the matter up with the next court. But within a week Doug complained again to Ringer, saying that he had given his *pro per* request, known as a *Faretta* motion, to Maxwell Keith, who had refused to file it.

"That's not so, Clark. We're not going to type up your junk," said Keith in the courtroom.

"See what I mean?" said Doug.

Doug could present his motion orally to Judge Leetham in calendar court, which would assign the case, Judge Ringer told him. "He has to hear that type of motion."

"And you had to, too."

"Oh, shut up," Judge Ringer said.

And an adjournment was taken.

The next day, Doug wasted little time in asking to address Judge Leetham about his relationship with Maxwell Keith.

"I am not represented at these proceedings," Doug said. "I don't know what this man is doing here. He is not my attorney. . . ."

"It's amazing," said Judge Leetham, a canny man. "The court notes that Mr. Keith has been at every hearing so far. And this is a shock to see him today, is it? Well, it is a shock I hope you recover from. Transferred forthwith to Department One twenty-seven for all further proceedings."

Later that day, in front of Judge Ricardo Torres, who would preside over the trial, Doug renewed his request.

Torres, the son of Mexican immigrants, was a fifty-two-year-old CPA and IRS agent turned lawyer. He had been passed over for years for a judgeship before being appointed to the superior court by Governor Jerry Brown only a year and half before the Clark trial. He was an imposing man with a quick wit and a reputation for swift decision-making. Sometimes a little too swift, thought his detractors, who felt he ruled from his guts rather than his head. That day he took the bench in an apparently genial mood.

Grumbling once again that he had declared a conflict of interest with Maxwell Keith, Doug brought up his *pro per* request. He still wanted to fire Maxwell Keith and represent himself, but now he wanted Penelope Watson to be cocounsel, even though Watson had told him that she had no desire to proceed in that fashion.

Maxwell Keith, anticipating being bumped off the case, said that while he was still counsel, he wanted to enter on Doug's behalf a plea of not guilty by reason of insanity. Which, he added, he had not discussed with Doug because Doug no longer was speaking to him.

"Therein lies the conflict, Your Honor," said Doug, making the most of his chance to create a good impression with the new judge. "I am not guilty by any regard, way, shape, or form. My counsel has been off on a tangent somewhere. He blew up in court yesterday twice, as a matter of fact." Here Doug became pious. "And loudly—and I apologize for the language—Mr. Keith yelled in court yesterday, 'I am not going to file your fucking papers.' He has told me to shut my fucking mouth on the record."

Maxwell Keith had used no such "vulgar language," protested Jorgensen, who also argued against Doug's being granted the right to fire Keith and proceed on his own. It would, he said, cause an unjustifiable delay.

After a question session during which Doug declared erroneously that Jorgensen had accused Keith of incompetence, Judge Torres decided that the latest *pro per* request was untimely. It was denied.

Keith still wondered about the not guilty by reason of insanity plea. That, said Torres, was strictly a legal issue up to the defendant.

"I refuse to even respond to anything that ludicrous from what is represented as my counsel," said Doug.

Carol Bundy's case was pending in Judge Torres's courtroom. Already he had heard a motion and read the preliminary-hearing transcript, of which he informed Doug.

"That is more than sufficient to convince me that I can't get a fair trial in this courtroom," said Doug.

Judge Torres disagreed. But if Doug or his attorneys wished to disqualify him, he would not be offended, he said.

Neither Doug nor Keith and Watson pursued the matter.

Earlier, Bob Jorgensen had moved to dismiss the accessory charge against Doug in the Jack Murray murder. It did not seem worthy of being tried with the other counts, he said. The motion was heard in chambers out of Doug's presence, which lead him to cry later that there was a conspiracy to convict him. Following the seizure of his letters, he said, Jorgensen had learned of the defense plan to accuse Jack Murray and was trying to thwart it.

In chambers, Maxwell Keith objected strongly to severance.

"That count will tend to show," he said, "there is more than a distinct possibility that someone else other than Clark committed these homicides."

But Judge Torres granted Jorgensen's motion, saying that Keith could bring in any such evidence during the defense phase of trial.

And so, in August, the final pretrial motions began, interspered beginning in September with the tedious process of jury selection.

By September 20, jurors were still being questioned when Doug complained again about Maxwell Keith, saying that he had done everything in his power to get rid of him.

"He is not prepared for trial now. He has no intention of preparing for trial. He's not interested," said Doug, who later in the day contended that Keith had been "antagonistic" toward a juror. "I don't see any reason for him flopping around in his chair, glaring. . . ."

"Your Honor, I object to this," said Jorgensen, who had no affection for the defense bar in general but found Maxwell Keith to be an intelligent and able lawyer.

"Shut up, you asshole," said Doug, whereupon he was removed from the court and placed in the lockup.

After a five-minute recess, he was brought out again and his litany of complaints and insults began anew. He considered himself "unrepresented" in court. Maxwell Keith was a "buffoon." Maxwell Keith was "dismissed."

"You don't get to call the shots . . . ," said Judge Torres.

"You railroad me. Fine."

"The minute you start to misbehave, then I have no option but to treat you in a forcible manner, which means—"

"You'd love it, wouldn't you?"

He preferred not to exercise his power, said Torres patiently. "You can do it the easy way for you and the court, or we can do it the hard way."

"Dump-truck way. Let everybody roll right along with Mr. Keith just dump-trucking. Let him dump-truck me."

"You know as well as I do that he is doing a good job."

"He hasn't done shit, Your Honor."

Rose Bird's state supreme court had the reputation for reversing convictions at higher than the expected rate based on inadequacy of counsel. Bob Jorgensen was convinced that Doug, expecting conviction, was doing everything he could to make a record for appeal. The insults Doug flung his way amused him, but he felt for Maxwell Keith.

"You've stuffed this man down my throat against my will," said Doug to Judge Torres. "You and Ringer. He's a friend of Ringer's. He's a dump truck. He comes in here, looks like he rolled out of Main Street Mission with his hair sticking out everywhere. Looks like he slept in his suit most of the time."

Penny Watson was doing a fine job, said Doug. He had selected her, and he was happy with her.

"I thought Judge Ringer selected Miss Watson."

"Bullshit."

"Didn't I tell you not to use profanity in this courtroom?"

"I am not in a courtroom. . . . You drug me in here, you put up with my profanity. I'll cease the profanity when I'm in *pro per*."

By now, Judge Torres had lost his patience.

"When I don't have jurors in here, I will gag you," he threatened. "I will slap something across your mouth and you won't say a word and I'll have you handcuffed to the chair if you get smart. . . . I'll chain your legs and have you—"

"I'm shaking, Your Honor."

Once again, Doug was removed to the lockup, speaking as he went.

"I'm not represented. I'm being railroaded. This is a railroad that you call a courtroom."

PART

FOUR

23

THE TRIAL BEGAN IN OCTOBER HEAT MORE THAN TWO YEARS AFTER the arrests. Leroy Orozco, who would sit at Jorgensen's side, walked the few blocks northwest from Parker Center, as he would every day, uphill through the smog and whine of city traffic. His briefcase contained the murder book filled with Jorgensengrams and evidence lists.

He and Jorgensen had spent hours comparing blood types to victims, and phone calls and work hours of Douglas Clark and Carol Bundy to the murder dates. Over and over they had dissected the murder scenarios and compared Carol Bundy's stories to the physical evidence of bullet holes and blood. Painstakingly they had gone over witnesses' statements, including Carol's. If she ended up taking the stand for the defense—which Jorgensen hoped she would—they did not want any surprises.

Carol's story had held up, even though there were some discrepancies: no bullet had gone through Marnett Comer's elbow or Gina Marano's sinus as Carol had stated; there was no sperm or semen found in Cindy Chandler's throat or Gina's anus. But Carol had also said that Doug gave her snippets of misinformation in order to undermine her credibility.

Leroy had wanted Jorgensen to call Carol for the prosecution. Get her talking on the stand after they'd built the case.

It was too risky, felt Jorgensen, aware of Carol's instability. If she were feeling loyal to Doug, she might deny everything. Also, the prosecutor had received his share of Carol Bundy mash notes. Because he had ignored her overtures, he worried that she might try to pay him back in court.

Department 127 was on the fifteenth floor of the busy criminal-courts building. The lighting was harsh, the atmosphere stuffy, and, as is often the case in windowless rooms, there was a feeling of time stopped. This feeling would become more intense as the trial crawled into the following March.

Bob Jorgensen, in aviator glasses and pinstripes, had prepared for his first day of this fight to the death: during voir dire he had asked prospective jurors if they had ever been dues-paying, card-holding members of the ACLU or the NAACP. Both of those organizations were against the death penalty, and he did not want members on the jury. None of the eight-woman, four-man panel had belonged.

He had made no secret to Orozco that he thought Doug was a less-than-human scumbag. "I want to nail the son of a bitch," he had said.

It was an odd courtroom scene, with Doug, lean, bespectacled, and pin-striped, reminding Orozco of Jorgensen's evil twin. Both men were possessed of a restless energy that sent them in different directions: in the early morning, Jorgensen logged on to his computer where he had abstracted virtually every California Supreme Court criminal-case decision since he had been admitted to the bar; Douglas Clark went to the streets in search of victims.

Doug's first move was to renew his request for *pro per* privileges with Penny Watson as his cocounsel.

Jorgensen was concerned. The area surrounding *pro per* was legally murky. He could envision the Rose Bird supreme court reversing Doug's anticipated conviction on the technical grounds that his request had been timely and *pro per* should have been granted. He had written to Judge Torres and later filed a motion. He wanted the court to ask Doug whether, if *pro per* were granted, he would seek a delay.

When Doug said that he would ask for a two-week delay to prepare for trial, Judge Torres counteroffered by saying he would grant Doug's motion to represent himself if Doug would proceed immediately without Penelope Watson.

He was not ready, said Doug, suggesting once again that Judge Torres was trying to "railroad" him.

222

Doug's motion was denied, and the jury was sworn in.

The Sunset murders was a complicated case with hundreds of pieces of evidence and a lurid and improbable plot line. In his opening statement, Jorgensen's goal was to let the jury know, as methodically as possible, the evidence with which they were to be presented, without giving them so much that they wouldn't believe him.

He was not, though, above grabbing their attention from the beginning as he moved into the shocking story of Mindy Cohen's second phone call from "Detective" Clark.

" 'I made love to them and it felt so good, felt so good,' " said Jorgensen, undoubtedly startling the jury as the killer's words spouted from him. " 'Now I want to do it to you. I came in the mouth of one of them. Now I want you, Mindy.' "

Almost professorially, for Jorgensen's inner fire did not translate into courtroom theatrics, he moved through the discovery of the bodies, the bloody boot print in the garage, and the blood spots on the back of Douglas Clark's ski painting—spots that had turned out to contain enzymes linked to Gina Marano. He mentioned Gina's missing red phone book, in which she had written Mindy Cohen's phone number, and the telephone-company records that showed the second early morning call to Mindy had been made from the Verdugo apartment. It was the call during which the killer had confessed.

The records would also show, said Jorgensen, that from Joey Lamphier's apartment, when Doug was there alone, someone had called Laurie Brigges, sister-in-law of Henry Brigges, who had given Cindy and Gina a ride the day before they were killed. From Lamphier's apartment, someone had also phoned, but not reached, the lawyer who had given the party where Mindy Cohen met Gina and Cindy.

After nearly forty minutes, Jorgensen was finished. Maxwell Keith reserved his opening statement, and the procession of prosecution witnesses began.

Jorgensen's plan was to present the crimes as chronologically as possible. On the first day, Charlene Andermann, the prostitute who had survived the April 1980 stabbing, took the stand. After her attack, Andermann had been hypnotized. A recent state supreme court ruling had declared the testimony of hypnotized witnesses tainted and inadmissible, and Maxwell Keith had filed a motion to have Andermann excluded. But Judge Torres ruled that

223

Andermann herself could testify, while any statements she had made under hypnosis would not be allowed.

The jury, then, would not learn of Andermann's belief that her attacker had told her his name was Don (or Ron), which was also Douglas Clark's "swinging" name.

On July 30, 1980, Andermann had looked at a photo lineup. It did not contain a photo of Douglas Clark, because at the time he was not a suspect. Tentatively, she had identified someone else, saying that the eyes were the same, but she could not be sure.

In August, at a live lineup where Doug again wasn't present, she had tentatively identified the same man, once more noting that because of the time lapse, she could not be absolutely positive.

On direct examination, Jorgensen led Andermann through her story, then asked her to point out her attacker in the courtroom. She pointed out Douglas Clark. Then she described getting in his car and driving to the side street where he held her down and stabbed her.

Over the two days of Andermann's testimony, Maxwell Keith was able to bring out the contradictions in her various statements. She had claimed she was picked up at a Safeway store. There was no Safeway at Sunset and La Brea—although there was a Ralph's nearby. She had identified her attacker's station wagon as a Country Squire with wood paneling, said he had a mustache and had worn, variously, a blue-and-red or a green-and-black Pendleton. Andermann also admitted that she had swallowed codeine with gin-and-grapefruit drinks on a day that she had tried to help police create a composite drawing of her suspect.

She was a brown-haired woman who showed the ravages of street life and still seemed somewhat confused about events. She also sniffled with a cold. Before turning her over to Jorgensen for redirect examination, Keith tossed in a sarcastic shot.

"Have you taken any codeine for your cold today?"

"No."

"I don't have anything further at this time."

Jorgensen and Orozco were not worried about what they considered minor contradictions. Clearly Andermann had been stabbed by a light-haired man in a blue station wagon. And there was a truthful simplicity to her manner, they thought.

She held up her middle and ring fingers, paralyzed from the stabbing which had severed a tendon.

"They don't go right," she said.

The man who attacked her had given a sick laugh of pleasure

when she told him he was hurting her. As she had recounted this during a pretrial proceeding, Douglas Clark had laughed.

"Was it the same kind of laugh?" Jorgensen asked now.

"Yes."

"Tell me, do you have any doubt in your mind whatsoever that the man seated here, Douglas Clark, is the man who stabbed you and told you, 'This is your last round, baby'?"

"No, I don't."

"Are you sure he's the man?"

"Yes."

And with that, a relieved Charlene Andermann was free to leave.

After Andermann, things moved at a surprisingly fast pace as witnesses described the movements of Cindy Chandler and Gina Marano before their deaths. Henry Brigges, seeming surprised to find himself in the middle of such drama, took the stand to tell of picking them up and giving Cindy a business card with his phone number and that of his brother, George, and sister-in-law, Laurie. Cindy's bloodied pink jumpsuit, which Detective Helen Kidder described to the jury as having been ripped or cut up to the crotch, had been entered into evidence by the time her shell-shocked stepfather, Andy Marano, appeared to describe the red address book that Gina had always carried and that had not been found with the bodies.

On the third day, a flustered Lydia Crouch took her seat to testify, as bouffant, hefty, and Texan as she had been on the night Doug met her at the Viking Bar. Orozco, watching her carefully, thought that he detected in her a residue of loyalty to Doug.

Lydia was still not aware of the details of the case, but with her appearance the trial began to take its shape. The key civilian witnesses would be women testifying against—and occasionally for— Douglas Clark. Women who, whether they knew it or not, had been his victims.

Jorgensen elicited several statements from Lydia that damaged Doug: he had suggested she buy a .25-caliber Raven automatic at the Diamond pawn shop in Van Nuys; he had shown her a photo of a car resembling Carol Bundy's Datsun and told her it had been in a hit-and-run accident—there had been red liquid dripping down the fender; and he had claimed that a cat had bled to death in the front of the Buick.

The "cat," Jorgensen surmised, was Cathy, killed the night before the car wash with Kevin Crouch. But he could not refer to her. Although Carol had been charged with her murder, Doug had not.

Helpfully to the defense, Lydia Crouch also said that Doug was at her house all morning on June 22 and that she had left to visit a neighbor only for about five or ten minutes. June 22 was the day of the first phone call to Mindy Cohen from the bogus detective. The call had never been traced.

Like Charlene Andermann's, Lydia Crouch's recollections of Doug's activities had shifted over the two years since Doug's arrest. But then again, Lydia had received a threatening phone call from a man who warned her not to testify against Doug.

A rumor had traveled through the courtroom that actress Jaclyn Smith was there. But the dark-haired woman in sunglasses was Janet Marano. She had been rising early and dressing carefully to come to court, determined to let people know that she was a normal woman who didn't have a filthy house and who hadn't raised Cindy and Gina to become prostitutes. She wanted to look at Douglas Clark and see what she had not been able to see on television: that he was a murderer. But she still didn't see it. All she saw was a blue-eyed innocent who could belong to her family.

Jenny Chandler, dressed in black and looking like Cindy, was in the courtroom with her mother, listening to Lydia Crouch's testimony. Every time Lydia described blood in the Buick, where Carol said he had killed Cindy and Gina, Doug turned around and smirked in Jenny's direction.

She left the courtroom in tears.

After the second phone call from the man who said he had killed Cindy and Gina, Mindy Cohen had fled to Lake Tahoe, where she hid out in a tiny apartment above a dry-cleaning store. Detective Gary Broda had flown there to play her a tape, from which she had identified Doug Clark's voice as that of the caller. The defense had wanted the identification suppressed on the grounds that the tape was unduly suggestive: Doug had been talking to the police about a woman having sex with a horse. They had also filed another motion based on the failure to have legal counsel present for Doug at what they considered a voice lineup.

This was just the kind of argument that Jorgensen would have sympathized with in his Berkeley days. Now it irked him as much as had a pretrial decision to sever the child-molestation charges from the murder counts.

"The defendant apparently has been unfairly treated," he said, "because he was charged with child molestation of which there is, of course, overwhelming evidence, photographs, and admissions. And he's now being unfairly treated because we happen to have a reliable witness who has his confession."

There was no justification on earth, he argued, for excluding Mindy Cohen's identification of Douglas Clark's voice.

"Mr. Jorgensen talks very well, but he never reaches the point," said Maxwell Keith.

"He also gets you stirred up," Judge Torres observed, overruling the defense.

It was October 12, the fourth day of trial, when Mindy Cohen took the stand with her curly rock-and-roll hair in a ponytail. Instead of her usual sexy clothes, she wore a "Little House on the Prairie" dress with a gray blazer over it.

Doug had seen Mindy, her style more relaxed, at his preliminary hearing. Now she looked as if she'd just come from bible study class. He was annoyed.

Jorgensen led her through the story of Mark's party and the first phone call from the detective. Then Mindy, fighting tears, told of the second phone call, in July, which had been traced to the Verdugo apartment.

"What did he say after he said, 'I'm going to do it to you, Mindy'?"

"He said he was going to get me."

After the first call on June 22, Mindy Cohen had been unable to remember the name of the man. She had said so at the preliminary hearing. During cross-examination, she admitted to Maxwell Keith that she had remembered the name "Doug Clark" after Gary Broda told it to her as he showed her photographs.

Keith was casual. Although Doug taunted him by calling him Clarence Darrow, he reminded Orozco more of Spencer Tracy playing Darrow in *Inherit the Wind*. He would toss a question out, walk away as if he didn't care, then turn back and pounce. He was of the old school and believed in operating within the law. Which, Orozco surmised, was the trouble between Keith and Douglas Clark.

While he was thinking of it, said Keith, didn't Mindy Cohen make a note of the time that the first phone conversation occurred?

"No, I didn't."

Keith had with him an envelope upon which Mindy Cohen had jotted notes after the call.

"You forgot about that, did you?"

"Uh-huh."

"Things are easy to forget. Isn't that right?"

"Some things," said Mindy Cohen, not about to be tricked.

At 10:20 the next morning, Maxwell Keith and Penelope Watson held an urgent meeting in chambers with Judge Torres. The day before, Doug had asked again to go *pro per* and had been denied. In the evening at county jail, he had told his lawyers that he planned to fire them both today and renew his request to represent himself.

Keith urged the judge not to grant his client's request. Doug was crazy, "As crazy as anybody I've ever seen or will see," he said, and not capable of making an intelligent waiver of counsel.

The only avenue to save his life was a diminished-capacity defense, Keith thought, or strong psychiatric testimony during the penalty phase of the trial. He and Watson had two doctors on call who had examined Doug. Please, Maxwell Keith begged, grant permission to introduce their testimony.

Later that morning, Judge Torres announced that he was going to grant Doug's request to represent himself but would revoke that privilege the minute he felt it was being abused.

The jury was about to be brought in and Maxwell Keith was still worried that Doug was too crazy to be able to sign a knowing waiver. Once more he pleaded for a psychiatrist.

"It is my understanding, Your Honor," said Doug, "that Mr. Keith has been removed from the case. . . . I don't feel it's proper for him to make a motion of this nature."

Judge Torres agreed and Maxwell Keith's motion was overruled.

24

THIS WAS WHAT DOUG HAD WANTED ALL ALONG. IMMEDIATELY HE seemed to bask in the attention. Veteran court watchers commented that he was the only *pro per* they had ever seen who seemed to know what he was doing. From watching Doug argue with judges during pretrial sessions, Jorgensen already knew Doug was clever. He did a job that was no worse than many other lawyers who prowled the halls of the criminal courthouse. But he also knew that Doug believed he could outwit the system. And Doug was not, thought Jorgensen, nearly as clever as he believed.

The prosecutor drew from Laurie Brigges the story of the "detective" whose name she thought was Clark who had called to give her details of the Chandler and Marano murders and ask if her brother-in-law Henry was "tall and fair."

Like Mindy Cohen, in her first statement to the task force, Brigges had been unable to name her caller. She had given the name "Clark" to her brother-in-law, who had phoned the police to try to find the detective. But before she spoke again to Henry, worried that she had made a mistake, Briggs had told police she thought the caller's name began with an "H."

In his first cross-examination, Doug brought out this information.

"So telling the police officers that it began with an H was a ruse of some sort, would you say?" he asked Laurie Brigges.

229

"I just wasn't sure. I thought possibly it could have been another name."

"Another name, but a name beginning with H."

"Possibly."

"Possibly." Doug paused for effect. "Let's try M."

"I don't know."

"You don't know? . . . Did you pick it out of thin air?"

"The letter H?"

"Yes."

"I must have."

This was good for Doug, Orozco thought. But then he spoiled it.

"I see," Doug said. "You're confident now that it was and always has been the name Clark on that phone call you had?"

"After speaking with my brother-in-law, yes."

Doug also made the mistake of repeatedly referring to the bogus officer as "Detective Clark." He reinforced the idea that he was the man who had called.

Jorgensen had grabbed the jury's attention with the Andermann, Cohen, and Brigges dramas. He then moved on to two weeks of expert witnesses, detectives, and the unnerved citizens who had discovered the bodies and bones of Marnett Comer, Exxie Wilson, Karen Jones, and Jane Doe no. 18.

Doug, who was turning out to be a pedantic cross-examiner, again blundered as he questioned Detective Frank Garcia. Because of the Jack Murray charges being severed, he had lost his planned defense. Now, without that to fall back on—and to obscure the facts pointing to his own guilt—he turned to requesting as many petty details as possible, often damaging his cause. With Garcia he brought out the idea that dead bodies had been inside a bloody garage.

". . . it's your opinion," Doug asked, "that something was dragged on the floor. Is that what I'm to assume?"

"Yes."

"What would it be that you would assume was dragged . . . ?"

"A body."

He also seemed to rather revel in questions about blood.

"Now these blood drops . . . were these caked-on stains . . . flush to the cement? Or—would you describe . . . some of these blood spots?"

"Certainly," said Garcia, happy to oblige. "They weren't blood clots laying on the cement. They were pretty well blended into the cement itself."

The next morning, over a number of Doug's objections, William Bodziak, an FBI shoe-print analyst, testified that the black Vulcan-brand boots Doug had been wearing when he was arrested were more worn, but corresponded to an impression taken of the bloody boot print in the rental garage.

Again Doug's approach was to appear, while obfuscating, to be seeking the truth. Had the boot-print photos been taken from a stepladder, he asked Bodziak, and what make of camera was used? Later he asked the criminalist who found sperm in Cynthia Chandler's vagina to inform the court how many cc's of vaginal fluid were in a vial and the concentration of spermatozoa to a cc.

"Was it plentiful?"

Not surprisingly, the criminalist did not recall.

Doug, though, scored by eliciting the information that had concerned criminalists as they stood in the garage and wondered whether to preserve the boot print or risk losing it by performing a conclusive test for blood: the decision to preserve the print meant that they could presume, but not tell the jury "without a shadow of a doubt," that the substance on the boot was human blood.

The trial continued, with Doug complaining that Watson and Keith had not turned over complete files to him.

"I did not want to take over this ship," he said to Judge Torres, "and have the departing crew take the compass and the coal bins, leave me without navigation material in the middle of the damn ocean going nowhere."

"They didn't want to abandon the ship," said Judge Torres. "You forced them out in the middle of the night. That's your decision."

The trial was beginning its third week when Doug's high-school sweetheart, Bobbi, took the stand, a drably pretty woman who was clearly a reluctant witness.

Jorgensen began by asking her about Doug's attire in 1980.

"Do you recall telling Detective Garcia that you had observed the defendant wearing women's underpants? And did you state, 'Yes. In fact he asked me. He asked me if he could have a pair of my panties'?"

"Objection, Your Honor, leading and also cumulative. She has already answered that question," said Doug.

"Overruled."

Bobbi was allowed to answer.

"When I talked to the officer, okay? I—I just don't know. I don't

231

know. I'm confused, because I know what I saw and it doesn't—I can't say that I said that to him."

It seemed as if Bobbi was trying to protect Doug. But the story of her Memorial Day weekend trip to Los Angeles two and a half weeks before the Chandler/Marano murders was important on key points having to do with the ski-painting evidence and the guns.

Doug had met her plane at Los Angeles International Airport, Bobbi testified under direct examination by Jorgensen, and they had taken an airport bus to pick up a blue station wagon. After checking into a motel they went to Carol Bundy's apartment, where Doug told Carol to get a gun.

"Before that, what did he tell her to go get?"

"I am going to object," said Doug. "This is leading. There was a conversation . . . he can enquire as to the conversation."

"Overruled."

Jorgensen repeated the question, and Bobbi answered.

There had been a conversation about bullets, she said. Doug had told Carol to get some. Carol had said she wanted to talk to him, and they had walked into the bedroom together.

The next morning, after a night in a motel, Doug and Bobbi rode on his motorcycle to his rental garage, where Bobbi noticed the ski-scene painting. She had tilted it to look at it, but had not noticed any blood spots.

After visiting the garage they had driven up north to Doug's parents' house, where they target shot. Then on Monday, Memorial Day, they returned to Los Angeles. Doug and Bobbi went to a nude-dancer bar and then to a motel, where Doug left Bobbi before returning with Nancy Smith.

"Did she do anything for you and the defendant in the motel?"

Doug objected and was overruled. He knew what the answer would be and he didn't want to hear it, Orozco thought. He was objecting too often, letting the jury know that he had much to hide.

Reluctantly Bobbi answered, saying Nancy had danced for them.

"Let me ask you this. Did you have mutual sexual activity?"

"Yes."

"Objection, Your Honor."

"Overruled."

The prosecution had love letters that Doug had written to other women. Now Jorgensen presented these to Bobbi ostensibly so that she could identify the handwriting.

Doug objected again, saying that Jorgensen was wasting the jury's time playing "hanky-panky" with witnesses. By showing his letters, Jorgensen was trying to impeach his relationship with Bobbi and sway her from the truth, "knowing full well this woman happens to be the one woman in the world that I love."

Unmoved by Doug's sentimental outburst—delivered out of earshot of the jury but within Bobbi's—Judge Torres overruled the objection. Bobbi identified the handwriting as Doug's and was ordered to return the next morning.

But before court adjourned, Doug wrangled with Judge Torres: he had filed discovery requests in the Jack Murray murder; by ruling them irrelevant, said Doug, the judge was strapping his hands.

Judge Torres gave Doug a lecture: his life was on the line and the case was too complicated for him to handle. "You've made a mockery of what you've done so far. I don't know if you realize it. I am sitting here listening. You refuse to cross-examine on what is really relevant. You go into things that are constantly hurting you."

"The truth can't hurt me, Your Honor."

If Doug got a guilty verdict and the death penalty, he would have no one to blame but himself, the judge said. He could rant and rave all he liked. It was not going to bother Judge Torres.

"Well, obviously."

"I'm not like One-twenty-six." Judge Torres was referring to Judge Ringer. "You have got a different judge. You are not going to get to me."

"I didn't get to Ringer. Ringer's own lack of nerve got to him or he'd still be on this case."

"It isn't going to bother my nerves."

The trial had begun as a battle of wills between prosecutor and defendant, lawyer and client. It was about to turn, as well, into a battle between defendant and judge for control of the courtroom.

The next morning in court Doug was at his most tedious as, in his cross-examination, he took Bobbi from the airport to Carol Bundy's apartment, to the motel and his rental garage, then on the journey toward his parents' house.

"Now, after having left the garage on the motorcycle with me—I assume we locked the garage, is that correct—before we left?"

"You left the garage some time ago," said Judge Torres, wearying, "and you were traveling on the highway."

By the lunch break, Doug was still on the road.

That afternoon, Jorgensen questioned Bobbi about Doug.

"Would you say you're in love with him?"

"Oh, yes."

"Do you intend to marry him?"

"A proposal has been made, correct."

And Doug questioned Bobbi about Doug.

"You testified to the prosecutor's question that you are in love with me."

"Correct."

When court adjourned, Bobbi was free to return to Indiana, not exactly, one member of the jury thought, a shining example of midwestern values.

Before the coroners took the stand, several of Doug's coworkers from the Jergens factory testified. Carlos Ramos told about discovering the guns on top of the boiler; and Bernie Kupiec, Jergens' security guard, told of Doug's 2:06 A.M. arrival at the plant on the tenth of August, the date Carol claimed he had hidden the guns after the discovery of Jack's body.

Another colleague named James Finnegan told the court that Doug had asked him to "hot load" .25-caliber bullet casings for him by refilling them with gun powder.

"Hotter loads means deeper penetration," said Finnegan.

After the man who bought Carol's Buick described turning up a bullet while rummaging for loose change down the back seat, the trial ended its third week.

Things settled into a routine. At lunchtime, Jorgensen usually ate an apple and an orange at his desk, and Leroy Orozco returned to Parker Center. At night, Leroy chased down last-minute evidence and checked with frightened witnesses to make sure that they would be in court. His wife, he told Jorgensen, was ready to call out a hit man because of his hours.

As a young man, Orozco hadn't been a saint. But even though he was devoted to his family, he felt he still paid for it. Patsy Orozco knew he drank beer with colleagues to unwind after work. During trial, there was no time for beer, and his wife became suspicious.

"Where have you been?"

"Working."

"Hmm. You don't smell of beer."

On Fridays the trial was dark and the detective and prosecutor met at a small French restaurant not far from the courthouse to eat and discuss the case. Jorgensen, in his Friday uniform of tan slacks and sports jacket, fussed over the menu and asked the waiter how the fresh vegetables had been shipped. Paper trays, he felt, destroyed their flavor. (Even Jorgensen's pig-outs were carefully controlled. After a week of nothing but broccoli, he would allow himself twenty-four pancakes for Sunday breakfast.)

When his Friday lunch arrived—he didn't touch red meat—he organized the food carefully around his plate and prodded it with little stabbing motions of his fork. Only after ensuring that his wine was exactly room temperature and making a to-do over the tasting did he begin.

Orozco always ordered Budweiser.

"Will that be room temperature?" he made a point of asking the waiter.

"No, sir. I'm afraid the Budweiser is chilled."

"Well, all right. Give me chilled then."

The men exchanged no personal confidences; instead they focused on the work to be done. So far, both were pleased. The case was almost entirely circumstantial, but circumstances, they thought, led inexorably to Douglas Clark—if the jury were not fooled by the blond hair and the pin-striped suit.

Now it was time for the coroners. Two days after Gina Marano and Cynthia Chandler's bodies had been found, deputy medical examiner Dr. Eugene Carpenter autopsied them. The bullet wound to Gina Marano's left temple had indicated that the gun had been held fairly close to her head. And Cindy Chandler's chest wound had a "burn-bruise" appearance caused by a gun "jammed right into the skin." Carpenter had detected no barbiturates in either body, but in Cynthia Chandler .02 percent alcohol was present. This was meaningless, as the body makes its own alcohol as it decomposes.

There was no evidence for or against postmortem sex.

"Sexual intercourse after death will not leave bruising," Carpenter told the jury.

It was now the turn of Dr. Joseph Choi, the forensic pathologist who had autopsied Marnett Comer, Karen Jones, Exxie Wilson, and Jane Doe no. 18 (or Water Tower), whose body, like Cathy's, had not been claimed.

Jorgensen marked a series of grisly photographs of Comer's mummified body to be entered as exhibits and shown to the jury.

"What do you mean by 'mummified'?" he then asked the doctor.

"Decomposed and dehydrated. And it is very hard, like leather type of skin," Choi said in his heavy Chinese accent.

There had been three gunshot wounds in Marnett Comer's chest, with one bullet remaining in the spine. It also appeared to Choi that Comer's stomach had been slit with a knife.

As for the other victims, a stippling pattern on the flesh of Karen Jones's head indicated that the gun muzzle was six to twelve inches away when fired. The bullet had penetrated the temporal lobe of her brain and her pituitary gland.

Now Jorgensen entered photographs of Exxie Wilson's decapitated torso and head. About fifteen to twenty cuts had been necessary, the doctor estimated, postmortem or while Wilson was in a coma.

"There were not one flat cut. They had many flaps like a saw tool. . . . Just by looking at it alone they just matched," said Dr. Choi, who managed to chuckle every now and then in spite of the unpleasant matters of which he spoke.

Wilson's brain had been frozen, Choi testified, and "icy to cut." The head appeared to have been recently washed.

The doctor moved on to Jane Doe no. 18. Based on the suturing of bones in the skull, she had been about twenty years old, or maybe younger, Choi thought. Her skeleton had not become completely bleached, so the doctor thought that she had been dead one to two months when she was found on that late August day.

The trial had been going on for nearly a month. Over the last weekend in October, Doug was busy in the county jail library. On Monday, November 1, before the jury was brought in, he approached Judge Torres to ask that as he was restricted to his seat and not allowed to approach witnesses, the same restrictions should be applied to Robert Jorgensen. A trial was a melodrama, Doug said. The ability to move and gesture was part of the scheme. Restricting him and not the district attorney created in the jury's eyes a presumption of guilt and "extreme dangerousness."

He made a good point, and Judge Torres suggested he stand at the podium. Doug agreed and the podium was moved to the middle of the courtroom. He still would not be allowed to approach witnesses.

Doug made another motion: he wanted a law clerk appointed. But his motion was denied. If Doug felt he could not handle the case, he would reinstate Maxwell Keith and Penny Watson, Judge Torres suggested.

There was another matter, about which Doug was furious. Investigators had served search warrants on Veronica Compton's Washington cell and Joey Lamphier's apartment, where they had discovered incriminating letters from Doug. Joey, he now claimed, was his "legal runner," and he had been writing to Veronica Compton as a potential witness as well as for personal reasons. Jorgensen had made an illegal seizure of his privileged "work product," and he wanted him off the case.

"Do you feel your *pro per* status is just getting too much for you . . . ? You can't handle the case, is that what you're trying to tell me?" asked the judge again, ruling Doug's motion frivolous.

The jury and Dr. Choi were brought in. But Doug, invited to continue his cross-examination, was angry about his lost motions. He would stand mute, he declared, throughout the rest of the trial. Out trooped the jurors, who did not hear Judge Torres announce that by standing mute Doug had effectively renounced his self-representation.

Over Doug's protests that Judge Torres was violating his constitutional rights under the Sixth Amendment, Maxwell Keith and Penelope Watson were reinstated. Court was recessed until 1:30 so that they could prepare.

When court reconvened, Doug threatened to assault Maxwell Keith, calling him his "so-called attorney" and mischaracterizing him as "making every effort possible to gain a conviction."

If he attempted any such assault, he would be removed from court, warned Judge Torres. Just in case, the judge had loudspeakers waiting in the lockup so that Doug would be able to hear the proceedings.

"Mr. Keith is not my attorney and does not represent me. Jury, be aware of that," Doug said loudly as the trial resumed.

That night, Doug did some research and no longer felt that he had had the right to stand mute the day before. By the following morning, he was asking to have his *pro per* status reinstated.

"Well, it is obvious to the court that the defendant wishes to place the court in a dilemma," said Judge Torres. He felt Doug was more interested in making a mockery of the judicial system than in defending himself.

Jorgensen agreed. He had letters Doug had written to Carol declaring his intent to create reversible error in case of appeal. But he also believed that under California law, as long as Doug behaved, he had to be accorded the right to self-representation and perhaps even had the right to stand mute.

Judge Torres relented. He would reinstate Doug's *pro per* privileges, he said. But if he misbehaved or caused delays, they would be revoked again.

When they entered the courtroom, the jury had no idea what to expect. A new body? More repulsive testimony? Douglas Clark or Maxwell Keith for the defense? Another one of Douglas Clark's women, over whom he seemed to have some kind of mysterious power?

Caught up in the surrealistic world of the Sunset murders, some of the jurors were becoming desensitized to the violence. But that seemed to happen to everyone; prosecution, defense, police, early in a case of violent murder were appalled. But as time went on the unthinkable became routine, and research and preparation lent detachment so that it was possible to crack the occasional joke.

But Jorgensen, faced every day with the disagreeable personality of Douglas Clark and the force of his destructive manipulations, began again to feel oppressed. Clark was one of the most vicious sons of bitches he had ever seen. He hunted down and shot his victims for the sheer fun of it. His evil, Jorgensen had come to believe, was of monstrous proportions, and it troubled him that the world would probably never learn of it.

His presentation of evidence continued.

When criminalist Doreen Music was on the stand to testify about the kill bag in the Datsun and the three bullet holes in the passenger door, Jorgensen tried to enter into evidence twenty-nine rounds of ammunition, a pair of handcuffs, chains, straps, and a dildo taken from the northeast bedroom of the Verdugo apartment.

At the word "dildo," Douglas Clark objected, and there was a conference at the bench with the prosecutor claiming that the items were relevant because of the "fetishistic, ritualistic" nature of these sexual killings.

But there was no foundation, Doug argued, for admitting the sexual apparatus. So far all that had been established was that the victims were prostitutes and some semen had been found with two of them.

"I will sustain the objection at this point," said Judge Torres, regarding the straps, chains, and dildo.

The handcuffs and ammunition were admissible, but the shotgun was also declared irrelevant and the jury was admonished to disregard whatever else they might have seen the prosecutor take out of a box.

It was Wednesday, November 3, by the time Theresa was called to the stand, so furious over the child-molestation charges being severed that she could have shot someone. She had wanted her chance to confront Doug in public. Not being able to made her feel

as if what had happened to her was not important. She was fourteen now, her little-girl plumpness turning into a thick wall of fat
that would plague her into adulthood without providing the psychological or physical protection it symbolized.

That day, Penelope Watson was wearing a reddish-pink dress
and had taken some ribbing from Leroy, who was aware that all
except one of the victims had worn red or pink. From her distorted
perspective, Theresa assumed the lawyer was Doug's latest girlfriend. Then she took the oath and swore to tell the truth, the
whole truth, and nothing but the truth.

As Jorgensen drew from her the story of her drives with Doug
and his interest in prostitutes, her voice was small and whispery.

"What would he ask them to do?"

"Suck his penis."

"Did you one night while you were riding with Doug and Carol
hear Doug tell Carol that he wanted to pick up a rowdy prostitute?"

"Yes."

Doug spoke: "Objection, Your Honor. He's leading the witness
blatantly."

"Sustained. Don't lead the witness."

"Would you tell us what you heard Doug say to Carol regarding
picking up the prostitute?"

"He wanted to pick up a rowdy prostitute who would then pull
out her knife and he wanted to shoot her."

Jorgensen entered into evidence a top, jeans, and the "Greensleeves" music box, which Theresa said that Doug had given to
her.

During cross-examination Doug asked, ". . . Are you sure these
were gifts from me to you personally?"

"Yes."

"Rather than from Carol Bundy to you?"

"They were from you."

He wondered if they had discussed the gifts.

"I asked you why the music box was all scratched up," Theresa
said.

"And what was said about that, if I may blunder into it?"

"You said you found it in a parking lot."

Had she been in the car willingly the night she watched him
with a prostitute? Doug asked.

Theresa said yes. Because she knew that even if she were angry
now, she had been willing then.

When she stepped down, after an hour and a half on the stand, her mother was waiting for her. Theresa felt like a puppy. Good girl. Here's a biscuit and a pat on the head.

During his direct examination of Arleigh McCree, the officer in charge of the LAPD Firearms and Explosives Unit, Jorgensen elicited two compelling pieces of information. "Hot loading" bullets by remaking them and filling them with gunpowder and new primer would, said McCree, give a gun "more killing power." This confirmed the earlier claim by James Finnegan.

"If," asked Jorgensen, "a person knowledgeable in the use of guns wanted a pistol that could be used to fire into a head without having the bullet come out of the head, is there any particular weapon that would be preferable?"

"Objection, Your Honor. Calls for a conclusion and speculation."

Doug was overruled and McCree was allowed to answer.

"If one wanted to make sure the bullet remained in the individual's head, the .25 would certainly be a very good one for that purpose."

"Thank you. No further questions."

Criminalist Warren Loomis had obtained bloodstain samples from the ski painting and had analyzed blood from Gina Marano. Her O-type blood and enzyme characteristics were consistent with the stains on the painting, Loomis told the jury, adding that only about one in two hundred people would have shared the six enzyme characteristics in common between one of the spots and Marano's blood.

But Doug questioned Loomis about whether the blood on the back of the painting had been refrigerated before being placed there.

"Prior to? I have no idea."

"And the same question for the blood swatches on the floor of the garage?"

"I have no idea."

"You can't rule out refrigeration of any of that blood prior to being placed where it was?"

"That's correct."

"That is sufficient. Thank you. No further questions."

Doug was making the outlandish point that in order to frame him someone had stored Gina Marano's refrigerated blood and then placed it on the painting.

When the first reports of Doug's arrest had appeared on television, a frightened go-go dancer named Donielle Patton had telephoned the task force. She had worked at the Outrigger bar on

Van Nuys Boulevard, where Doug had been a regular visitor between August of 1979 and May of 1980.

His sex life was becoming boring, he had told Patton, and he was attempting "sadomasochism, leather, and physical abuse" to reach orgasm. He also visited Hollywood to pick up prostitutes. They made him feel superior because they were beneath him, he said.

So far, the only civilian testimony to suggest necrophilia as a motive had been Mindy Cohen's. But Doug had spoken of it to Patton as well, and the prosecution wanted her to tell the jury.

Patton was so fearful, that the night before she was to appear, Leroy Orozco went to her apartment to make sure she would show up. When he arrived, Patton was nude. Discreetly, he waited outside while she put some clothes on. Just as discreetly, because the impression that a go-go dancer might make on the jury was always of some concern to Leroy, he asked what she was going to wear the next day. She produced a miniskirt. That wouldn't do, Leroy told her.

The next day Patton testified in a skirt of moderate length. She also fingered a rosary. Judge Torres allowed Doug's remarks about prostitutes into the record. Patton was also allowed to testify that Doug had claimed to be bisexual and had offered her money if she would accompany him to bars to pick up men, then watch him have sex. (Patton had refused to go.) But Doug's sadomasochistic habits were irrelevant, Judge Torres declared.

In May 1980, Doug had come in looking excited, his eyes bright, according to Patton, who continued over Doug's objections. He had found a new way of reaching sexual gratification, he had told her: he slit women's throats while having sex with them and ejaculated on their bodies.

"Did he describe their behavior as he slit their throat?" asked Jorgensen.

"Objection as to relevance, Your Honor," said Doug.

"Overruled."

Donielle Patton asked for a Kleenex. Remembering what Doug had described made her cry. After a pause, over Doug's further objections, she continued.

"He said that—that, um, he got off to a jerking motion with their body. He found that to be a new high."

In May of 1980 the Outrigger had closed. But before it shut down Doug had offered Donielle Patton eight hundred dollars, which she declined, to take a trip with him and Carol Bundy. Later, in July and early August, Patton had spotted Doug on his motorcycle near her apartment and the store where she shopped. He just sat there and stared at her. When she called the police, they told her they could do nothing.

On cross-examination, Doug brought out that in Patton's original interview with the task force she had described him as fantasizing about slitting girls' throats.

She had used the word "fantasy," Patton explained, because she had not believed that anyone would commit a horrendous crime like that and tell someone about it.

Toward the end of Patton's testimony, Doug asked her why she had withheld some information until this trial.

She knew that Doug was receiving copies of her statements, said Patton. And she had been afraid, because at the time he had her address.

"Would it surprise you today, Donielle," said Doug, "that I have your current address and I have your current telephone number and I have had it ever since August the eleventh—"

Patton, terrified, again began to sob.

"No further questions," said Doug.

But he had not stopped in time, thought Orozco. Doug did not seem able to control himself for long enough to stop damaging his cause. It was a game, one of the court reporters thought, to see what he could do and get away with.

Jorgensen's case was beginning to wind down. Later the same day, Joey Lamphier was called, slim, brown-haired, and more conventionally attractive than Doug's other girlfriends. She would be the last of Doug's women to speak for the prosecution. During their three-year romance, Joey said, she had seen Doug wearing women's underpants. He also had women's clothing, including a black slip, gloves, panties, and one or two pairs of shoes.

Before trial, Joey had told Jorgensen about seeing Doug wearing women's underpants with a hole cut in the front through which he let his penis hang. Now she said she thought there had been one instance of that but she could not be sure.

But Jorgensen had letters Doug had written to Joey in which he accused her of not recalling certain things that could prevent his death. The word "recall" was in quotation marks: Doug had been asking Joey to lie for him. Why would she not bend and say she "recalled," he had asked? Could she face her conscience if he spent the rest of his life in prison?

"You are playing with putting me in jail forever," Doug had

written, "to die a horrible choking death eventually in the gas chamber. And shaming my family forever."

Joey's mythical future child had received a maudlin letter from Doug, similar to the one he had written to Tammy Spangler. In it, he described the baby's birth after his own death—which he suggested would be attributable to Joey's obstinacy in not "recalling."

In court, Joey confirmed for the prosecution that on June 16, the day of the Laurie Brigges call, Doug had called her at work to tell her he was at her apartment and about to use her phone. She also confirmed that Doug had owned lace-up work boots—described by Charlene Andermann—and had carried a small metallic gun.

Originally Joey, like Carol Bundy, had identified Doug's gun as being the nickel murder weapon. But today, she "recalled" that it was chrome. She had thought the gun was nickel, said Joey, until she went to a gun shop to check and realized her mistake.

Under Doug's recross-examination, Joey agreed with him that her statements had been "manipulated, twisted, and abused" by the district attorney.

"And right now you are lying in my behalf in any manner to try to rescue me from some evil deeds I did?" asked Doug.

"Absolutely not."

Doug turned to the day of the bloody car wash with Kevin Crouch. Joey now helpfully recalled Doug's arrival at her apartment that day between twelve and two with the Buick, which was not bloody or wet. They had bought gas at the corner Mobil station and she had given a receipt with the Buick's license plate on it to officers.

"You've never seen it again, have you?"

"No."

Furthermore, asked Doug, hadn't she told Officer Leroy Orozco more than he and his partner wrote down? And wasn't that what he, Doug, had been pressuring her to recall?

"Yes."

After Doug's recross, Jorgensen requested further examination on the grounds that Doug had opened up new matters.

Judge Torres refused. "Mr. Clark will do that forever," he said. "The court is simply not going to allow it. . . . Mr. Clark simply doesn't understand cross-examination. I have explained it to him over and over again."

Jorgensen was left without the opportunity to elicit the fact that the gas receipt had been for Joey's car and not the Buick. Joey Lamphier was excused.

Doug's original taped statement to the task force was important to the prosecution because it showed Doug to be lying. Judge Ringer had ruled the tape admissible, but during trial Doug reintroduced a motion to have it quashed. His motion was denied, and after half a day of wrangling over exactly which portions of the tape would be admitted, Detective Mike Stallcup took the stand to answer questions and read sections of the interrogation. The jury heard that Doug had described trolling for hookers in Hollywood. They also learned that he had identified Cindy Chandler's picture, had claimed to have her phone number in his wallet, and had said, "I really cared about that girl. She was a good kid. She wasn't a hard whore. She was just great. And when I read about it and I thought it was her, it scared the fuck out of me because she had my phone number."

Through the transcript, Jorgensen was able to let the jury know that Doug had denied knowing the whereabouts of the guns, had denied knowledge of the wooden box in which Exxie Wilson's head had been found, and had denied giving Theresa any gifts.

"Nothing," he had said. "Not a thing."

Often, when Doug appeared to be blundering through his cross-examinations, he was deliberately trying to bring in material the court considered irrelevant but that he considered either pertinent to his Jack Murray defense or detrimental to Carol Bundy's character.

As he questioned Mike Stallcup, Doug asked if the detective had seen photographs of Carol and himself with Theresa.

He had seen about fifty or sixty pictures with Doug, said Stallcup, and two of Carol Bundy.

Doug was leading up to part of his defense: he had feared Carol, who had threatened him with the photos to ensure his cooperation after Jack's murder.

That afternoon, the prosecution called its final witness, Leroy Orozco, there to let the jury know that he had found Cindy Chandler's name and phone number on the card in Doug's wallet. Jorgensen moved on to Orozco's search of the Verdugo-apartment file cabinet and his discovery of the Exxie Wilson newspaper article.

As he continued with other items for Leroy to identify, Doug objected and Jorgensen approached the bench.

"Your Honor," he said. "I have here a magazine, the significant portion of which is a comic strip entitled 'Hooker.' "

But dragging in his reading matter violated the First Amendment, Doug protested.

"I mean, you can't be held accountable for whatever books you read. I may read Harold Robbins or I may read any other best-seller out of *The New York Times* best-seller list."

"You wouldn't put this in with the best-sellers, would you?" asked the judge.

"Wait a minute. If you remember, in *The Carpetbaggers*, the man cut off a woman's breast and made a purse out of it. Anybody that reads that, can they bring that up in a rape or sex or robbery or any other crime?"

Doug's objection was sustained and the trial continued, with Doug questioning Orozco about the "Cindy" and "Mindy C." pencil notations in the wallet.

"Have you ever worked a criminal case involving forgery?" Doug asked.

"It's been some time back, but yes," said Orozco.

"You have. It's a whole lot easier to forge in pencil than it is in pen, is it not?"

"I have no idea."

Orozco did not share Jorgensen's feelings about Douglas Clark representing ultimate evil. He simply thought he was a jerk. Doug had consistently refused to provide a handwriting exemplar. After court one day, Orozco had trekked to county jail to try one more time. The sheriffs had brought Doug to the watch commander's office.

"Shouldn't you be home eating a taco?" he said to Orozco. Once again he had refused to give a writing sample.

The first of December was spent entering more items into evidence, with Jorgensen presenting another magazine that Orozco had found in Doug's filing cabinet.

"I have a paper clip," said Jorgensen, "on a cartoon strip which depicts a man who takes a chicken, decapitates the chicken, and masturbates into the dead carcass of the chicken. People who enjoy Charles Dickens have Dickens novels in their homes. . . . Likewise, the defendant, who has a vast collection of grotesque pornography in his home, can be understood to have an interest in that kind of material."

Judge Torres asked Jorgensen if he were trying to draw an inference to the Exxie Wilson murder. "That is just not reasonable," the judge said.

The chicken cartoon was not admitted.

There was additional learned discussion about a book called *Oralism*, which contained underlined passages about someone named

Hedvig who had applied her lips to a pistol which discharged, inundating her face and her bosom. There was a "double entendre" there, Jorgensen acknowledged. But even so, Doug's "morbid interests in firing pistols into women's heads during sexual encounters" made it relevant, he thought.

Oralism was not admitted, and Jorgensen moved on to the book of pornography that contained the picture of a head impaled upon a stick.

Doug stood before the bench leafing through the volume.

"I'm looking at the thing for context," he said.

The page with the severed head was admitted, as were photographs of Exxie Wilson's headless corpse and one of Doug, grinning, holding the Newberry's pine box during a session at Parker Center where he, Maxwell Keith, and one of his investigators had been allowed to view evidence. Doug had mailed the photos to Veronica Compton and they had been seized from her Washington cell.

Exhibit 225, seized on the search warrant at Joey Lamphier's apartment, was described as "the crotch part of a pair of underpants." Doug, arguing against the crotch being admitted, claimed that it was "work product" and protested that it had been sent by an "alive and well" girlfriend in New Zealand with the purpose of comparing secretions to those of alleged victims' underpants.

The crotch was allowed, as was a letter from Joey Lamphier to Doug telling him that she "would never turn against" him. She had also warned that Doug didn't stand a snowball's chance in hell against Jorgensen, and Doug complained that the remark was prejudicial.

Judge Torres disagreed. The jury had seen Keith and Watson's defense and watched Doug, he said. They could form their own opinion and agree with Ms. Lamphier. While he was on the subject, Judge Torres said again, why did Doug not let Keith and Watson take over the defense?

"Because they are going in one direction, and that leads straight to the gas chamber. And I'm going in the other direction, and that leads to the streets, whether you know it or not."

"They are your only chance to escape the gas chamber at this stage of the game, Mr. Clark."

The following morning, out of the presence of the jury, Doug argued over admitting incriminating letters he had written to Veronica Compton and Joey Lamphier. Judge Torres seized the moment to explain to him where, from his point of view, the trial stood.

"The evidence is overwhelming, beyond a reasonable doubt at this point, that you committed the six murders of these girls."

He pointed to the ballistics evidence tying the murders to Doug's gun, then to statements Doug had made in letters that Gina Marano bled a lot; that he knew Cindy; that freeway lights were visible from one of the dump sites; and that a body lay in the hills for thirty days.

"Nowhere else except from your writings do these things come out. So the only thing the prosecution has not established is the motive for you killing these six girls or your intent. These documents reveal that."

They were allowed in, including a letter referring to "Art Garfunkel balling (deceased) Theresa Russell" in the movie *Bad Timing*. But a letter reading "Places to Fuck Doug into Orbit"—they included an autopsy table and the hood of an Eldorado—was not.

Doug had also written a letter describing how he had obtained a court order to view evidence. His goal had been to get his fingerprints on the sex books seized from the Verdugo apartment, rendering the preexisting prints useless as evidence.

" 'Failure to preserve.' they were *handled* by *me*. (neat huh?? . . .)"

The letter was admitted.

After placing the 231st exhibit into evidence, the People rested their case.

It was December 2. Doug began his opening statement at ten minutes past three, saying that the Sunset murders case was "a case of twos": two double murders, two guns, and two Carol Bundys.

"There's a Carol Mary Bundy and there's a Carol Ann Bundy. And Carol Mary Bundy is not quite sure at times, I believe, which she is."

Her confusion had begun, he said now, early in 1980 when Ted Bundy married a woman named Carol Ann:

"Carol Mary Bundy in California, clear across the continent, launched with her lover, Jack Murray, this string of murders."

Jeannette Murray would take the stand and the jury would learn, Doug told them, of Carol and Jack's "intense love relationship" that lasted until the night Carol pulled the trigger of Doug's gun and shot Jack in the head. Carol had killed Jack and had tried to frame Doug for that murder, but she had not succeeded.

Lydia Crouch and others would testify that he and Carol had not been lovers, Doug went on, and evidence would be introduced to show that Carol and not he had been at the Verdugo apartment a few minutes away from where Karen Jones had been found on June 23.

"You'll learn that in fear of arrest for Jack Murray's murder, I played right into the hands of the two murderers who did these crimes. Thank you."

The following Monday, Doug stood before Judge Torres demanding a list of items from Jack Murray's van.

They were not relevant, said Judge Torres, unless Doug could call a witness who would make them so.

As usual, Doug lost his temper. "This railroad train of yours is going to have to come to a screeching halt. These items are relevant. I'm asking for them to be brought over here."

He wanted the handcuffs found in the Verdugo apartment.

"Denied."

But the handcuffs had already been admitted into evidence by the prosecution. Doug crowed, a child in a pin-striped suit. "You just ruled them irrelevant. Now what are you going to do about it? You ruled them irrelevant."

"I'm waiting for your next item is what I'm going to do. I'm not going to even give you an answer on such a silly request as that."

" 'Silly request' is the trap snapping shut on your ankle. You just stepped in it, Your Honor."

But that morning was a victory for Doug. Because of his discovery motion, a total of forty-three new items were made available to the defense, as well as other evidence mentioned in the Chandler/ Marano and Exxie Wilson property reports. The victory, of course, was limited. Because Jack Murray had not been the Sunset killer, the items would bring Doug no closer to proving his own innocence.

Doug's first task was to try to undermine the credibility of Charlene Andermann. A Cedars-Sinai nurse presented a medical form stating that Andermann had said she was in a motel room with a client when she was stabbed. (Later a Cedars-Sinai doctor confirmed that Andermann said she was attacked in a car.) The nurse was followed by a substance-abuse counselor who testified that in July 1980, Charlene Andermann had picked someone from a lineup and "made a statement that she was sure that was the man" who attacked her.

Later Doug questioned Anthony Guarino, the investigating detective in the Andermann case, asking him, "Has Miss Andermann given you any false names during the course of your investigation?"

Yes, said Guarino. She had used the name "Goldstein" at the hospital.

"It was a Cedars-Sinai Hospital," Guarino went on to explain. "She thought she had to be Jewish to enter."

The courtroom erupted in welcome laughter.

A little after twelve o'clock, out of the presence of the jury, Judge Torres again warned Doug about his manner of questioning witnesses.

"My patience is running out with you, Mr. Clark. I am telling you that . . . I am telling you now that my patience is running out."

"I didn't think you were capable of being unbiased in this case, and—"

He was capable of running the courtroom, said Judge Torres. And he was also capable of stripping Doug's *pro per* privilege.

"You keep threatening. You keep threatening that. Are you trying to intimidate me? Well, you goddamn can't do that. You have threatened me, you have browbeaten me. Will you just back off and do your job?"

"All right. Your *pro per* privileges are revoked. I want to see the attorneys at one-thirty."

He wasn't a psychiatrist, Judge Torres said after lunch. But he felt Doug was unable to admit that he couldn't handle the case on his own. Instead he had misbehaved so that the judge would take it away from him. And unless he apologized, his *pro per* privileges would remain revoked.

"You are asking me now to kneel or kiss your feet, and I don't think I will be doing that," said Doug.

"You won't apologize?"

"I don't feel the court has an apology coming. I feel I have an apology coming."

The defendant had dug a hole and buried himself, said Judge Torres, and he didn't really think Keith and Watson should come to his rescue by taking over.

"You're wishy-washy . . . ," Doug accused, saying that Judge Torres was looking for a way out of his "ridiculous ruling" through an apology. The court was incompetent, insisted Doug, and he could not falsely back down from his opinion.

Maxwell Keith and Penelope Watson were ordered to step back for the defense, and Jorgensen was apprised of the new circumstances.

He wanted to reopen his case, said Jorgensen. He wanted to present another witness.

"I understand she's been subpoenaed over here by the defendant, and I think she's in the lockup here today. It's Carol Bundy."

25

AT LAST THE PROSECUTION'S SELF-ANOINTED STAR WITNESS WAS GET-
ting a chance to shine. The only thing was, Jorgensen did not have
to reopen his case. She was about to testify for the defense. Obviously hoping that Carol would commit perjury for him, Doug had
subpoenaed her and Maxwell Keith decided to follow through.

As Carol took the stand, her latest attorney, Dvorah Markman, at
hand, some courtroom observers thought that it was with a certain
amount of vindictive glee.

As, over the next few days, Maxwell Keith drew out the story
of her affairs with Doug and Jack Murray, Doug glared in Carol's
direction. He was enraged to see her dressed in a beige linen suit
with a bow-tied blouse followed by a series of what struck him as
Mother Hubbard outfits. She was the picture of middle-class stability as she sold him down the river.

Immediately before her testimony, Carol had been given use im-
munity by the district attorney's office, which meant that if she
told the truth, it could not be used against her at her own trial.

And under direct examination by Maxwell Keith, Carol told everything, beginning with meeting Doug at Little Nashville, her at-
traction to him, their shared fantasies of capturing and subduing
young women, and her growing knowledge that this was more
than Douglas Clark's dream. She also told about Jack Murray and

the money that he had stolen from her safety-deposit box. Alternately she wept, laughed, and pulled herself up into a haughty pose of detached discomfort over the unseemly nature of the subjects under discussion.

Wanting to reveal the Carol Bundy beneath the prim middle-class facade, Keith peppered her with questions and got results.

"Did you ever see a head without a body in the Verdugo apartment?"

"Yes, I did."

Keith wondered if Carol had played with the head.

"I handled the head and played with it, yes."

"Made the head up."

"Mr. Clark wanted some cosmetics on it. He had—"

"I didn't ask you what he wanted. I asked you if you made the head up."

"I applied cosmetics to the head."

"Did that make the head look like a doll?"

"Yes."

"Did you later dispose of the head?"

"Yes."

Had she considered herself mentally ill at the time? Keith asked.

"I object," said Jorgensen. "That is irrelevant and calls for a conclusion on the part of the witness."

"Sustained."

Keith also wondered if Carol had been present when Wilson's head was cut off the body.

"No, I was not."

Doug's contention was that Carol had cut off Exxie Wilson's head as well as Jack's. Jorgensen had asked the task force to investigate both decapitations. Based on the coroner's evidence, he and Orozco were satisfied that they were performed by different people. The points of decapitation, the types of knives, and the cuts themselves varied. But as the Murray charges were no longer part of Doug's case, Carol was not allowed to answer questions about Jack's murder.

Keith moved on, asking Carol if Doug had "treated her like dirt."

He had, she said.

And at times had she been "mesmerized by his charm"?

"Mr. Clark had virtual total control over my personality and my behavior, my wants, my desires, my dreams while I was with him."

"And how did Mr. Clark have total control over your behavior, your wants, your desires, your dreams and character?"

"Sir, if I knew that, I probably wouldn't be here."

Had Doug used anything other than the power of his personality to gain control over Carol? Keith wondered, implying that Carol could have walked away.

"It was his personality or traits of his personality that blended with traits of my personality that was responsible for the situation," Carol said, explaining that she was a masochist who fantasized about humiliation and pain.

Their relationship had been "fairly normal" in the beginning, though, Carol told the courtroom.

"With the possible exception that Mr. Clark is probably the most extraordinary lover I've ever had in my life . . . How can I say this delicately? The man is talented. He's extremely good in bed."

She became kittenish. Carol was, in fact, not unlike one of her own plump, Garfield cat cartoons, whose large, round eyes resembled hers behind her glasses.

"I'm sorry, Doug" she said. "I don't mean to embarrass you. . . ."

Carol continued. There had been occasions when one or the other of them would perform oral sex, and the recipient of the act would call a friend or a random phone number to "talk about sexy things."

Suddenly, though, Carol seemed overcome with coyness. "You're embarrassing me asking these questions," she said.

"Oh, come on now," said Maxwell Keith.

"Your Honor," said Jorgensen. "I object to counsel's editorial comments."

"I don't think that was an unreasonable comment," said Judge Torres.

Carol dropped several bombshells for the jury, including the fact that Doug had given her a pair of bullets with which to make earrings. She also told of Doug's claim that he had taken Exxie Wilson's head in the shower and masturbated with it. She thought it was a fantasy, she said, going on to explain that another of his fantasies was having a young woman straddle him while Carol shot her in order for Doug to feel the death spasms.

"And were you present at any of the necrophiliac activities?"

"At no time did I ever see him perform sexual acts with a dead person, no."

"Did John Murray ever do that in your presence?"

"No."

"Did Mr. Murray ever fantasize in your presence regarding sexually oriented matters?"

"No. Mr. Murray had no imagination."

Surely Maxwell Keith wanted the jury to hear the word "fantasy" as often as possible. The more they heard it, the more likely they would be to think that Doug and this mentally ill woman had fantasized committing the murders. But the jury had already heard that semen was found in Exxie Wilson's throat. Carol's story was credible.

As she told more, it became clear that what she said was supported by the evidence: the bloody garage floor; the slit in Marnett Comer's belly; and Gina Marano's blood on the painting, about which Doug had laughed.

All this was in front of the jury already, but it had lacked a story line and a motive, which Carol gave, carefully calling the victims "young ladies" and referring to Exxie as "Miss Wilson." Doug didn't like it if the girls gave bad blow jobs, Carol said; Doug didn't like it if the girls were rude; Doug didn't like it if they used prophylactics. And so Doug had killed them. Just as, he had claimed, he had murdered about fifty people since he was seventeen.

Maxwell Keith continued to play up the idea that this was make-believe. "When Doug told you this, your reaction was, this is just another nut running around telling me stories. Is that correct?"

"I thought it was somebody who had an ego problem, was trying to build up his sense of self-esteem."

Did she believe, asked Keith, that she was losing her mind?

"I object. That's irrelevant. Incompetent."

But Jorgensen was overruled.

"My own particular opinion is that for many years I've been emotionally and psychologically unstable. During periods where things are relatively calm, I can cope well, I'm able to speak well, and appear on a normal basis. When conflict and stress reach a certain point, then I lose contact with reality. And no, I do not believe under such circumstances that I am sane. . . . At this moment I'm fairly stable. I cannot tell you that next week I will be."

Through her new lawyer, Carol had changed her not-guilty plea to not guilty by reason of insanity. Maxwell Keith raised the issue but was stopped from asking questions about any psychiatric examinations Carol might have had.

Arguing with Judge Torres that if psychiatric reports corroborated what Carol said about herself, they could be relevant to the defense, Keith said, "There's a well-known psychiatric diagnosis known as folie à deux, which means that when two people get together who are mentally unbalanced, the two of them just make each other worse by reason of their unfortunate condition."

A good point, Judge Torres thought. But best kept for the possible penalty phase of the trial, during which the jury would determine the sentence.

On December 13, Douglas Clark appeared in the courtroom in jail clothes, fuming. When he had lost his *pro per* privileges he had also lost his daily showers and his court-ordered telephone calls. He had not been able to phone Maxwell Keith, he complained. The week before, his cell had been searched and his legal notes seized. He had refused to dress today because he had not showered, and he blamed everything on Judge Torres.

"It's open season on Clark in that jail. I don't get shit over there and it's your doing. . . . I'm not going to play games with you. I'm not going to sit here and have the record not reflect what you are doing."

Ignoring his abuse, the judge agreed to send Doug back to shower and change. Court would resume at 1:30 P.M., he said. But Doug continued to argue, calling Judge Torres a "petty little twit" and demanding, "What about the telephone calls?"

"Nothing else is changed. . . . Take him out."

"I don't know if I'm going to go along with this."

"I don't care."

"You are an asshole. You know that? You push a man just so far. You ought to be defending parking tickets in Tijuana."

"Bring the jury out."

Due to circumstances beyond anyone's control, the jury learned, they had the morning off to finish their Christmas shopping.

In his opening statement, Doug had stated that the dates of the Chandler/Marano and Wilson/Jones murders corresponded to two double murders that occurred during Washington State killer Ted Bundy's murder spree. But even though Maxwell Keith would not be able to produce the witnesses or evidence that Doug had promised, with his first question of the afternoon he followed up on the idea of Carol having a Ted Bundy fixation. Doug, showered, was at the defense table.

"Mrs. Bundy . . . have you ever used the name Carol Ann Bundy?"

"No, I have not."

"Have you ever thought yourself to be Carol Ann Bundy?"

She was hardly aware of Ted Bundy's existence, said Carol, until after her arrest.

A few minutes later, she became upset discussing her overwhelming "sense of guilt and responsibility."

"Was it your overwhelming sense of guilt and responsibility that caused you to laugh when you were describing killings to the police on August 11, 1980?"

Her behavior had been inappropriate, but she was out of control, said Carol primly. "I've already stated that during times of extreme stress that I tend to lose track of reality. . . ."

"Was it your overwhelming sense of guilt that caused you to tell the police on August 11, 1980, that it was fun to kill people?"

"You already asked that question, and I handled it as well as I can."

"No, I asked you if it was your overwhelming sense of guilt that caused you to laugh and giggle about killing people. You answered that. The next question is, was it your overwhelming sense of guilt that caused you to tell the police what fun it was?"

Carol's lawyer objected, was overruled, and Carol was allowed to answer.

"I would not say that a sense of guilt made me giggle or laugh. Killing is not fun. It wasn't fun to me then. . . . If I thought killing was fun, I certainly don't think that I would be telephoning the officers asking them to come and arrest me. . . . I do know that the statements that I made to the police regarding Mr. Clark's activities and my involvement with Mr. Clark was accurate. I did not falsely accuse Mr. Clark of murders, nor did I falsely confess to murders."

Jorgensen had a little smile on his face. Carol was doing well, Orozco thought. She was doing everything he and Jorgensen had hoped for.

On August 11, Carol had told police that she thought Doug wanted to be caught, and Keith asked her the basis of her belief.

Well, understand, she didn't have a great deal of criminal experience, answered Carol. But it seemed to her that "a criminal who wanted to succeed would not select as a partner an obese, half-blind, mentally erratic woman who happens to be diabetic and rather unpredictable . . . especially someone who also has a compulsion to be honest."

"Who has a compulsion to be what?"

"A compulsion to be honest."

"Do you also have a compulsion to kill?"

"Objection," said Carol's lawyer.

"Overruled."

"No."

In court Carol had said that Exxie Wilson's head was on the kitchen sink when she first saw it, and Maxwell Keith quoted the transcript of her original statement to police in which she said: "He goes to the freezer and there's this round plastic bag. Now we had already discussed the possibility of doing it. And I looked at that round plastic bag and I thought, Oh, shit."

"Did you say that?"

"Yes."

Hadn't Carol told the court on a previous day that she was repulsed and revolted by Exxie's head?

"I was essentially turned off of it, moderately repulsed. I wasn't so revolted to run into the bathroom and throw up, as you asked the other day."

When Doug told her he was going out to "take care of business," did she tell him not to? Keith asked.

"I don't think I said, 'No, Douglas, that's being a bad boy. You mustn't do it.' "

"Well, what did you say?"

"Probably nothing at all."

Carol had told the task force that the murders became "a joint venture where we were both enjoying it," and Maxwell Keith threw this at her now.

She had not considered it a joint venture to begin with, Carol said. But toward the end, she had.

"Not that I was a willing participant, but that I had been brought into it and I was trapped in the situation and there wasn't any way of getting out. And so I was a reluctant partner. I was in it—I wasn't forced in it by having a gun at the back of my head specifically, but I felt pressured to do it."

There was a long pause, then Maxwell Keith said, "That's a lie, isn't it, Mrs. Bundy?"

"No, it is not a lie."

To Jorgensen's growing annoyance, Keith kept referring to the uncharged Jane Doe no. 28/Cathy murder without stating which murder he was discussing.

"Do you find it difficult to get a dress off a dead girl?" Keith asked.

"I've only done it one time. It was difficult. . . ."

256

"When you were taking the dress off this dead girl, were you very cool and calm?"

"I think stunned is a better word for it. I was not excited or as nervous as I would have anticipated being. I was just kind of numb more than anything else."

Effectively, Keith was chipping away at Carol's mask of propriety. At the bench, Jorgensen expressed "outrage" at his mode of questioning, which, the prosecutor suggested, Keith "clearly intended to be argument to the jury and not to elicit any meaningful testimony."

"I take that as a tremendous compliment, sincerely," said Maxwell Keith, aware that he was getting to the prosecutor.

"I think it is a compliment of your ability, I'm not disputing that," agreed Judge Torres. But if he heard any objections regarding Jane Doe no. 28 or Jack Murray, he would sustain them. The question about Carol taking a dress off a dead girl was stricken and the jury admonished to disregard it.

By the time Jorgensen began his cross-examination, Carol had spent three and a half days on the stand. Again he led her through the story of how she met Doug, her purchase of the guns at his request, his lie about being an "ex-felon" who could not own firearms, and the test firing of the Ravens into a telephone book at Balboa Park.

"Did he tell you that he wanted a woman to kill for him?"

"Yes, he did."

"Did he tell you who that woman was to be?"

"Yes."

"Who was that?"

"He said that I would kill for him."

Jorgensen was also able to let the jury know through Carol's testimony that two days before she took the stand she and Doug had ridden on the same sheriff's bus from the court building to the prisoner holding area. Doug had asked her to say her name was Carol Ann Bundy. He told her that it would bolster her NGI plea.

There was something pathetic about Carol to people who watched her testify. She was drab. Her eagerness to recount details of her erotic life with Doug made her seem the mesmerized nurse-housewife that she and Doug had planned to present. He was a dominant personality, she said now. And in some of their sexual byplay she viewed herself as his slave and wanted to see him as her master. "In the early and midterm part of our relationship, there was much exploration of bondage, the emotional-psychological aspects of this. . . . I wanted him to have control, total control of me and the relationship."

Jorgensen turned to details of the "Nick" incidents in late April or early May, in which Doug had claimed to have killed the hit man with whose girlfriend he had been having oral sex. Carol remembered Doug telling her that he and the woman had struggled for the knife, cutting her hand, and there had been a pause of some kind during which he asked her about her family.

"Had anyone disclosed to you the contents of the testimony in this trial on Charlene Andermann?"

"No, I'm not aware of anybody's testimony other than my own."

Carol was in the middle of the story about the Chandler/Marano murders when Jorgensen asked her if Doug had described Cindy Chandler's clothing.

Doug objected, saying the question was vague.

"Mr. Clark," said Judge Torres, "you are not supposed to be making these objections. Mr. Keith—"

"Your Honor, regardless. Objection: vague as to when."

"Mr. Keith, you better tell Mr. Clark that if he doesn't keep quiet, tell him what the court is going to do."

"I think my attorney ought to get his act together."

"Bailiff, take him out of the courtroom."

The jury was also removed, one of them remarking after the trial that watching the bickering between counsel and defendant was like watching a television show.

Half an hour later, outside the presence of the jury, Judge Torres asked Maxwell Keith to find out if Doug planned to behave or to disrupt things and listen from the lockup.

Keith was not his representative, protested Doug. He had had enough and he wanted to return to jail.

Once again he was removed from court.

The defendant would stay in the lockup, said Judge Torres, and Penelope Watson should go in every half hour to see if he had changed his mind.

"Please don't do that to her," Maxwell Keith said.

"Wants to make sure I don't nod off," said Penelope Watson.

The jury was brought back to the courtroom to listen while Judge Torres explained the situation: "As you can see, Mr. Clark has decided not to be present during these proceedings, and he can hear everything that is being said in the lockup where he is at this time."

There came a loud pounding sound on the courtroom wall.

"As witnessed by his acknowledgment," Judge Torres said, to the accompaniment of hearty laughter in court.

"Let's proceed."

There was further banging.

"Oh, dear heavens," said Carol Bundy from the witness stand, as if she had never before been exposed to the slightest hint of violence.

Rage over Carol Bundy's testimony, the jail's lack of cooperation with his attempts to prepare his defense, and the stripping of his *pro per* privileges, could have been the reason for Doug's growing lack of control. Maxwell Keith would claim that his client could not hear the proceedings. But years later, Doug would say that rather than being out of control, he deliberately had goaded Judge Torres to get him to reveal bias.

For whatever reason, the pounding on the wall continued, with the judge cautioning Jorgensen to stay near the microphone so that the defendant could hear. During lunch recess, Doug was brought handcuffed into court.

"What's this bullshit," he said to Judge Torres, "having me brought out here in manacles, you asshole?"

"All right, gag him. Sit him in the chair and gag him."

"What's the cause of this?"

"Sit him in the chair and gag him."

"Oh, you're so full of shit you stink."

"Put the gag on."

Doug proceeded to call Judge Torres a "sleazy cocksucker," "a Tijuana taxi driver," and "a gutless worm."

A blond and muscular bailiff came into the court carrying a leather gag, which he placed over Doug's face to the delight of Leroy Orozco, who clapped, and the distress of Maxwell Keith, who later registered an objection and declared it "indecorous." Bob Jorgensen shook Leroy's hand.

Gagged, Doug kicked at a table, then kicked again, overturning it. "Get some help up here," cried Judge Torres. "Get some help up here, get some help up here."

Now two bailiffs entered the courtroom to restrain Doug and fix the gag so that he could not be heard. One of them, imaginatively, produced a sanitary napkin with which to stifle the curses.

"The court is not going to put up with this nonsense. He is not going to come into this courtroom, insult me and call me—"

259

"Fuck you, Judge," came the muffled sound from behind Doug's gag as he was once more removed to the lockup.

That afternoon, Jorgensen introduced the subject of Doug's attempts to get Carol to commit perjury.

Earlier that year, Carol explained, she had been feeling angry toward the district attorney's office and had given Doug two suggestions about how to implicate Jack Murray with respect to Gina Marano's blood on the painting. One was to say that the painting had been at the Lemona Avenue apartment instead of the garage. The other was to say that she had borrowed Doug's garage key, which Jack had then stolen.

"He wanted me to come up with an idea, some way that would frame Jack Murray for that particular instance."

The suggestions were untrue, said Carol, and Jack Murray was in no way involved in any murders that she knew about.

Doug wanted the jury to hear the tape of Carol's police interrogation, and Maxwell Keith was looking forward to seeing Carol squirm. On Monday, December 20, the jury listened, following a transcript, as Carol told the story of Doug and her murder of Jack; her sorrow about how abruptly her "career" as a killer had ended; and the planned defense that she was just a Valley housewife under the spell of a charming man.

Broda had asked her if she were remorseful.

"I don't know if I can put it that way . . . ," Carol had said as if it were an odd question. "I don't know if you can call it remorse or guilt or—any of those things. But I'm—just wasn't handling the situation. I'm falling apart. . . . I'm in love with somebody who's a mass murderer."

What "pissed" her off to the point where she decided to tell the police, Carol had said, was Doug's telling her that she was a motor mouth and that she was going to screw up.

"So this isn't a screwup. This was my own choice and voluntarily. I mean, this wasn't because I slipped up and was careless about something that I'd said or done."

Too, Doug had been switching to hitchhikers because the street girls were uptight. "Ultimately, he may just decide to go to just ordinary straight women for no particular reason." Eventually, said Carol, he was going to hurt her. He had fantasized about killing Joey, whom he supposedly loved, and about having Bobbi straddle him while Carol blew her away.

"If he can fantasize about that sort of thing, other than his word, what guarantee do I have that I'm going to see tomorrow?"

On the Betsy/Claudia and Kilgore tapes, Carol had made ambiguous statements that seemed inconsistent with her August 11 arrest tape, and Maxwell Keith wanted the jury to hear them. Doug had killed "probably about twelve or thirteen" people since she had known him, she had told Kilgore; she had been involved with eight or nine of them, including "the two girls, the one that he cut the head off with: I played around with the head with him on that and the fat girl that he dumped off near NBC studios." She had also used the word "we" when she discussed the killings.

Judge Torres had allowed the August 11 interrogation tape but would have refused to play it if the request had come from a less experienced lawyer than Maxwell Keith, he said. The material was simply too damaging to the defense. So, he felt, were the Betsy/Claudia and Kilgore tapes. He ruled against admitting them.

In the afternoon, Maxwell Keith confronted Carol with a letter in which she had described her "damnable reputation" for telling the truth.

"Well, let me assure you of one thing: I never tell the truth. You can believe me," Carol had written. "Actually, I'm the same as everyone else. I'll lie through my teeth when it suits me."

In another letter she had criticized Doug's long hair and goatee, which she had seen on television. A middle-class jury would love that, she had mocked.

"Shit, if it happens we have to go against each other, remember, I look innocent. Impression is worth as much as facts.[. . .] Clean up. You generally were cleaner than me. Don't change now."

Discussing strategy, Carol had told Doug that in exchange for help at her own trial, she would give him enough "damaging material" to destroy her "and send Jorgie to studying his asshole looking for nervana."

But when Keith asked Carol about how she would benefit from her testimony, she told of rejecting the prosecution's offer of a plea bargain.

"If both people are responsible in a situation, I think that both people should face their responsibilities. . . . I couldn't exchange one minute of Doug's life to save one minute of my own."

On recross Jorgensen asked Carol what she meant by her statement, "I never tell the truth, you can believe me."

It came from a "Star Trek" episode, she said. It was a joke. A paradox that Captain Kirk and Mr. Spock had programmed into a computer in order to drive it mad.

On the twenty-first of December, court broke for the Christmas holiday. Carol sent a card to Judge Torres.

"Inappropriate? I hope not," she wrote, going on to say how much she admired the judge's "presence" and "personality." Alas, she said, what a shame that they could never share the delight of a cup of coffee.

"Merry Christmas, Carol B."

After the holiday, Doug returned with a toothache and threatened to "raise Ned" if the trial continued while he was in pain. In front of the jury, he called Judge Torres a "jerk," a "goddamned asshole," "a spineless bastard," "a fat cat," "an asshole," and a "stinking faggot."

Later the same day, Carol Bundy was allowed to step down after testimony that had been devastating to the defense. Where could they go next? Orozco and Jorgensen wondered. From the beginning, they had debated whether or not Doug would testify.

"He can't," said Jorgensen.

"He's got to," said Leroy. "To tell his side of things."

"May we approach the bench?" Maxwell Keith asked. ". . . may the court please, my next witness will be the defendant, Mr. Clark."

Keith had advised Doug that it was not in his best interests to take the stand; Doug had insisted.

"Oh boy. We're going to have some fun now," Jorgensen said to Orozco. It was the face-to-face combat that Jorgensen had been waiting for. But first there was direct examination by Maxwell Keith, during which Doug, alternately arrogant and folksy, predictably tried to evade the evidence with elaborate plot twists and contradictions.

As he could hardly have denied the second Mindy Cohen phone call—it showed up on the Verdugo-apartment bill when Carol had been at work—Doug now admitted making it. But he said he'd been seeking Cindy Chandler to take her to his brother's wedding. Out of "common courtesy," he had given his name to Mindy. When she became alarmed, he had hung up. He had also called Laurie Brigges and Mindy's lawyer boyfriend, Mark. But only at Carol's suggestion, when he had been looking for furniture movers.

What had he been doing on June 11, the day Cynthia Chandler and Gina Marano were killed? Keith asked.

"Everything I did that day? Well, I presume I breathed, I probably ate. . . . I can tell you what I didn't do. . . . I didn't dance in the Bolshoi Ballet, and I didn't murder anybody."

Lydia Crouch had things wrong. He was already at her apartment when she arrived home on the night of the Chandler/Marano murders. Carol, he theorized, had stored Gina Marano's blood and squirted it on his ski painting. After Jack Murray was dead, sensing that Carol was going to frame him for the Sunset murders, he put the guns in his desk at work and had no idea how they got up on the ledge by the boiler. He had not moved into the Verdugo apartment until June 27, he had never seen Exxie Wilson's head, and he certainly had not killed her or Karen Jones.

"Was Carol possessive of you?" asked Maxwell Keith.

"Not quite an accurate term, no."

"What would be an accurate term, do you feel?"

"Possibly jealous and vindictive, I would say. Jealous of my relationships and vindictive towards my other female friends."

Maxwell Keith was curious about the blood in the Buick, so Doug told his dying-cat story.

". . . I put the cat in the car, [it] kind of dragged itself halfway under the seat and croaked on the way between Joey Lamphier's alley and Vineland Animal Hospital."

Was Doug sure that the Cynthia Chandler he had known was the same girl who had been killed? asked Keith.

Doug gave a foolish answer. When he saw the picture of her alive, he had not been sure, he said. But when he saw the crime scene and coroners' photographs, he was "fairly darned sure."

For the night of the Charlene Andermann attack, Doug produced an alibi. He had been out that evening with Joey and had written checks to a dancer.

"It was my habit to write a complimentary statement of some sort under the payee section, such as, 'lovely lady,' or 'terrific girl,' or 'foxy chick,' or whatever."

Two ten-dollar checks were offered as evidence, one of them endorsed to "one really fantastic lady." The dancer herself, though, never appeared for the defense.

As an explanation for why he had moved back in with Carol Bundy to the Verdugo apartment when he claimed to find her "disgusting," Doug told the jury about Carol's behaving like a "hot and cold running maid."

They had their differences, he said, but they ironed them out.

"She had to assure me that she would cease and desist in the

263

molesting of [Theresa] . . . ; that the new apartment would be separate bedrooms, separate bathrooms, and separate refrigerators."

He had also insisted that Carol return all the photographs she had taken of him in compromising positions with the child. She said she would, but did not.

It was he and not Carol who had been staying at the Lemona apartment the night of the Wilson/Jones murders, Doug went on. After studying the phone records, he had realized that Carol had called him from Verdugo Avenue and awakened him in the middle of the night.

"I rose, stumbled out into the front of the apartment, found the phone, picked it up, and there was no one there."

By Wednesday, December 29, the trial had been going on for nearly three months. At the end of the day, Judge Torres joked, "Are we in session tomorrow?"

There was a collective cry of "no" from the jury.

"Have a Happy New Year, all of you. Have a safe and happy New Year."

26

THE NEXT YEAR WOULD BEGIN WITH JORGENSEN'S CROSS-EXAMINATION of Doug, for which he had been waiting eagerly. Beforehand, Orozco and the prosecutor held a strategy session. Go for the throat, Orozco advised. Start right off, bam: "Have you ever worn women's panties, Mr. Clark?"

Jorgensen considered it. That might alienate the jury, he decided. He didn't want them to think he was trying to bury Doug.

"They probably hate him as much as we do by now," Orozco said.

When trial resumed on January 3, Jorgensen decided instead of attacking to dig at Doug to get him to reveal himself.

"Mr. Clark," he said, "do you remember what the weather was like on the twenty-second of June, 1980?"

"Clear, sunny, approximately eighty-five degrees at one-twenty, two o'clock in the afternoon."

"In 1980, what was your annual income?"

Instantly Maxwell Keith objected on the grounds of irrelevance and was sustained.

The lawyers approached the bench. Jorgensen felt that Doug was lying about giving big tips in dancer bars. He also felt sure Doug had written the dancer checks to create a false alibi.

"I'm confident," Jorgensen said, "that I make considerably more money than the defendant, and I can't afford to go tipping anybody twenty dollars a night."

"Maybe you don't have the same priorities he does," Judge Torres said.

"That's probably true."

Jorgensen rephrased his question and Doug said that he made "about twenty, twenty-two, twenty-four thousand."

"How much money did you make from insurance fraud, Mr. Clark?"

Maxwell Keith moved for a mistrial and was denied.

"Was the burning of the Pacer involved in any way in insurance fraud, Mr. Clark?"

"Not unless Jack Murray collected on it after he burned it."

"Jack Murray burned it?"

"You bet your buttons he burned it."

"Jack Murray is dead, isn't he?"

"You bet."

Jorgensen wanted to impeach Doug's statements that he had no interest in sadomasochism. Over Maxwell Keith objecting that the trial was "not a course in Krafft-Ebbing," Jorgensen read aloud from Doug's letters to Veronica Compton. " 'Let me crush your sanity under my heel, let me lash your tender breasts, torment you to the edge, and love you beyond life itself as I thrust you over the brink into blood lust and murderous vengeance [. . .] feel the painful invasion, lash and teeth of gnomes and witches.' "

His letters had been altered, said Doug. Judge Torres ordered his remark stricken.

The more that Doug tried to talk himself out of the murders, though, the more entangled he became in his lies.

To distance himself from the June 23 Wilson/Jones murders, he had claimed that Carol moved into the Verdugo apartment before he did. But on June 16 he had the utilities turned on, and on the eighteenth and nineteenth he placed calls from there to his parents and Joey Lamphier's office.

While Carol committed the murders with Jack, Doug had contended, he was sleeping on the floor in the empty Lemona apartment. But supporting Carol's story that she was still at Lemona, the phone bill showed a June 27 call to her friend Richard Geis in Portland.

Doug had also told conflicting stories about the June car washes. Jorgensen read him his own notes: " 'Car wash, let them go for June twenty-first. Then refute. Then admit on my testimony to June fourteenth. Tell it exactly as it went down and very doubtful in one hundred-degree Fahrenheit heat Wednesday blood would be wet on the following Saturday P.M.' "

"Did I write that?"

"Yes."

"Apparently I wrote that, yes, quite some time back to my attorney, uh-huh."

Jorgensen, loving every minute, also quoted from Doug's earlier statement in which he claimed that Carol had been with him on June 22, the day that he moved out of Lydia Crouch's.

"No, that's definitely, definitely not what was testified to," said Doug.

"Oh, somebody forged the transcript here, Mr. Clark?"

When the court admonished Jorgensen not to editorialize, he apologized.

"He is grinning when he is apologizing, Your Honor," said Maxwell Keith.

"The record will reflect that he grinned when he apologized. The record will reflect that Mr. Clark is grinning."

Again the courtroom erupted in laughter.

A few minutes later, Jorgensen began to read another of Doug's poems and Doug objected that the prosecutor butchered his work. "If it's going to be read . . . I would prefer to read it."

It was titled "Idle Hands of the Devil's Workshop" and was not one of Doug's better efforts.

"Now what witch's spell," he read, "just what in hell! I exclaimed with no small fright./ This woman found the key, and secrets shall tell, that I'd burned on moonless night."

"Doesn't that say buried, Mr. Clark? B-U-R-I-E-D? Buried?"

"Yes. 'Buried on moonless night.' Thank you."

Doug then treated the court to a pedantic explication worthy of a high-school English lit class.

The "secrets" he referred to were "not dead bodies lying around the Los Angeles County area" but "the secrets that everybody locks the deepest into their id, personality, and psyche."

"Are those wholesome romantic secrets?" Jorgensen asked.

"Pardon me?"

"Are those wholesome romantic secrets?"

"Definitely not in your opinion."

As he wound up his cross-examination, Jorgensen confronted Doug about peppering his testimony with Jack Murray's name.

"As a matter of fact, you've been doing your very best to lay it on dear dead Jack, have you not?"

"Bet your buttons. He did it, he ought to wear it."

Doug must not have been expecting Jorgensen to quote from yet another of his letters to Veronica Compton about Carol:

" 'She's thinking deal. If she just lay it on dear dead Jack, I'd be clear and then assist her. But no, she's so P.O.'d at me for some fucking reason she can't see how she's hurting herself. If she nails me I'll retaliate so the DA fries us both. If she gets smart we both come out better off.' "

All Doug could do was, once again, make an elaborate inspection of the document for forgery and leave the long-suffering Maxwell Keith to try to pick up the pieces of his client's shattered credibility.

The night that Exxie's head was dropped, Doug contended, and Jorgensen did not believe, that he had been in a bar called the Hello Doll at a farewell party for a dancer—owner of the panty crotch—who was returning to New Zealand. He had written her a check dated June 27, he said, and had left the bar in the early morning hours. On redirect examination Maxwell Keith introduced the check and Doug's alibi, then went on to address the separate issue of whether Doug really had tried to persuade Joey Lamphier to perjure herself.

He had to "meet fire with fire," explained Doug, and had been "contemplating trying to subtly influence Ms. Lamphier into offering what would be knowingly false testimony by my knowledge, but not by hers." He had failed in his attempt, he admitted.

By January 10, Doug must have realized that he was also failing in his attempt to lie his way out of the murders. He began the day by refusing to answer Maxwell Keith's questions. Keith was "incompetent" and "unprepared," he reiterated.

Doug had turned tail, thought Jorgensen, but was following through with his plan to suggest incompetence of counsel in case of conviction. Jorgensen had letters to Carol in which Doug spelled out such a plan. He also had a letter in which Doug had praised Maxwell Keith's intelligence. The letters would be irrelevant to the jury now, but would be available to the state supreme court in the event the case reached appeal.

The defense continued with Doug no longer on the stand. But there was no defense. A voice expert had already testified out of turn that people's ability to recall was diminished by stress. The Sybil Brand librarian stated that Carol Bundy did not have library privileges and had not checked out the library's one Ted Bundy book, as she had claimed. A composite artist, a policewoman, and a police hypnotist brought out the inconsistencies between Charlene Andermann's statements before and after hypnosis, her difficulty creating a composite, and her tentative identification of the other suspect. And criminalist Doreen Music testified about finding a sealed bottle of Lidocaine in the bottom drawer of Carol Bundy's nightstand.

A check dated June 21, 1980, made out to an auto-parts store, was entered to prove Doug's contention that on the day of the Kevin Crouch/Buick car wash he had picked up a rebuilt starter for Carol's Datsun. And another auto dealer identified a service order dated June 30 to check and repair a Datsun flywheel. Carol Bundy had signed the work order. But this did not seem to add up to anything.

On the nineteenth day of the defense case, a lethargic Nancy Smith confirmed the story of dancing nude for Doug and Bobbi at the motel in May. She had also engaged in oral sex with Bobbi while Doug watched, she admitted.

Maxwell Keith turned to the time Nancy had spent at the Verdugo apartment. Had she thought Doug and Carol strange? he asked. Nancy said she couldn't say.

On cross-examination Jorgensen asked her again.

"What do you consider strange?" replied Nancy Smith. "I have to know what you consider strange, first, before I can answer it."

"Would you consider it strange for the defendant to take out a photograph album containing photographs of a little girl and masturbate and climax on your chest?"

"Um, yes, it's along the lines of strange, yes."

"Did he do that?"

"Yes, he did."

This confirmed Carol Bundy's and Donielle Patton's testimonies about Doug's sexual habits.

On January 13, with a flurry of expectation in court, Veronica Lynn Compton took the stand, powdered, black-haired, and looking, Leroy thought, as if she'd been sent straight from the coroner's office. Jorgensen had prepared by reading what he considered her miserable letters until one o'clock in the morning. But Veronica was a witness in the Hillside Strangler case across the hall and had decided that one trial was enough. To the audience's disappointment, exercising her right under the Fifth Amendment, she refused to answer questions on the grounds that they might incriminate her.

In one way or another, all of Doug's women who were key witnesses had let him down during the trial. Veronica Compton was simply the last. When she left the stand, she took with her whatever hope Doug might have had left to gain perjured testimony.

That afternoon, the defense rested with the promises of Doug's opening statement unfulfilled. No one had appeared to claim that he and Carol had never been lovers, and he had failed to present the Sunset murders as a Ted Bundy copycat case on the part of Carol and Jack Murray.

After a brief rebuttal, the court began receiving more exhibits into evidence, with Jorgensen taking some teasing over the women's underpants.

"I guess Mr. Jorgensen wanted to handle them," said the judge.

"It wears off on you after a while, Your Honor," said Jorgensen.

The lawyers asked for a long weekend to prepare their final arguments—Jorgensen did not want to have to miss the Raiders game and said he needed extra time to compete with Doug's finely honed poetry. He couldn't compete, said Judge Torres dryly. Unsympathetic, he denied the extra time.

27

As Doug had tried to extricate himself from one of his lies, Jorgensen had written on a scrap of paper and passed it quietly to Leroy Orozco. "O what a tangled web we weave when first we practice to deceive," it read.

Over the weekend the prosecutor had tried to organize Doug's conflicting stories into some kind of order. He had given up. The tangled web would be the theme from which Jorgensen prepared his own purple prose to weave between the bare facts of the evidence.

He began by apologizing to the jurors for having led them on a tour of a sewer, the "native habitat" of Douglas Clark: "A disgusting realm of cruelty and depravity of whose existence four months ago you probably only had the vaguest suspicion." From that sewer, said Jorgensen, Douglas Clark "regularly emerged from darkest night, pale, red-eyed, nervously alert, to prowl our main streets in his cowardly search for weak and defenseless prey."

He would try, said Jorgensen, not to repeat the "grotesque" matters to which the jury had been exposed. The evidence of guilt was so overwhelming that he was not going to go over it piece by piece.

Obviously, though, Jorgensen had decided he had to address the Charlene Andermann contradictions. "Insofar as we know," he began, "she was the last one on whom the defendant would use anything as unreliable as a knife alone."

It was likely she "erred" over the wood paneling on the car and her attacker having a mustache, he admitted. While Andermann had described the car as a Chevy and officers' reports had said it was a Pontiac and a Ford, Carol Bundy's wagon was in fact a Buick, a GM car easily confused with the other makes.

There was also Andermann's firm identification of Doug and Carol Bundy's story of Doug's "false heroics" when he staggered, bloody, into her apartment late in April. True, there was Doug's alibi check to a dancer on the night of the Andermann attack. But where was the dancer, and why hadn't the defense questioned Joey Lamphier, who allegedly had been with Doug, about that night?

Moving on to the murders, Jorgensen brought up a letter Doug had written in which he described Marnett Comer as always wearing "sexy size 6" bikinis.

"He knew her size," said Jorgensen, "because he took her panties from her corpse and added them to his collection of dead girls' underwear."

Working his way through Doug's stories, Jorgensen pointed out that he had denied calling Brigges and Cohen, then had changed his mind when he realized that telephone bills made the calls indisputable; on August 11, Doug had told police that Cindy's phone number was in his wallet; later he said he had not written it down. He then claimed that he had not said that. He had also refused to give a handwriting sample, a further indication that the writing was his.

The objective facts supported the thesis that Doug had moved into the Verdugo apartment before Carol, Jorgensen continued. But why tell conflicting stories about that time period between June 21 and 27? At first Doug said he had the Buick overnight before the car wash, then he said he picked it up in the morning. Then he claimed to have left it at Carol's. Then he said he hadn't left it at Carol's. Carol was with him when he moved out of Lydia's. Then Carol wasn't with him.

"He had to fabricate for himself a story that would place him apart from Carol Bundy and as far away from the Verdugo Street apartment as he could for that time period."

The prosecutor moved on to the 3:08 A.M. phone call from Verdugo to Lemona and Doug's claim that he had picked up the phone to find no one there. It had been a seven-minute call.

"I don't need to tell you that that's balderdash," said Jorgensen.

272

Doug had just murdered Karen Jones and Exxie Wilson, "and he was telephoning his partner, Carol Bundy, to tell her about it."

Jorgensen turned to Doug's interest in necrophilia, "as described at insufferable length in his writings."

However insufferable Jorgensen found them, he had used the writings himself at insufferable length, and now he read again a pseudo-poem from another letter to Veronica Compton:

"be off on your last journey." . . . he orders this abject waif . . .
"Please, no," begs the quivering chin and full soft lower lip.[. . .]
Now-submerge my lovely fool . . . bathe in death's river . . .
Ha Ha! his evil desception revealed is pure evil, demented, vicious and uncompromising-

Probably, said Jorgensen, the words described the way the defendant dealt with his victims before he killed them.

Playing on Doug's own words, Jorgensen wound up:

"Ladies and gentleman. I trust that every one of you has perceived the secrets Douglas Daniel Clark has buried on moonless nights. That you, too, know his every deed . . . That you, too, have heard those dying sighs, that you have found the bones all dried and bleached, and you, too, know it all. And I trust that you will soon return with a verdict that this vile, cowardly butcherer of little girls so richly deserves, guilty of all charges and guilty of special circumstances."

Maxwell Keith was known as a shrewd and articulate man, but as the trial had progressed, papers had begun to flutter from his grasp. He had rummaged in his briefcase for items never found. He fumbled for words. He even, on occasion, apologized for himself mid-sentence as if trying to deflect the cries of "fool," "buffoon," "incompetent," and "inebriate" from his client. His was a classic response to abuse.

Cursed with too much evidence and no defense, and unfortunately with his notes at home, as he had not expected to argue that day, Keith rambled as he tried to save this man who claimed to despise him. As the evidence was circumstantial, he argued, it was just as easy to draw inferences in favor of innocence as of guilt.

Doug "may have acted up a little" in court, said Keith, but he had been under severe pressure. From the circumstantial evidence of watching Doug conduct part of his own defense with no legal training, the jury could draw the inference that he was extremely intelligent. And because of his superior brain power, it was not reasonable to accept that Doug would have acted the way he had been accused of acting. It was not reasonable to drive around with dead bodies in cars. Or to hide weapons in his workplace.

On the other hand, Carol Bundy, also intelligent, was obese and mentally ill. It was more reasonable to think that she had committed these acts with someone other than Doug. Carol had wanted revenge, suggested Keith, and had taken the witness stand hoping for a plea bargain.

Keith moved on to the discrepancies in Carol Bundy's testimony: a bullet had not penetrated Gina Marano's sinuses. No bullet went through Marnett Comer's elbow. The semen in Exxie Wilson's throat produced the result of A-type blood, while Doug Clark was O type.

Carol had done a good job, he said, of trying to appear as a pleasant, overweight woman "aghast at all these goings on" and trapped by Doug's Rasputin-like power. But if Carol had been as afraid of Doug as she said she was, said Keith, Carol would have left.

Yet by listening to the tape of her conversation with police, the jury had received the impression of "someone who had no compunction about killing, whatsoever."

It would be dangerous, Keith said, to convict Doug on the basis of Charlene Andermann's identification; as for the writing in his wallet, it did nothing but point to innocence; the holes in Marnett Comer's sweater and the holes in the "Daddy's Girl" T-shirt did not match; and Donielle Patton's credibility was "dubious."

Returning to his theme that these were not the crimes of a thinking man, Keith appealed to the jury for acquittal. Obviously not expecting that, he suggested "hypothetically" that the crimes were murder in the second degree—crimes of passion—and not first degree, premeditated murder.

When it was Jorgensen's turn to make his final argument, he began by reminding the jury that statements from attorneys were not evidence. He then went on to refute Keith's arguments.

A criminalist had testified, he said, that the semen in Exxie Wilson's throat indicated that type A blood was present, or a mixture of A and O, which could have been a combination of Wilson and Clark's blood types; the nonmatching holes in the "Daddy's Girl" T-shirt and Marnett Comer's sweater were a "red herring," because "obviously there were holes in Marnett Comer's body where the defendant shot her."

Considering the bloody boot-print evidence so strong, he barely bothered to tackle Keith's challenge to it. Then he moved to Keith's contention that semen in Cindy Chandler's vagina had not been incriminating because she was a prostitute.

That was only Douglas Clark's statement, Jorgensen said. "I suggest that no one in his right mind will believe most of the things the defendant said, and there is no particular reason to believe that this little sixteen-year-old girl was a prostitute."

What could be believed, said Jorgensen, was that the defendant had intercourse with her dead body.

"Douglas Clark carried in his car a blanket with which he covered his hideous cargo," said Jorgensen. "His attorney, Mr. Keith, also has a blanket which he likewise uses to cover his hideous cargo. Mr. Keith's blanket is his own gentlemanliness. And beneath it he seeks to hide the hideous cargo he's been forced to carry throughout this trial, his client, Douglas Clark."

Because Doug wrote doggerel verse and whole sentences, Keith had inferred that he was intelligent. But did that make him a reasonable man? Jorgensen asked.

"Some of the most evil men in history have been very intelligent men, but they have had the most dreadful, defective character[s]."

Doug, Jorgensen said, was thrilled not only by killing but by identifying publicly with his murders: "He may have wanted to be caught. . . . I believe he wanted attention. He wanted the notoriety our society affords to the Angelo Buonos and the Lawrence Bittakers and the William Bonins. Unfortunately for him, he did get caught, but somehow the fame he sought eluded him."

On the morning of Friday, January 21, the jury began deliberating, going home over the weekend and in the evenings with admonishments not to telephone each other to discuss the case. They had also been told not to take an immediate vote but to look at all the evidence.

When they did take a vote, two of them voted for acquittal while the rest looked at them in disbelief. To the majority, everything seemed to fall into place. They began to go over and over the evidence. Carol Bundy had been credible and pitiful to them, coming across not as a sociopath but as a sad woman who needed attention, the last in a procession of deluded women over whom Douglas Clark had exerted control.

Some of the jurors at first had been taken with Doug and what they saw as his disarming, boy-next-door looks. His personality fascinated them. Others were not so taken and found him chilling. By the end of the trial, they had not wanted to catch his eye. His look disturbed them.

At least two jury members felt sorry for Maxwell Keith as the key recipient of Doug's abuse. But because of Doug's allegations, the jury as a whole speculated about whether he drank as Doug charged. They found nothing tangible to support the accusation.

The guns, Carol Bundy's testimony, Doug's lies and behavior in the courtroom, and the criminalists had made it clear to most of them that Doug was guilty. Discrepancies in Charlene Andermann's and Lydia Crouch's testimonies did not seem important. The women had been under stress.

After five days' deliberation, the jury reached a verdict. On the morning of January 28, the bailiff announced that they had found Doug guilty of all six counts of murder as well as attempted murder and mayhem in the Charlene Andermann attack. He was also found guilty of the special-circumstances allegations.

Franklyn and Blanch Clark sat in court with Doug's ex-wife next to them. Doug turned around and looked at them.

"Hi, Mom," he said, and he winked.

28

THE PENALTY PHASE WOULD DETERMINE WHETHER OR NOT DOUG would go to the gas chamber. This was the prosecution's last chance to present other crimes or evidence from Douglas Clark's background for the jury to consider in addition to the crimes of which he had been convicted.

It seemed almost too much to have to begin again with bones, sheriff's deputies, and the coroner. But that's what Jorgensen did, presenting evidence about the discovery of Cathy and Jane Doe no. 99, the young woman believed to have been the "package" in Tuna Canyon. (Like Cathy and Water Tower, she had not been identified.)

Carol Bundy reappeared to tell of the hunting trips to Oxnard and Anaheim, of Doug's "disdain toward ordinary people," and his and her own beatings of Chris Bundy. Then at the end of the second court day, Jorgensen asked that yet another of Doug's letters be received in evidence and read to the jury. In it Doug had said he was going to "win and walk," and he called Jorgensen a "cock-sucking effeminate rotten cheating bastard." The prosecutor and Detective Gary Broda, Doug wrote, walked "on 'Closed Cases' up a staircase of ruined lives." Some day they would reap their reward. Doug planned to hire an investigator "and nail these two fags in a fucking '69' so one blast (case) nails 'em both."

Maxwell Keith and Penelope Watson also were entitled to an opportunity to present mitigating factors in a last chance to try to wrest sympathy from the jury.

Doug had not wanted his family to testify. When Maxwell Keith, none of whose clients had ever received the death penalty, insisted on putting them on, Doug asked that the record show that it was against his wishes.

And so Blanch Clark, motherly, dowdy, and seemingly bemused, told of Doug's difficult birth following a car accident, her migraine headaches, and Doug's attentiveness. Her third son had been a good, kind boy who was no trouble in school, she testified. He had not acted strangely, except that in Europe he drank wine instead of water. No, there had been no problems in Switzerland. She and her husband had brought Walter and Doug home because "they had to have their American history and all this."

"I gather this is all a terrible shock to you," said Maxwell Keith.

"Yes, sir. It certainly is."

"Do you feel he should die in the gas chamber for what he's been convicted of?"

"I can't believe you're asking me that question."

"I'm asking it, though."

"Absolutely not."

Franklyn Clark followed his wife, still a man of military bearing, seeming a little rigid. Perhaps his wife tried to compensate for that by making excuses for her children, thought a jury member.

Penelope Watson, who had delved into Doug's background, questioned Franklyn. The younger three children, he said, had gone to boarding school when he could afford it because he had "always been one that felt education was a very desirable thing in anybody's life."

Like his wife, Mr. Clark did not remember any problems in Switzerland. Nor, for that matter, did he remember the content of Doug's reports from Culver Academy. What with working twelve-to fourteen-hour days, which couldn't just stop because the children were on vacation, his times with them had not been all that great. Doug had been "talkative," he agreed, but "just as normal in the household as the rest of them."

"Did you tell Mr. Henry [one of Doug's earlier lawyers] something to the effect that you had a problem with Douglas dressing in women's underwear that you couldn't handle?"

"No."

"And that's why you sent him to Culver?"

"I did not."

"I have no further questions."

It was now time for what the courtroom had been waiting for with interest: the psychiatric testimony that would, everyone hoped, explain all that had gone before.

Gloria E. Keyes, M.D., was on first, a Howard University Medical School graduate now affiliated with Martin Luther King Hospital. When Dr. Seymour Pollack, who had examined Carol Bundy, assigned her to the Clark case, Dr. Keyes had been a forensic psychiatry fellow at the USC School of Psychiatry and Law.

She had interviewed Doug in a mess hall with him handcuffed to a steel bench, then in a prison cell with the door propped open. By the time of trial she had spent more than a hundred hours on the case (this estimate was loudly disputed by Doug) and had talked to Doug's parents, his sister Carol Ann, and his brother Walter. She also had notes from Penelope Watson's interview with Walter.

Over Doug's objections and threats of a lawsuit, Dr. Keyes testified that she had diagnosed him as having a personality disorder, a number of psychosexual disorders, and shared paranoia (once known as folie à deux).

"Did you find Mr. Clark, when we speak of personality disorders only, to have a psychopathic personality?" asked Maxwell Keith.

"In my reference, I use antisocial personality. . . . It's a more contemporary and euphemistic description," said Dr. Keyes. But it was the same thing, and included impulsivity, social-norm deviation, and job-performance problems; there was no documentation that one was born with it.

Dr. Keyes, who had received "widespread reports" of Doug's contempt for other people, had also found him to have a narcissistic personality, which manifested itself in grandiosity, putting other people down, and having a shallow capacity to relate to others.

It was paradoxical but true, Dr. Keyes continued, that Doug suffered from low self-esteem, even though his denial was strong that there was anything wrong with him.

"He thinks he's sane?"

"Yes, he thinks he's sane."

Did she believe, Maxwell Keith asked, that Doug was a very sick human being?

"Impaired or dysfunctional" were more comfortable terms for her, said Dr. Keyes, who felt that Doug was also self-destructive:

279

he did not restrain himself in court when it would behoove him to do so.

"Do you have any specific things that happened in Doug's childhood that you believe constituted the onset—"

"Objection," said Doug. "Calls for hearsay."

"—of Doug's psychiatric personality?"

There was a recess, and Dr. Keyes did not answer the question. Afterward Keith posed it again.

"The parents," said Dr. Keyes, "denied that there was ever any problem at all in his upbringing or in his childhood, that he was a good student and that there was no behavior problem."

The only hint of friction had been an offhand comment by Franklyn that Doug "finally got it together" when he studied to become a steam engineer. It was clear, said Keyes, that the father had not been pleased by the way his son was turning out.

"Is it your opinion that Mr. and Mrs. Clark, Senior, particularly, were not being entirely candid with us?"

"I think that that is true."

In her conversations with Walter Clark, Doug's brother had seen himself as a family black sheep who came home with a grade of ninety-seven and was ignored. Walter had always felt as if he wasn't part of the family and must have been adopted. Doug, on the other hand, would lie about almost anything, Walter thought, and had been praised or sympathized with for getting into trouble. Dr. Keyes had received a report that Doug had told Walter he was interested in cleaning up the streets of prostitutes. But her memory was vague and she was unable to detail it. She did, though, mention Penelope Watson's passing on to her Blanch Clark's advice to Walter: she did not want him to expose any family secrets.

Dr. Keyes moved on to Doug's relationships with women. In spite of an appearance of independence, she said, he consistently exhibited dependency by letting the women take care of his expenses. He was also a paraphiliac: he responded to a "constellation" of deviant sexual preferences that included fetishism, in which a male uses women's clothing as a masturbatory object. Although the records had reflected it, said Dr. Keyes, Blanch Clark had denied catching Doug with her garments as well as his sister's.

Normal behavior, said Dr. Keyes, showing herself to be on the conservative side, was male and female sex. But Mr. Clark had maintained that his behavior was not abnormal, and perhaps society was wrong.

Maxwell Keith wondered if Dr. Keyes found Doug's letters to Veronica Compton "bizarre."

"Well, there was a very rich fantasy life," Dr. Keyes said carefully, adding that fantasy led to problems only if people acted out against others. In this case, Doug's fantasy life served his purpose of masturbation. This, combined with the acting out of fantasies, indicated his feelings of incompetence, fear, and anxiety around adult sex.

Doug had become upset by the word "necrophilia," even though he denied indulging it and denied the murders. Because of his objections, Dr. Keyes had agreed to call it "atypical paraphilia."

Although there was very little literature on the subject, she said, some people considered necrophilia to be a "blatant psychotic manifestation." Doug, though, did not exhibit any kind of psychosis or delusion.

If a child's ego did not develop normally, Dr. Keyes explained, and he did not learn to relate well to a parental figure, as the child grew older he would feel and react to people as if they were inanimate objects, as in necrophilia. There was an "ego splitting" in which part of Doug appeared normal but another part was "primitive and undeveloped."

"Do you find Doug to be something of a pseudo intellectual?"

He could have been a real intellectual if he had wanted, said Dr. Keyes. In jail, his verbal IQ had tested at 123, high for someone who hadn't been to college. His performance score was 106, giving him a full-scale IQ of 118, which was better than average. But he was a low achiever, who manipulated rather than worked steadily to achieve something.

At first he came across well socially, said Dr. Keyes. He dropped big words and quoted Shakespeare. He was widely traveled and could be articulate and engaging. But then he didn't carry through.

Now Dr. Keyes got around to discussing "shared paranoia," formerly called folie à deux. It referred, she said, to a belief that went back and forth between two people. In this case, it was between Douglas Clark and Carol Bundy, whose weaknesses and strengths fed into each other.

Maxwell Keith read Dr. Keyes a letter Doug had written to Carol in which he declared himself "fucking very damn near the smartest, most brilliant but uneducated SOB you'll ever hope to meet." He had told Carol that simply by using his "mind's bright star" he could change her from "mediocre housewife" into whatever she wished.

"I don't like you peons, okay . . . ?" Doug had written. "I don't want you, I don't need you. I cannot stand being around you."

That, Dr. Keyes agreed, was an example of Doug's grandiosity and narcissism. It was a delusional system, not in the sense that he was hearing things that did not exist but in the sense that it was a fixed, false belief with no basis in fact. Women got caught up in this "I'm great" approach because they were vulnerable.

"Not that a lot of men don't do that, you know. That's usual."

But with Doug the behavior was extreme, and it would be difficult, said Dr. Keyes, to separate Doug's mental and personality disorders from the acts for which he had been convicted.

Jorgensen's cross-examination was brief and prosecutorial. He wanted to know if Doug was sane, if he knew what he was doing when he committed the murders, and if he intended to commit them while knowing they were wrong. Dr. Keyes answered yes to all the questions, saying as well that in spite of her talk of delusions, Doug was in touch with reality and did not hallucinate.

"But he actually protects himself from being psychotic by acting out his desires and fantasies, isn't that true?"

"I think that's an explanation, yes."

"In other words, if he weren't out killing people, he would have this severe mental disorder. But this is an escape valve."

"That's speculative. Yes, uh-huh."

Jorgensen wondered if Doug had expressed remorse.

"He always maintained with me that he never did it, so if he never did it he never would, of course, acknowledge remorse."

By the time she stepped down, Dr. Keyes had been on the stand for a day and a half. She had, of course, diagnosed Doug, but she had not explained him in the sense of being able to say what had happened in his life to make him do what he had done.

Next was Dr. Donald Lunde, a clinical associate professor of psychiatry at Stanford Medical School and author of *Murder and Madness* and *The Die Song, A Journey Into the Mind of a Mass Murderer.*

Penelope Watson questioned him.

Multiple murder, Lunde began by saying, was as old as human behavior, homicides, and criminal trials and was unrelated to current phenomena such as television or a breakdown of the family. Dr. Lunde agreed with Dr. Keyes's diagnosis of antisocial personality and paraphilia. But he also thought Doug suffered from sexual sadism. This was a "rare condition" and insufficiently studied: people awaiting trial and the results of an appeal tended not to cooperate, Lunde explained, and later they were killed.

Although Doug and the Clark family had not cooperated with him, Lunde had studied his own small group of white males who, like Doug, were of above average intelligence and had an interest in police work. From the ages of about five, six, or seven, they had been obsessed with weapons, and later with sexual gratification and their own sexual performance.

Most of them, Lunde said—again from an early age—had an almost complete fusion of their sexual and aggressive drives, combining lovemaking and killing in their fantasies.

"We don't know why it is or how it happens. We just know that it's there. . . ."

Was that typical for Mr. Clark, Watson wondered, and had Lunde found an object at which Doug's hostility was directed?

His hypothesis, said Lunde, which had been impossible to pursue at length because of the lack of cooperation, was "that there is in this man, and has been from an early age, some incredible rage that also involves sexual feelings toward his mother."

The doctor had asked Doug to describe his mother, and the words he had used were almost identical to the words he used to describe the women he had brief relationships with later in life. His perception of her, as a boy, had been "short, fat, kind of blond hair."

Doug, Dr. Lunde had said, had gone for an unusually long time without admitting his guilt.

If it was Jorgensen's last opportunity to try to send Doug to the gas chamber, so it was Doug's to try to undo the psychiatric testimony and persuade the jury of his innocence.

It was not in his best interests to testify, Maxwell Keith warned yet again. Proving the psychiatric diagnoses of grandiosity and self-destructiveness, Doug took the stand anyway to answer Maxwell Keith's questions.

He tried to dismiss the stories of his cross dressing—he had simply played dress-up at the age of four, he said; he denied being expelled from his Swiss school, which he deemed "overrated" and "a mini-concentration camp"; and the only problem he remembered from India was spending his ten-rupee allowance to get "blind stinking drunk" on hooch.

When some of the employees were fired, it had disturbed him, said Doug. That was when he realized that people with Ph.D.s and three-piece suits weren't worth a damn.

"I found out that most of them that I knew were pseudoplastic frauds, really. Unhappy with their lives, had no particular goals, other than to succeed on a yardstick that I didn't accept."

He had gone into a slump and started questioning all the values to which he'd been exposed, including the status consciousness and racism of the military.

"Did you have any conflicts with your mother?" Keith asked.

"None whatsoever."

"How about your father?"

"No, huh-uh. No. We—as a matter of fact, we are not a family that believes in, for instance, like corporal punishment. We don't, you know, go in for kid beating. This is why I cracked up when Carol was relating all that crap about Chris."

He had hit Chris with a big, broad belt, Doug said, at Carol's request.

"And if you have ever been whipped with a narrow belt or a broad one, you best choose the broad one. It doesn't hurt at all."

What about his view of prostitutes?

"I don't see any difference at all, as a matter of fact, between a streetwalking prostitute and a lawyer in their ethics or their morals."

The court spectators laughed. Then, after a perfectly timed pause, Doug said, "I don't mean that demeaningly to the prostitute."

There was more laughter.

"You're down on lawyers, too, aren't you?" asked Keith.

Now Doug told his saga to the jury of Judge Torres being Carol Bundy's judge, of Max Keith's unwelcome attempt to file an NGI plea, then Jorgensen's dropping the Jack Murray charges.

"I said, 'Leave that in, because that makes everything to do with Murray relevant so we can prove who killed these people.' " He looked at Keith. "And you agreed with me."

Why, asked Keith, did Doug think the death penalty would be improper in his case?

That was difficult, said Doug. "If in fact I had done what I'm accused of doing, if the verdict were correct and I were sittin' right there, I'd be thumbs down. I'd vote for the death penalty. . . . Pardon me. Had a lump in my throat here. Tough subject from this point."

Pushing his emotion aside, Doug pressed on. As he said, in the jury's position, he would have voted for death himself had he not learned of "the pollution" in the district attorney's office that had cold-blooded killers testifying against each other in exchange for reduced sentences.

"Will Bundy face the death penalty? Doubt it. She'll worm her way around [it]. . . ."

The death penalty was "an obscenity," said Doug, even though he had voted for it.

"If I could afford it, I could have the assistance of counsel. *If* I could afford it. And Penny and Max sat in the back of the court-room knocking down some six hundred bucks a day and I couldn't talk to them by his [Torres's] order. . . . Money. That's what it comes down to. Money and votes."

Give him time, said Doug.

"Give me five years and keep your eye on the press."

Doug was through, and so was Maxwell Keith. It was four o'clock in the afternoon and court was adjourned.

When Doug's ego had pushed him to take the stand a second time, Jorgensen had been disbelieving but pleased. He still worried about overdoing the case. But if he asked the right questions and allowed Doug to talk, he'd talk himself right into the death penalty. It was the moment Jorgensen had been waiting for.

He started casually, asking him his opinion of lawyers. As he understood it, Doug hated Karl Henry, Jorgensen said.

"I don't hate anybody."

"What are your feelings about Mr. Henry?"

He was incompetent, said Doug, "a money-grubbing shyster attorney that's very, very impressed with himself." Paul Geragos was "four times worse." As a group, he felt that court-appointed attorneys were "just a step above ambulance chasers," "a bunch of rejects" slopping along taking their appointments and accepting the "dole of half normal pay."

Jorgensen reminded him that Geragos and Keith were two of the most highly regarded criminal lawyers in the state. He went on to wonder if Doug included Carol's lawyer, Dwight Stevens, in his assessment.

"He wouldn't come to see me. . . . I don't think even you would decline an invitation with me. Which, by the way, you have had the entire case."

"Mr. Clark, I wouldn't get within a hundred yards of you."

Judge Torres protested. "Mr. Jorgensen, please. You are within a hundred yards of him."

But Doug overruled the judge. "I would like to respond. I walk behind you all the time, Mr. Jorgensen. If you think that letter was a threat on your life, I would have killed you sitting right there. I could have done it. I could have done it many, many times. If I had any animosity toward you and felt you should die and it was my somehow given urge to kill you, you'd be dead."

"Mr. Clark, you only do that to helpless girls who have no weapon."

"You're about the same as that, a helpless effeminate person without a weapon."

If he didn't get a reversal of the case on appeal, did he intend to try to escape? Jorgensen asked.

"Oh, horseshit, Jorgensen. I could have escaped a long time ago if I ever felt like it."

Jorgensen brought up Doug's being fired by the Department of Water and Power and his threatening them with a shotgun.

"That's another pipe dream. Never happened."

In 1978 or 1979, had he gone to a different job in a blood-soaked shirt?

The gate guard who had alleged such a thing hadn't even worked there at the time, said Doug.

"Mr. Clark," asked Jorgensen. "How did that hole get in the clerk's enclosure?"

"What hole?"

Doug got down from the witness stand and made a studied examination of the court clerk's cubicle. He then tried to shift the blame to the defense table.

"It looks to me like the corner of this table knocked a nasty hole in the wood there. Yes, yes indeed."

"Did you see someone kick that table into the wall?"

Keith objected and was overruled.

He had kicked the table one day, Doug admitted, when he was being "needlessly manhandled."

Hadn't he also called Judge Torres "vile names" even though he had testified yesterday that he did not accept American racial prejudice?

"Did you say, 'Fuck you, Torres'?"

"I think that's highly relevant evidence, yes. I think that's definitely highly relevant evidence of somebody's guilt in murder cases."

Jorgensen turned to the psychiatrists' diagnoses.

"Gobbledygook" and "double-talk," said Doug. "Psychiatry is a kindergarten sport. Maybe a thousand years from now, two thousand years from now, they'll know something about the inner workings of the human mind. They are wandering around in the dark."

When Jorgensen turned to the murders, able now to discuss Cathy, with whose murder Doug had not been charged, Doug decided to give his version of the story. In it, as in Carol's, he had gone into the Hughes Market on Highland Avenue in Hollywood to buy cigarettes. When he came out Carol had engaged Cathy in conversation and had worked an arrangement out with her for twenty dollars.

"Did you have the two guns in the car that night?" asked Jorgensen.

"I don't think the two guns were there. As I recall, there was one at least. . . . I hadn't seen the chrome one for quite a while."

"Where was the nickel one?"

"In Carol's purse. I guess she had it on her. I don't know."

"How did you happen to know that?"

"Well, I was going to get through the chronological events. . . ."

"I just wanted to know how Carol had that gun."

"I am explaining that."

"Had you seen the gun in her purse?"

"No, I hadn't. As a matter of fact, I had asked her not to carry handguns around because it's an offense to carry it in her purse. . . ."

They had pulled into the empty Mobil station. Cathy had got into the back seat with the space on either side of the Buick too narrow for him to get out. "Clumsily" he had climbed over to the back to neck with Cathy. She had knelt on the passenger-side floor to lie in his lap with Carol's "beady glasses staring" at them.

"And so I was trying to ignore Bundy and I looked up and she had the gun and it was pointed right at me. And she looked—well, I should say her facial expression looked normal but her demeanor wasn't normal. And I saw this gun pointin' at me and I'm looking at her and I'm thinking, 'What the hell?'

"And then, bang, the bullet cleared—now, this is what throws me. I'm not sure that the bones they found are Cathy's because that bullet went in the back of her head. . . . Now wait a minute. We were in the bench seat. It would have been slightly to the right maybe of the midline in the back, but the bullet came clear through her head and hit me in the stomach."

He had on a blue work shirt that the LAPD had tested for blood. He couldn't understand why it hadn't come up positive.

"Maybe if you sent it to the FBI they might know how to do the test better than you guys."

Doug began to overdo it here. Thinking he was next to be killed,

287

he had freaked out, wet his pants, become speechless, broken down, collapsed. Cathy was panting and thrashing around and he could almost, but not quite, reach the gun. He tried to pull Cathy on top of him to protect himself from Carol, who just sat there, calm.

"All right," said Jorgensen, loving it. "Go ahead and tell us the rest of the story."

Doug could only recall "vague snatches." Pulling out of the Mobil station. Driving up Highland Avenue.

"I must have climbed over the seat and got the car started . . . I really can't tell you why at that point I was doin' what Carol told me. . . . She was in total control. I know that. I just didn't have any way in the world to stop."

"Was it unusual for Carol to be in control of you . . . ?"

Doug started on about the Theresa photographs and Jack Murray again.

"Wait a minute. I don't want to go into that. I want to talk about the night Cathy was killed."

Doug continued. He was behind the wheel with Carol in the passenger seat with the gun. "I wasn't totally convinced that I couldn't overpower Bundy. A good right cross to the mouth probably would have stopped her. . . ."

But Carol was threatening that no one would believe he had not killed Cathy.

"We drove. I remember parts of it. Bundy climbed over." He must have been wanting the jury to know that Carol didn't always wear linen suits because he said, "She was wearing her stretch pants and sweater-type thing. Her usual outfit."

All he remembered was Carol telling him to keep driving as she thrashed around in the back, stripping the girl's clothes off.

"Was she also giving you instructions as to where to drive as she was doing this?"

"No. This is the odd part. She just said, 'Drive.' So I kept on just driving."

Carol climbed back into the front seat. Again he could have assumed control by knocking her glasses off and taking the gun. But, said Doug, "I didn't trust the goddamned LAPD to think before they act. . . . And she proved it."

Eventually they found a dirt road. "There was no creek across the road. This is malarkey."

But Carol hauled the body out of the car, told him to back up, and they drove home.

"Why didn't you report the murder to the police?"

"I think the proof is in the pudding. I think the case had pretty well borne out that LAPD . . . twist things around, take the easy way. Don't investigate. They never bothered investigating Murray even with the evidence that we put forward in my letters."

"So, long before the LAPD and I and all of the others involved framed you in the murders that you have been convicted of, you were sure that they would frame you if you even tried to report a murder to them, and that's the reason you didn't do it. Is that correct?"

No, Doug said. He just could not take the chance that people would believe Carol Bundy. And that was what had happened. Carol had convinced the jury that she was honest.

After the lunch break, Jorgensen continued with the Cathy murder and Doug's contention that a bullet had gone through her head and hit him.

"Do you recall Dr. Choi's testimony regarding the bullet wound to the head of Jane Doe twenty-eight?"

"Yes. I paid particular attention to it because it seemed to conflict with what I recall as the exit of the bullet. . . ."

"He didn't find an exit wound, did he?"

"Well, that's my point. I don't know the internal working of a skull. I didn't have biology."

". . . Dr. Choi did, however, find a fracture in the upper part of the skull where the bullet had apparently struck and stopped, didn't he?"

"That's an opinion, yes. That is a possibility, certainly, uh-huh."

And things went on from there.

"Mr. Clark," said Jorgensen. "You know this jury has found you guilty beyond a reasonable doubt and to a moral certainty of every one of these murders?"

"No kidding."

"Now, don't you have somewhere in your soul, if you have a soul, any glimmering of a feeling of conscience? Any glimmering of a feeling of remorse or—"

"If I had a violin, I would play it, Mr. Jorgensen. You are not impressing me. You may be impressing the jury . . . I think between you and me and the fence post that you and I know that I'm not the killer."

"No, Mr. Clark. The People know just the opposite."

Robert Jorgensen had no further questions and neither had Maxwell Keith. Penalty-phase arguments were set for the next day.

The California Penal Code had included capital punishment since 1872, with lethal gas replacing hanging in the 1930s. But no one had been executed in the state since 1967, when Governor Ronald Reagan refused clemency for thirty-seven-year-old cop killer Aaron Mitchell. In 1972, California voters had affirmed an initiative to enforce the death penalty. In 1976, it had been reenacted by the U.S. Supreme Court, then reaffirmed by California voters in 1978. The condemned were beginning to pile up on San Quentin's death row as prisoners spun out their automatic appeals for as long as possible.

But proponents of the death penalty were hard pressed to show that it acted as a deterrent. Murder rates in Florida, Louisiana, and Texas actually rose in the 1970s after bans on capital punishment were lifted; it cost less to keep prisoners locked up for life than to have the states pay for the round of appeals that followed a death sentence; too, the death penalty was applied inequitably, with the percentage of black condemned prisoners far outstripping whites, and some criminals escaping the death penalty altogether for crimes considered worse than those committed by condemned men.

In 1980, California Governor George Deukmejian had ridden the wave of law-and-order Reaganite politics into office to replace Governor Jerry Brown. It seemed as if it would not be long before the condemned actually began to die again in the state.

On the first day of penalty-phase argument, Jorgensen told the jury that any plea for mercy based on the morality of the death penalty was irrelevant: "The punishment dictated by the law, which is the collective voice of the People of the State of California, is death."

As the jury might have become desensitized, he warned them, they should remember the moment when they first realized that in front of them was a man who took a young woman's body to a parking lot, sliced off her head, and took the head home and put it in the freezer.

"I don't deny, ladies and gentlemen, the death penalty is a great punishment. But does it even come close to the wrongdoings of this man?"

This man, Douglas Clark, was waiting to speak, once again, on his own behalf. He stood at the lectern, this time quietly protesting his innocence and shamelessly invoking America, the flag, even apple pie. They had to do their duty, he told the jury, and vote for death—as he himself would vote if presented with the evidence in this case.

He quoted poetry. "Down, down, down, into the darkness of the grave gently they go/ The beautiful, the tender, the kind." And he just happened to mention that there had been a death penalty on the books when Christ died on the cross.

But whoever killed these victims deserved the death penalty: "You're not dropping a bomb over Vietnam and annihilating a hospital. You're just putting your name on a death warrant. You're just putting your name there so that Deukmejian can put his on it. He has worked long and hard to be in a position where he could personally do it. He said he will. We put him in there. Let's do it. That's my vote."

Maxwell Keith was up next to say how moved he was by Doug Clark's argument. Moved, and yet not in agreement. Whatever Mr. Clark's faults, frailties, or psychological problems, he was, said Keith, a human being who was not born that way.

It would have helped, said Keith, if the Clark family had told what they knew.

"But, good God, ladies and gentlemen, something happened. Whether it was one set of psychotraumatic events or a series of things that progressed and developed from early childhood through adolescence, I don't know. But something caused Mr. Clark to become the sort of person that you have found him to be."

Doug Clark wasn't going anywhere, argued Keith. And he should be kept alive, studied. Doug was self-destructive; he was crazy; his paraphilia reached beyond the pathological almost to the unthinkable. He had exhibited a virtual death wish, and his activities might well be uncontrollable, otherwise it defied the imagination, said Keith, to believe that someone could indulge in them.

"Ladies and gentlemen, I ask you. Should we, do we put our sick to death . . . whether they're sick in the mind as is Doug or sick in the body as with someone with cancer?"

No, said Keith. We try to make them well.

"Do you for one minute, ladies and gentlemen, think that Mr. Clark's death will solve anything? Do you think his death will benefit society? Do you not think you should show mercy towards this defendant because he is a human being and we are a civilized society?"

Doug was not entitled to the jury's sympathy for what he did, said Keith, but to their mercy and sympathy for what he was.

"Kill him, ladies and gentlemen, if you will. Do so, but ask yourselves, will that bring back any of the victims in this case . . . ?"

It was Jorgensen's turn for a closing argument and he told the jurors that Maxwell Keith had urged them to "disobey the Constitution and the laws of this state and this nation" by asking them to vote for life without possibility of parole. His assertion that Doug was sick was not supported by the evidence. And even if the evidence were there, it would not be a mitigating factor.

"I concede that the defendant is an intelligent and an evil human being. The rest of Mr. Keith's contentions I dispute because they are demonstrably false. . . . Douglas Clark absolutely refuses to follow the single most basic rule of civilization. He kills whenever and wherever the fantasy strikes him. A civilized society cannot permit such behavior. If it does, that society itself will be destroyed."

The jury should not be swayed by arguments calling for them to exercise discretion, show mercy, be sympathetic, feel guilty, or ignore the law, Jorgensen said.

"The law requires and justice demands that . . . Douglas Clark pay with his own life."

Penelope Watson had the last word about Doug. "I'm not going to tell you I like him," she said. "I'm not going to tell you he's my friend. I'm not going to tell you I respect him. I'm not going to tell you he's a genius. But I am going to suggest to you that you don't kill someone just because he's a son of a bitch."

The jury were not the sovereign people of California, as the district attorney had suggested, said Watson, and they did have discretion, which she asked them to exercise.

"So what caused the Doug Clark you've seen in this courtroom for the last five months to become the way he is?" Look at Doug's parents, Watson suggested. "I can understand that this might be an embarrassment to them. Somehow I don't understand, no matter how embarrassed you are, how you can let your child die. . . . What family secrets are there? . . . What occurred? I don't believe for a minute there was nothing."

When Doug's mother was in court, Watson went on, his behavior became more outrageous.

"I don't know if you watched him while she testified and observed his attitude towards her and his demeanor. But I suggest to you that it wasn't an exchange of love."

How, she wondered, did that combination of sexual drive and aggressive drive happen?

"You may very well not care if you ever know how or why Doug Clark, white, middle class, advantaged, intelligent, almost middle-aged, supposedly the most considerate of children, landed in Department One twenty-seven convicted of six counts of murder. But I suggest to you that it's important. . . . It's worthy of study."

If he were the only one on earth like that, Watson went on, maybe the jury could say, "Let's kill him."

"But he isn't the first, and he's not going to be the last."

Save his life, she asked, not for him or his family but "for the rest of us."

It was Thursday, February 10, when the jurors retired to deliberate.

By about 10:30 the following morning, three of the jurors were holding out for life without possibility of parole. The others were in favor of death. Jury foreman Angela O'Neil requested the entire testimony of doctors Gloria Keyes and Donald Lunde. The court reporter went into the deliberation room to read it. At 4:04 P.M. that day, court adjourned for the weekend.

At 11:40 A.M. on the following Tuesday, Douglas Clark and his attorneys waited in the courtroom. The jury had reached its decision. As the clerk read, Doug stood, apparently nonchalant, hands behind his back.

He had been sentenced to death on each of the six counts of murder.

"The violence," said one juror afterward to a local paper. "The terrible things he did to those girls—it's unforgivable. We have the victims to think about."

On March 16, the day of sentencing, court reconvened for the last time in the case of Douglas Daniel Clark. On the grounds that Doug's privilege to act as his own counsel had been improperly revoked, Maxwell Keith made a motion for a new trial. Judge Torres denied the motion. He also shot down an appeal for a modification of the death-penalty verdict. "Each victim was executed while in a helpless position" and "the defendant showed no remorse," he said, going on to note Doug's lack of mental disturbance and antisocial personality.

"Why don't you cut the bullshit and get to the sentence," said Doug, who was wearing a striped tie with his three-piece suit.

"Mr. Clark, please."

"I know you've got your soapbox. Why don't you stop the crap and get to the sentence? We don't need all this bullshit. I'll waive it. I don't need to know why you decided to do this, Rick."

". . . that he is selfish, has no regard for others, no social conscience, has an explosive personality, and has an extreme violence potential."

"I can't stand your soapbox."

Again, Maxwell Keith spoke against the death penalty, saying that it was barbaric and uncivilized and capricious. He also took issue with Torres's opinion that Doug was not mentally disturbed. "I find that from my association with Mr. Clark for over a year and a half that he's the sickest person I ever saw. Assuming he committed these offenses, which he denies."

Doug whispered something to Maxwell Keith. His client, said Keith, wanted to make a statement.

"I don't want to hear from Mr. Clark. Thank you."

"So much for the Constitution, eh, Judge?"

For the attempted murder of Charlene Andermann and the mutilation of Exxie Wilson, Judge Torres intoned, Doug would receive twelve years and eight months, which would be stayed pending appeal.

"Stand up, Mr. Clark."

Doug stood up.

"All right. The court will now arraign him and read this judgment of death."

The penalty would be inflicted, Judge Torres said, within the walls of San Quentin at a time to be fixed in the warrant of execution.

"Upon this judgment becoming final, said warden is further commanded on the time and the date hereafter fixed by order of this court, state prison at San Quentin, California, to carry out this judgment then and there putting Douglas Daniel Clark to death in the manner and means prescribed by law. . . ."

Doug spoke: "I want the execution within ten days."

He could write to the supreme court, said Judge Torres.

"You are dead, Mr. Clark," said Maxwell Keith.

"Thanks to you, you fool."

Finally Judge Torres gave the order. "Take Mr. Clark and deliver him to San Quentin."

"Keep them flying, Rick!"

Doug was led away.

PART
FIVE

Epilogue

On May 2, 1983, the day that Carol Bundy was to go to trial, she withdrew her not guilty by reason of insanity plea and, weeping, pleaded guilty to two charges of first-degree murder in the killings of Jack Murray and Jane Doe no. 28.

Daphne, Doug's one-time girlfriend, had been waiting to speak as a character witness for Carol.

"She was controlled by Doug," Daphne said to the woman next to her.

"Bullshit," said Jeannette Murray.

Carol escaped the gas chamber. But on May 31, 1990, Judge Torres sentenced her to two consecutive twenty-five-years-to-life terms in state prison, plus an additional two years for the use of a firearm. It was the maximum possible sentence. Her first eligible parole date would be in 2012 and the prison system would have the option of keeping her in for life.

Assistant District Attorney Ron Coen watched as Carol was taken from the courtroom. He was disappointed, because he had been looking forward to stomping about pointing his finger and crying out for justice. He had firmly believed that Carol was involved in all the Sunset murders, but felt he could prove only two. Justice had been served, he thought, but it would have been a fun case to try even if his kids could have won it.

His favorite line of Carol's would remain, "You're treating me like I'm some kind of criminal."

When Carol's former lawyer Joseph Walsh read in the newspaper about Carol's plea and sentence, he was shocked. But if others associated with the Sunset murders also thought the sentence brutal—and some did—Carol, as usual, idealized her situation. In a letter to Judge Torres, she complimented him for the "gentle" way he handled her case and told him that she agreed with his "just and fair" decision.

"Society," Carol wrote, "must segregate those persons unable to conform to its requirments. I *am* a decent woman. Why else was I unable to get away with my crimes?"

She enclosed a sketch. It was the plump, Carol Bundy-like Garfield cat smiling and holding a placard that said, "Thank You!"

Vicky Peters, long since estranged from Carol, felt that her older sister had been born without a conscience. Carol posed as meek, yet she was controlling, thought Vicky. But a victim could be guilt-free. She pictured Carol in jail, thinking, Safe at last. No more decisions to make.

Vicky had stayed with Carol and Grant in Van Nuys when Chris was two and Spike was not yet conceived. One day when she was baby-sitting, Chris fussed and wouldn't go to sleep. Vicky took a wooden spoon and paddled his little behind until bruises came up on it. Let the psychiatrists look at that, she thought. He had been irritating, but really she had beaten Chris because he was Carol's. Every bit of anger that she had stored up inside her over the years came out on that baby's bottom. And later she felt so much guilt that she never again lifted a finger to a child.

Someone had to break the chain, Vicky thought, so after Carol pleaded guilty, she wouldn't take the boys. She had heard they were going to a loving home, and she was afraid of what she might do to them. Gene's way was to deny everything, and Vicky's was to admit to it. Eventually, she would not even spank her dog.

But as far as Carol was concerned, even Carol didn't know Carol, Vicky decided. She was a hologram, projecting what she thought someone wanted to see. You reached for the image and there was no substance.

"It's no fun playing with someone else's dolls," Dr. Kaushal Sharma said later about Carol Bundy's murder of Jack Murray. "If your friend has six Cabbage Patch dolls you want one of your own."

298

Sharma, Dr. Blake Skrdla, and Dr. John Stalberg, the forensic psychiatrists who examined Carol Bundy pursuant to Judge Torres's order, had found her to be legally sane but suffering from a variety of personality disorders.

Carol had become desensitized to violence, Dr. Sharma believed, during her association with Douglas Clark, which had primed her for her murder of Jack Murray. Her involvement in killing came, he thought, from an unusual "psychopathological need and sexual deviation."

Some of Carol's answers to his questions were "inconsistent and conflicting," Sharma concluded. Even though her story of the Sunset murders was supported by the evidence, he thought that much of what she said about her own background might not be true, including her story of being molested by her father.

Dr. Skrdla, who agreed that Carol was competitive with Douglas Clark and saw her as exhibiting antisocial features, said later that he believed her story about her father's abuse and found it "inexcusable." At the same time, Carol may have identified with her father. Her role in the murders, Skrdla thought, could have been a repetition compulsion: a reenactment of childhood trauma that was an attempt to understand or integrate the problem.

It did not surprise Skrdla that Carol claimed to enjoy killing. Rather than face reality, people in an uncomfortable or unpleasant situation may eroticize it by turning it into something pleasurable.

Douglas Clark reinforced all Carol's problems, Dr. Skrdla thought. If she had not met him, her life might have taken a different course.

Her murder of Jack Murray was "purely defense," Carol had told police, so that Doug would not discover she had confided in Jack. But to Dr. John Stalberg, she gave a slightly different account, saying that the killing was not premeditated, but that she had gone "out of control" when Jack ordered her to have oral sex with him. Carol's story of the crimes, Stalberg felt, would have been more accurate when her defenses were down. Although she had told him "he controlled me" about Douglas Clark, she had told the police that Doug did not coerce her and her involvement was voluntary.

Like Dr. Winifred Meyer, who had examined Carol earlier and declared her psychotic, Dr. Sharma did not believe that Carol was any more controlled by Doug than Doug was by Carol. They were, Dr. Sharma thought, made for each other.

While Dr. Skrdla did not find Carol flirtatious, Dr. Sharma did. Ask Carol about her favorite food, joked Sharma, and she would tell you about her favorite sexual position. She had pressed him to divulge details of his own sex life, which he had refused to do. To Sharma, her eagerness to expose her life secrets was a form of "emotional flashing." Carol enjoyed being shocking and would increase the details when he did not seem shocked enough by something she said.

There was a level, though, to Dr. Sharma, on which Carol was the Valley housewife she claimed to be. She was not an evil person. If she were a neighbor, anyone would be happy to have her over for Thanksgiving dinner, thought Dr. Sharma, who felt it was a misconception that only evil people do evil things.

Dr. Winifred Meyer later addressed the issue of Doug and Carol decapitating their victims and saving the heads. She saw it, as well as Doug's keeping victims' clothes and jewelry, as a form of denial in that it was a way of keeping the victims alive. Dr. Meyer also addressed the variations in Carol's story, which included confusion about where she first saw Exxie Wilson's head and when Doug first told her he had killed Cindy and Gina. The discrepancies were a manifestation of her psychosis, said Dr. Meyer, during which Carol, childlike, would have seen things from a different perspective from moment to moment. That perspective on events would remain psychotic, even if Carol were no longer so.

There was also the possibility that Carol enjoyed teasing people with variations on her theme, as her one-time lawyer, Joseph Walsh, thought.

That was true, Carol would admit later on. She had always been a mousy person, and the idea that people puzzled over who was the real Carol Bundy made her feel important. She wanted people to wonder over the extent of her involvement in the murders. If she were an enigma, at least people were thinking about her.

In an autobiography that Carol wrote for Dr. Blake Skrdla, she described a pattern of disturbance that began before puberty.

Her first memory of bloody violence was of an occasion when her father brought home a pair of chickens and chopped their heads off in front of her. The chickens had continued to flap around as Carol ran screaming into the house. She had refused to eat them.

At age eleven, she began stealing from stores, and at the same age made her first unsuccessful suicide attempt by trying to ingest iodine.

Her account to Dr. Skrdla of her mother's death had the ring of pulp fiction, as if she could write about it only by distancing herself.

In it her father left to take her mother to the doctor and returned home alone:

> Tears were in his eyes when he came in the house. "Mom's dead," he said. "Mom's dead!"
> "What? No!" I screamed and ran to him. He held me tightly. "What happened?"
> "She had a heart attack. She went into a coma in the office. They gave her a shot right in her heart but she never even woke up!"
> He was frankly crying now. I was confused and in a daze.

After her father molested her, Carol began exposing herself by running naked in the street late at night. At fifteen she became a sexual voyeur, peeping in people's windows. While still in her teens, although never a streetwalker, Carol began accepting money for sexual favors.

Her marriage to Grant Bundy, a homosexual, surely was doomed from the beginning. In fact, according to Carol, things were fine until she became pregnant with Chris. Then Grant began to belittle, insult, and slap Carol, and later he punched her. Once Carol left Grant for an "attractive butch lesbian" but dropped her after spending thousands of dollars on her. Carol had begun cutting work and found herself generally influenced by the woman's bad habits.

She had an "intense rapport" with her father, she had written to Skrdla, using the same words she used to describe her relationship with Douglas Clark.

"Dad was only human [. . .]," Carol wrote. "Now, all these years later, I can say I still think he was a great guy!"

But Carol possessed a "deep reservoir of hostility" toward both her father and Jack Murray, a hostility she denied, Skrdla noted.

Ten years after the murders, Carol would continue to deny anger, saying that if she held any bitterness, it was so deeply buried that she was not in contact with it.

While on San Quentin's death row, Doug married a heavyset woman named Kelly Keniston. Her letterhead reading "Information Clearinghouse of Criminal Justice," she made the rounds of talk shows protesting her new husband's innocence. With Doug's case still on automatic appeal, Carol, too, began helping him, even though she knew that his goal, as always, was to discredit her. She helped, she said, because she still liked Doug, even though she couldn't define for the world why she did.

301

She gave her legal and psychiatric files to his lawyers from the public defender's office. And in 1990, at the California Institution for Women at Frontera, where Carol had been since leaving Sybil Brand, she met with Dr. Dorothy Lewis.

Subsequently, Dr. Lewis, a professor of psychiatry from New York University School of Medicine and a consultant for Doug's appeal, prepared an affidavit for Carol. At the age of eighteen months, when she suffered convulsions as the result of a virus, Lewis concluded, Carol had sustained brain damage as evidenced by her strabismus (or wandering eye). Based on additional information, Dr. Lewis also concluded that Carol had not been competent to withdraw her plea of not guilty by reason of insanity.

Doug spoke of a session in San Quentin, with Blanch and Franklyn present and the family still insisting that Doug had a normal childhood. According to Doug, Dr. Lewis tried to hypnotize him. When it did not work, he offered to hypnotize himself. Then when Dr. Lewis began to ask what Doug considered leading questions about child abuse, he told her to "Get the fuck out the door."

Like Doug, Carol was hoping to get her case reopened. She had trusted the police and prosecutors to look after her, and then they hadn't, she thought. She also thought that Doug had taken her to the brink of insanity. Another couple of weeks and she would have been gone. She had never hated him for blaming her for the murders, though, because she thought his behavior predictable.

August 22, 1990, was Theresa's twenty-second birthday. She opened an envelope and found a card from Douglas Clark. Sorry she had to get caught up in things, he wrote, but it would all be over soon. Theresa ran from her mother's house, hysterical. What did he mean, it would all be over soon? Would she be dead?

In November 1990, Doug wrote again. This time he explained what he meant. He had proof that Jack and Carol were the real killers. There was going to be a new trial and the police and DA would be "desperate to fabricate anything they possibly can to take the place of evidence they got caught faking last time around."

If he'd had the strength to walk away at the first sign of the "improper love" he felt for Theresa, Doug wrote, he would not have the "guilt and pain" in his heart that he did now.

He rewrote the story of the evening they picked up the prostitute, to make it Theresa's responsibility. If they had been home alone, he wouldn't have been able to resist her: "So, instead of sex with you, I hired HER.[. . .] I know it sounds totally absurd to say

I fell in love with an eleven year old girl.[. . .] I ached inside.[. . .] If you HAD been 18 I'd have asked you to marry me in a minute."

Doug went on to tell Theresa that Carol had copied the crimes of Ted Bundy, who had killed women in a sorority-house massacre. Kimberly Leach, another of Ted Bundy's victims, had been twelve years old.

"We firmly believe the story she created about some sort of shotgun massacre at a Mexican bar and slipping and calling you TWELVE . . . was her warped plan to create the sorority house (bar masacre) and then, killing YOU as the twelve-year-old girl. Thank God you did not turn 12 until after her arrest. You know, I think, that she did not like you."

If Theresa was now the woman he had expected her to become, Doug wrote, he knew at his next trial she wouldn't "let lies protect Carol and kill an innocent man."

Theresa phoned Downtown Robbery-Homicide. Then she called the district attorney's office to find out about being put in a witness-protection program. She made plans to change her name and her social-security number and disappear. She had read the letter a couple of times and decided it was bullshit. Wrong, wrong, wrong. While she was amused by Doug's use of melodramatic words and his chummy tone, addressing her as "ya," instead of "you," she interpreted the reference to Ted Bundy's victims as a warning. Doug had managed to get Carol to kill for him and now he had a wife on the outside.

Carol had worried that, as an adult, Theresa might have ended up under a street lamp on Sunset Boulevard. She would have felt terrible, she told herself, if what she and Doug did influenced her behavior later in life.

Theresa was not on Sunset Boulevard, but she was working for a telephone-sex call-in line for which she had created nine different characters. In a play-acting group in the outside world, she also developed an alter ego whose mother was a prostitute named Greensleeves. At work she refused to have anything to do with pedophiles and screamed into the phone at them to get help. If she heard of a man molesting his daughter, she wanted to pick up a carving knife and put it through him.

As a teenager, she had considered suicide, and went through stages of not sleeping at all to sleeping fourteen hours a day. She read and watched on television everything she could about child molestation to try to understand what had happened to her. For a while, she considered herself "twisted," with an attitude that walked four feet in front of her.

When therapy didn't help, eventually she formed her own peer-counseling group. At twenty-two, with a child's face lost in folds of fat, she spoke of keeping a knife in her car to protect herself when she picked up hitchhikers.

Theresa had a recurring dream. She was a doll in a box. Someone took her out to play with her, then put her back, shutting the lid. The box, she insisted, was dark, but was not a coffin.

Three days after Carol's guilty plea, her ex-husband Grant, aged forty-six, was found sitting in front of the television set in his Canoga Park apartment dead from an overdose of pills. He had lung cancer and Parkinson's disease but, thought his mother, Carmeletta, if he and Carol had only worked on their problems together Grant would have lived.

The Bundy boys, waiting in the Midwest for their father to come and take them back to California, heard the news when they got home from school.

It was ironic, Chris thought later, that Carol had sent them away for their protection. They were shifted from home to home, and ended up abused. The boys were told that Carol had killed Jack Murray in self-defense as he tried to rape her and that she had been misled into not fighting her case. As they had been unaware of Carol's affair with Jack, the boys had no reason to disbelieve the story.

In 1987, when Chris was sixteen and Spike thirteen, a Christian couple flew the boys out to visit their mother for the first time since she handed them over to Grant in June of 1980. Spike thought Carol hadn't changed a bit and still had a great sense of humor. But Chris had trouble talking to her. She didn't seem pleased enough to see them, and she didn't seem sorry enough about what had happened. After he left the prison, he went for a walk and ran back to the Christian couple's house thinking he was being chased by a demon. When he got inside he felt better, but then he thought he saw red eyes looking at him through the window.

Back in the Midwest, Spike, tall and blond, green-eyed and clever, began, according to a relative, to lie and act out. Chris helped him get into a group home away from the abusive family atmosphere. There Spike began to get A's in school and plan for college. After high school, Chris, whose grades were also good, joined the army to pay for his own college education.

During basic training he considered killing himself using razor blades, but didn't. He was halfway across the bridge, he thought, so why bail out now?

In Korea he learned to dance, taught by a Korean woman with whom he fell in love. He felt happy for the first time he could remember. Still, he had problems with authority and hated the army. He missed America, and when he came back, still in the service, as handsome as his mother was plain, with a movie-star smile and bright blue eyes, he became a lifeguard at the pool on the army base.

Sometimes people told him he had charisma. He didn't like that. It reminded him of Douglas Clark. Chris felt dirty inside about what had happened, and he knew that it was Doug and Carol who had dirtied him. He would never get over it, he thought, even though he believed he had come to terms with it.

As a little boy he had felt like Luke Skywalker with Doug as Darth Vader, a mad Mr. Know-it-All, his mouth always working as he tried to bend Chris to his will while Chris refused to bend. And it probably was no accident that Chris seemed pleased when the army sent him to war in Saudi Arabia. At last Chris Bundy had his chance to fight someone he thought of as a "madman," even if Saddam Hussein was a substitute for the madman he would have liked to have been strong enough to fight ten years before.

Chris had the faintest look of Carol if she had turned out all right, instead of awkwardly, the way she did. It was only his coloring, an expression or two, a way of placing his feet when he walked, the likeness fleeting until he did an imitation of an abusive relative, arm swinging as she slapped at Chris's face and held the belt with which she whipped Spike.

That was when Chris truly resembled his mother as Carol stood in an airless cubicle of an interview room at the California Institution for Women imitating her own mother, Gladys, arm swinging, tongue planted firmly in the corner of her mouth as if for leverage, legs apart for stability as she held the belt with which she had whipped Carol.

Jeannette Murray continues to work for the telephone company and until a recent promotion had two other jobs to help support Bryan and Jessica. The children do well, and Jessica is head cheerleader at her high school.

Shortly after Douglas Clark's new wife, Kelly, was on *Geraldo* blaming Jack for the murders, Jeannette appeared there to say that

305

she would like Doug to go to the electric chair with Carol Bundy on his lap. Jeannette wanted to be the one to push the switch.

"The nightmare is not over," she said. "It won't be over until he's dead."

After the murders, the Marano family split up.

"The therapists. They think they've got it down pat," says Janet Marano. "Bereavement: this many months of this, this many months of that. Months? What about years? What about forever?"

In 1981, Judith Marano, then twenty-two, traveled back to California from the East to put flowers on Cindy and Gina's graves. She took photographs and smoked a cigarette, because Gina had given her one on her eleventh birthday. At the Marano house, the tree where the children cut switches for their own whippings had been chopped down.

Something was resolved. Although Judith would continue to think of Gina every day, she would no longer project her anger onto the whole world. At the age of sixteen, she had been diagnosed with her first bout of manic depression. Their family life had been unjust, she thought still. But she wanted to end the cycle.

Justice, she was convinced, would not come from putting Douglas Clark in the gas chamber. To her, he was dead already. There could be a resolution in the world, she believed, only when there was a resolution in families. If he were right in front of her, all she would want to know was, why did he do this?

Says the older woman who remembers Doug from the Culver Academy, "I know what Doug did was terrible, but I can't help remembering the boy he was and feeling sad."

Karen Jones had a little boy. He grew up with one of Karen's sisters and is deeply loved by the Jones family, who visit Karen's grave often.

During the Sunset murders trial, Leroy Orozco was promoted from Detective two to Detective three. When it was over, he quietly closed three stabbing murders that predated the case. One of them happened near the Department of Water and Power in the north Valley where Doug worked. The murder-vehicle description resembled that of Beverly Clark's pickup truck.

Although Orozco thinks Doug might have exaggerated when he boasted to Carol of killing around fifty people, he also believes that Doug could have killed at least twenty-five, starting with strangulation and graduating to stabbings, then gunfire. For ten years, Orozco has had his retirement speech prepared. He still works at Downtown Robbery-Homicide, as do Detective Frank Garcia and

Lieutenant Ron Lewis. Detective Richard "Mike" Stallcup has retired and works for a probation department in a small town.

Douglas Clark's enemies, Detective Gary Broda and Robert Jorgensen, are dead. Broda died in 1986 of Lou Gehrig's disease, and
Jorgensen in 1988 of a cerebral hemorrhage at the age of fifty-six.
He did not get back to Utah and still worked for the district attorney's office.

Helen Kidder is now a bomb technician and lieutenant in charge
of the Criminal Conspiracy Section of the LAPD. She had trouble
dredging up the emotions of 1980 and no longer thinks that Lieutenant Ron Lewis is a horse's ass. Peggy York is a lieutenant-
commander in charge of the Wilshire Division detectives.

For months after the trial, Juror Lenz Meylan had disturbed
nights as the events of the Sunset murders ran through his head.
In court, Doug was his own worst enemy, Meylan thought. Nothing would have made a difference during the guilt phase. But what
would have happened, he wondered, if during the penalty phase
Douglas Clark and his family had cooperated with Maxwell Keith?
Would the jury, which had looked for mitigating evidence, have
decided that he was not in control of his actions and spared his
life?

Several times a year, Meylan drives across the San Rafael bridge.
He glances at the looming presence of San Quentin and he wonders
what's happening to Doug Clark. Doug has rationalized everything
to the point that he's convinced himself he's innocent, Meylan
thinks, and he's on a mission that he'll pursue to the day he dies.

"I say over and over again," says Meylan, "he's going to outlive
us all."

In his later years, Franklyn Clark took up the hobby of collecting
and making porcelain dolls. In 1991 he died of cancer. Blanch Clark
says of Doug: "I'm positive he was not guilty. He was misjudged."

Carol Ann, Doug's sister, agrees. The psychiatrists and lawyers
tried to help but did not tell the truth, she says. Doug's birth was
not difficult, Blanch was not in a car accident, and there were no
incidents with women's underwear. Doug, she insists, was "in the
wrong place at the wrong time" and is innocent.

"I think he was always feeling sorry for women who turned to
prostitution. The bible says very clearly that sex and violence lead
to death, and Doug touched the very borderline edge of it. It almost
took his life."

Carol Ann doesn't visit him; it's too depressing. But they speak on the phone and she asks, "How do you live with this, deal with it?"

Her brother tells her he has found God.

"And I don't think he's lying. Although he's very good as a talker. He's delightful that way. At night he goes to sleep and feels Jesus's arms wrapped around him. So I believe him, you know."